Investing
in student
buy-to-let

howtobooks

Please send for a free copy of the latest catalogue:

How To Books
3 Newtec Place, Magdalen Road,
Oxford OX4 1RE, United Kingdom
email: info@howtobooks.co.uk
http://www.howtobooks.co.uk

Investing in student buy-to-let

Ajay Ahuja

howtobooks

I dedicate this book to my mother.

Special thanks to Ellie and my family, Anjana, Tom and Rosa.

I would also like to acknowledge with thanks my many conversations with David Delaney about property investment, Zach Chaudry about how to make a million!, Mandip about how to collect rent on time, and with Fred about how to even collect rent! Thanks also to Emily Shah for giving me the idea in the first place, Gavin for his in-depth questioning, Damian for his even more in-depth questioning and Giles and Nikki for their continued belief.

About the researcher
Having spent much of my time providing the business scope, I must state that I am indebted to the research input offered by a colleague. I would like to thank Kashim Uddin, whose hard work and persistence have seen the project through from start to finish. Since he has recently completed a research-based Masters degree in the sciences, his well-nourished analytical skills and versatile creative input have been of huge importance in the delivery of this book. Although he is still in his infancy of business appreciation, his enthusiasm for this book has been more than welcome and we'll hopefully see some more of his work in the near future.

Published by
How To Books Ltd, 3 Newtec Place
Magdalen Road, Oxford, OX4 1RE, United Kingdom.
Tel: (01865) 793806. Fax: (01865) 248780.
email: info@howtobooks.co.uk
http://www.howtobooks.co.uk

First published in 2005

British Library Cataloguing in Publication Data
A catalogue record for this book is available from the British Library

Cover design by Baseline Arts Ltd, Oxford
Produced for How To Books by Deer Park Productions, Tavistock, Devon
Typeset by Pantek Arts Ltd, Maidstone, Kent
Printed and bound in Great Britain by Bell & Bain Ltd, Glasgow

NOTE: The material contained in this book is set out in good faith for general guidance and no liability can be accepted for loss or expense incurred as a result of relying in particular circumstances on statements made in the book. The laws and regulations are complex and liable to change, and readers should check the current position with the relevant authorities before making personal arrangements.

Contents

Introduction

The government intends to have 50% of 18-30 year olds in higher education by the year 2010. With the buy-to-let market seemingly saturated, a steady and buoyant student buy-to-let market still offers the potential of good returns.

There are multiple reasons why the student buy-to-let market is a worthwhile investment. UCAS, the university applications agency, has seen a year-by-year increase in applications. The increased student numbers are fuelling a rush to build.

It is a well known fact that in today's competitive market, universities are struggling financially, which is having knock-on effects. In addition to the increased numbers of students, massive student housing shortage and lack of investment in new housing initiatives offered by the universities mean that the benefits of private investment have never been better.

In some student cities throughout the UK, you can see the private developers building high-rise student apartment blocks as they have latched onto this investment opportunity. Just the other day, I was at Manchester Piccadilly station and apparently out of nowhere a modern, high-rise student apartment block had sprung up to obscure the usual view of the city!

University town = students = £££!!

Well, not necessarily. This book will provide an intensive look into letting out your property to students. By the end you will feel much more confident about:

- what type of student you want
- which area
- and what kind of property will best fit your situation.

The idea of this book is to assist you in your choices and to act as a guide to the market. There are roughly 200 institutions of higher education in the UK. Some of these are in cities where the number of students exceeds the number of local residents. You will find details of these in the book.

Institutions which for various reasons, such as not enough students or projected number of students, do not make the investment worthwhile or sustainable, have been discarded from the book.

Students typically reduce costs by sharing and minimising personal expenditure. Consequently, student houses can bring higher than average yields by maximising the available space. On a less rosy note, one must also take into consideration the responsibilities of renting to students, such as higher maintenance, furnishing costs, and increased wear and tear, when compared to renting to a professional couple, for example.

The location of the property will also be a deciding factor in your purchase. This will be not just on a national level, primarily chosen by you, but on a more local level which will be dictated by the campus location, access to local amenities, nearness to bus stops, etc.

All these issues will be addressed in detail throughout the book, showing you how to buy the perfect property and reap the benefits of student let property.

Chapter 1
Why Invest in the Student Market?

What's so good about student properties?

The first good thing is that the market will always be there! Secondly, if you play things right, you can achieve higher yields than if you were to let the house out as normal. For example, if I were to let out my three-bedroomed terraced house to a couple with two kids in the area of Withington/Didsbury in Manchester then my average gross income would be say £433 per contract month. However, if I were to let it out to students, I could convert the bottom reception/lounge and rent it out as a house with four bedrooms. For an average rent of £50 per week, I would receive £866 per month – basically *double*! This increased yield can be achieved with the commitment and correct attitude required to attract the right student for the right property.

What sort of profit can you expect?

In any property investment, I always apply the same rule of thumb. Here it is no different, I call it the **rule of ten**. It's very simple to remember when looking at properties. Simply calculate the annual rent and multiply it by ten – this gives you the purchase price. So if you see a three bed, two reception roomed house and you know the room rate is £60 per week then the calculation is:

$$4 \times £60 \times 52 \times 10 = £124,800$$

So if you see the house advertised for £110,000 then go for it! If it's advertising for £150,000 then forget it. Speak to letting agents or look in the local press for typical rental values for the area that you are looking at. This yield is also stated as a **payback period** – the length of time it would take to own the property if you reinvested all the income earned to replenish your savings. You would calculate it like this:

$$\frac{1}{\text{Gross yield}/100} = \text{payback period}$$

This equates to ten years. Ten % is a like-for-like comparison to a bank or building society rate. So if your bank is offering 4% you know that you can earn 2.5 times as much from investing in property. But this assumes that you have funded the whole property purchase out of your own funds. Usually this is not the case. When you borrow to finance the purchase the returns are significantly higher.

It's surprisingly easy to manage a property outside your area once the property is set up right. There are many areas that offer you a return of 10% or greater and student properties can do the same.

Sometimes for student rental, the **average** gross yield per year is calculated as:

$$\frac{(42 \text{ weeks} \times \text{room rate}) + (10 \text{ weeks} \times (\text{room rate}/2)) \times \text{number of bedrooms}}{\text{Property purchase price}}$$

As you can see, the average has been calculated by charging **half-rent** during the summer period. This is where the landlord will charge 50% rent during the summer to reserve the property for the start of the academic year and is more commonly known as a **retainer**. During this agreed period, you are not to let your property to anyone else as this counts as rent. For more information see Chapter 4 on legal issues.

The VarsityLets scheme offered by Bradford and Bingley guarantees full rent for the year, meaning that the yields are increased. How much in demand or desirable your property is will have a considerabe effect on this average, i.e. if my house has all the latest mod-cons, full speed internet access, large bedrooms, newly fitted bathroom and so on, then I would feel extremely confident in charging full rent 52 weeks of the year and can adjust profit and yield figures by +1 or 2%. If I have a squalid property with a hazard-prone shower unit and rusty old kitchen hobs, then I would expect it to be more desirable if I charged rent for term times only.

As an arbitrary example, we look at a three-bedroomed house[1] at a purchase price of £145,000 in Bristol. We can see the differences where average yield 1 is the formula used above and average yield 2 is full 52 weeks rent for such a property. If the standard room rate is £52 per week, then the figures come out as shown.

---

[1] A three-bedroomed property plus front reception converted to bedroom, equalling four bedrooms in total.

Median room rate	£52
Average yield 1	6.7%
Estimated annual profit 1	£1,296
Average yield 2	7.5%
Estimated annual profit 2	£2,128

In general, when looking through the listings in Chapter 5, the yield and profit given are considered as a calculated minimum/average and should be weighted roughly + 1 or 2% if the landlord decides, and has the capability of charging full rent for 52 weeks as demonstrated above.

The example, for Bristol, shows that the average expected yield range is between 6.7% for a three-bedroomed house, but could be as high as 7.5% if 52 weeks full rent is charged. In this example, I personally would choose not to invest in Bristol.

What about capital appreciation?

Capital appreciation is the amount the property rises in value over time. I never include the gains by capital appreciation in my calculation of yields because it is an unknown figure at the point you make the investment. If there was any certainty of the capital appreciation of a property then the purchase price of the property would include this gain. As there is a lot of uncertainty over capital appreciation because of the numerous variables involved it is very difficult to predict when house prices will rise. And remember the gain is only realised when you sell the property, and the difficult thing with any investment is knowing when to get out and sell.

I see capital appreciation as a bonus. I focus on the investment as it stands. If it makes money now it will almost certainly make you money in the future. If the property prices crash – who cares! You are still making money as the rent rises with inflation and the mortgage payment is still the same. If property prices increase again – great! You can realise that equity by remortgaging or by selling and buying further properties! This way there is no downside risk and only upside potential.

Admittedly there is a lot of money to be made in capital appreciation speculation, but it should be left to the professional property investors. They have the time to research the market and can stomach the loss if there is a property price crash.

Chapter 2
Finding the Right Property

What to look for when viewing a property

Do not believe the myth that a property is only worth buying if you could see yourself living there. The fact is you *aren't* going to live there. What you should ask is whether *students* would live here.

Matching the right property with your target group is of crucial importance. The image of three or four undernourished and impoverished students, willing to live in a shoebox for three years, is a stereotype that has disappeared with the last decade.

This does not mean that every student would like a penthouse suite with a jacuzzi; nor does it mean that the trusted old formula of a three-bedroomed house with a standard sofa, kitchen table, etc. would not be adequate.

What is important is asking yourself how a potential student buy-to-let purchase can be made as competitive as possible within its local setting. For example, if you know that the latest student developments offered by the university will have full access to hi-speed or broadband internet in every room, then you must provide at least the same.

The best way to find out the demand and suitability of property is to speak to both the university students' union and the university student housing office. I have found that this way, from one perspective you'll get ideas through the student representation and from the other, a more commercially focused response and suggestions.

When viewing a property check for:

Carpets	You have a legal duty to provide floor coverings. If there are no carpets then you will have to pay for new ones.
Kitchen	Is the kitchen big enough to accommodate a small dining table? This is attractive if there is only one reception room and it turns the kitchen into a kitchen diner.
Smallest bedroom	If the smallest bedroom is smaller than 6ft 6ins in any direction then it is not a bedroom! You need to be able to get a bed in a bedroom hence this room can only be considered as a study or a baby's room. You need to consider this when thinking about what type of tenant you are looking for – if you are looking for two professional people to share a two bedroomed flat then the second bedroom must be bigger than 6ft 6ins.
Bathroom	Is there a fitted shower? A bathroom is a lot more desirable if there is a power shower. If there are two bathrooms then the property is very desirable, even if it is only a shower room.
Heating	Is the heating system old? This can be costly to replace. If possible get it checked prior to purchase. It is your legal duty to provide heating and to issue a gas safety record.
Electrics	Are the electric sockets old? This will tell you that at some point the whole electric system will require rewiring.
Service charges	If it is a flat you will have to pay service charges. Ask the agent if they have any details of the service charges. Some places have exorbitant service charges that render the whole investment unprofitable. Avoid listed buildings as they have frequent redecoration policies that can be expensive.

If the property is in a reasonable condition then buy it. If demand is good there should be no problem letting it out as long as the property is in reasonable condition.

Furnished or not?

The normal procedure for students is to start searching for next year's room within a few months of starting their course. In the majority of cases, they devote a significant amount of time to finding that right house. In addition to factors such as location, price, etc., a key factor in attracting the right student for your property is how you furnish your house.

The answer to the furnished or not query is, almost definitely, a big yes! A more appropriate question would be *what are the necessary furnishings required to attract the right student?* You must remember that for students, this will probably be their first time searching for a house or room to rent and they will take a tacit interest in the furnishings and fittings upon viewing a house. The key is not to overload the house with junk-shop furnishings and rusty, worn out cookers or freezers. The higher the quality of the property and its fittings, the better chance you have of finding responsible students to look after your property.

These are some key questions that I have asked myself:

- Is the cooker safe and does it need replacing?
- What kind of settee can I get that will be reasonably priced but welcoming?
- What items does the student tenant expect to find in the house?
- Should I provide a television?

As there is a requirement to furnish student houses, similar questions should be an integral part of the way you approach the student market. Some key furnishings related to student accommodation include the following.

Kitchen appliances	In general, a fridge-freezer and cooker are always basic requirements. Often microwaves, washing machines, tumble dryers and to a lesser extent dishwashers are also provided.
	Again, you must remember that the product needs to attract the desired student tenant. For example, if you decide to purchase a washing machine, make sure that it is a durable, long-lasting machine intended for heavy usage. It's no good buying one that, despite being very cheap, could cause annoyances and headaches five months down the line.
	Microwaves tend to be a good buy as they add to the aesthetic appeal of the kitchen and can cost as little as £30 for a decent one.
	Another important yet often neglected aspect is the availability of workspace. You could have a kitchen with a new hob or dishwasher, yet no space to butter a slice of bread. This could get frustrating for the tenant and may mean they use your sparkling white new dishwasher or microwave as a cutting board for their Sunday roast!
Sofas/couches	With student properties, it could be that the front room reception gets converted into an extra bedroom, meaning that the second reception becomes a living-cum-dining room.
	A good sofa, one that looks appealing to the eye and is fairly comfortable, will suffice. An overly expensive leather sofa is not a necessity.
Bedding	If it is a small bedroom, then obviously you'll only have space to accommodate a single mattress. But if it is quite a large bedroom, try to get a double bed if your budget allows. A double bed will always look more appealing than a single bed, regardless of the tenant being a student or not, and the cost difference between the two isn't too much.

Television, Sky, digital	This is where it gets a bit tricky. Is it worth it and can I afford the expenditure? I recall that in my student days (which were ages ago!), a few of my friends had landlords that provided the set-up for the Sky or cable network and my friends just paid for the monthly billing. I'm a bit wary of installing Sky in student properties, but I know others who have done so and there hasn't been much of a problem for them to date. You should also consider that you might not always have a student tenant from July to September, so you may have to bear the brunt of the costs.
	TV sets are really cheap these days. If you feel that the prospective tenants you are looking for will look after the set, this will add to the attractiveness of your home.
Internet	This will undeniably make your house appealing to all students as computer and internet usage has become a mandatory part of university studying. Should you be able to incorporate a way of accessing the internet from every bedroom in the house, the marketing appeal of this will be a huge pulling factor.

Location

As the market swells with buy-to-let investors, you must choose the best area within your budget to ensure that the potential profitability of the location is worth your money, time and dedication. For example, in my humble opinion – and I am sure others would agree – there are very few spots in London that would generate enough yield to compensate for the huge initial investment for a student buy-to-let.

Just glancing at the yields calculated in the listings, the not-so profitable areas include Bristol, Cambridge, Liverpool and Oxford due to the low yields. As I said earlier, I see capital appreciation as a bonus. If it makes money now it will almost certainly make you money in the future. In areas like Liverpool, as buoyant as the student market is, the whole city is plagued with buy-to-lets. Rent prices cannot keep up with increased house prices and standstill or general reduction of rents is due to this saturation, producing relatively low yields. Despite this, if you can still pick up a bargain in a potential or existing student area, then go for it. If it means that with your purchase you can offer competitive rental rates and still make a profit, then it's worth a look.

By contrast, the University of Brighton and the University of Bournemouth have a lack of student housing available and the universities encourage landlords to register with them in order to let out to students. The general high house prices will deter those that cannot afford the huge initial outlay, but there are still some good returns on the right property, if it is within your reach.

When considering the location of the property, it may work to your disadvantage to go for something straightaway based on how cheap the properties are in a certain area. If that area is not in demand by the students, then it's not really worth the effort. Studies[2] have shown that 20% of the 700,000 student lettings offered by the traditional landlord sector in the UK are unfit for letting. You don't want to add your house to that by buying a block of houses in a run-down area or an area that is renowned not to be student friendly.

From my experience, the best areas are immediately next to or near the campus or university lecture halls, followed by houses on or near bus routes leading to the university and town centre. These houses tend to have better capital appreciation, followed by those that are maybe two to three miles away from campus.

[2] A news report on student housing, www.guardian.co.uk

Chapter 3
Finding the Right Student Tenant

Finding and attracting the right student tenant for your house depends primarily on two factors:

1. The property.
2. You!

The property

Getting the right tenant will be mainly determined by the type of property you have. A two-bedroomed city apartment may do the trick in attracting the affluent students but could put limitations on the competitiveness of the property in the student market.

What I have found to be most adaptable and suitable are two-bedroomed, three-bedroomed and four-bedroomed houses and in some cases, even a five-bedroomed or more house. My reasoning for this is simple – if I can't find students to let it out to, then I could just as likely let it out to a family who are looking for such a property to rent.

The most popular, it would be safe to say, is the three-bedroomed terraced house which becomes a four-bedroomed property once the living room or dining room gets converted into a bedroom.

You

When I heard the word 'students', I used to automatically have an image of three chain-smoking, beer-swilling layabouts who would never pay me the rent! How accurate or not I was in my generalisation is not important. What *is* important is how I want to run my property and what types of student tenants I want in there.

First and foremost, you have almost definitely bought this book as you are comfortable with letting your property out to predominantly 18–22 year olds.

Secondly, the kind of stereotype described above is in all honesty outdated and similar pictures could be painted of people from different walks of life!

Let's not ignore the fact that if you let out to students, then you must be comfortable with the idea that three, four, five or even 12 or more (!) students in one house will inevitably lead to more wear and tear. You may have to refit the kitchen and bathroom every three to five years and lay new carpets every two to three years. The washing machine will be subject to heavy use and will need upgrading regularly.

Finally, bearing in mind that there is no longer a one-size-fits-all way of life within the student market, you must have a good idea of what type of student you want as your tenant. In general, student rent fluctuations are pretty flat compared to residential and professional lettings and it is fair to assume that the standard prices of rooms vary from £40 to say £80 a week.

Advertising

The best way of advertising your property is by:

- using online accommodation websites directed at students;
- liasing with and providing your information through the university housing office;
- contacting and advertising your property through the Students' Union (a list of these is provided at the end of Chapter 7) and through the local newspapers.

Another more creative way of promoting your property is by sticking up information about it throughout the campus, but check to see if this is permissible with the university authorities first. Maybe the university library has a noticeboard or something similar whereby the students can take your contact details from a handy A4 piece of paper.

Every university has an accommodation office that will help students to find suitable privately rented accommodation. They also have other useful local information. The best way to find out how things work for each university area and private tenancy is to get in contact with the specific university's accommodation office and get more information. All contact details have been provided for each university.

Some universities offer an **affiliated landlord scheme**. What this means is that they will let out your property as a **university accredited** building – giving the student a sense of security. For you, this is a definite plus in obtaining a student tenant – but will also be at a cost or fixed fee. It does not necessarily mean that they will collect the rent for you, nor will they show the prospective tenant around the house. For these kinds of services, look at 'letting agents' below.

Every student union also has a housing officer who is equipped to deal with everything from unhappiness with the room offered to problems with rent and advice on contracts or other legal difficulties with private landlords.

Advertising in the local and university press

This is an effective way of advertising. It is best to advertise in a paper that is delivered free locally or is easily accessible to the student population. The main things you should include are:

- **Area**. You must state clearly where the property is situated. You don't want annoying calls asking where the property is exactly and having to regurgitate the same information. Similarly, students will probably make less effort to contact you if they don't know where the property is.
- **Furnished**. State what furnishings are included and mention important items like washing machine, dishwasher, hi-speed internet access availability, etc.
- **Number of bedrooms**. You must put the number of bedrooms the property has as then readers will know if your property can accommodate them.
- **Price**. You must put the price in any advert. I always quote my properties as weekly rent e.g. £80 per week. This way the tenant assumes that the rent is £320 per month (as they think there are four weeks in a month when there are actually 4.33 weeks in a month) when in fact it is £346 per *calendar* month. Your property will appear cheaper than other properties that are quoted per calendar month. If you price your property at £79 rather than £80 the impact is even more significant. You should also make clear what is included in your rent. For instance, some landlords include water rates or electricity bills, others don't.
- **Features**. If it's got a new bathroom then say so! Anything that is not standard in a property, like a garage, separate dining room, large garden or new carpets, will attract more interest.

■ **Telephone number**. Do not give your mobile number only! You will get fewer calls as everyone knows that a five-minute call to a mobile costs a small fortune, especially to the people you are trying to target. Put a landline as well as a mobile.

To find out about the local newspaper in the area of the property you have bought or are thinking about buying visit www.newspapersoc.org.uk.

Student websites

A number of landlords advertise their property through student websites, many of which are available in the listings relating to that particular town or city. This is great as all students these days access the internet and their first port of call may be browsing the web to see if anything comes up.

In addition to this, the students' union of each particular university may be able to give you a comprehensive guide of where to advertise, or may even provide information on how you can advertise through them or their website links. A list of students' unions has been provided at the end of Chapter 7.

Using a letting agent

Using a letting agent is quite a costly way to find a tenant. They usually charge one month's rent plus VAT. However, they will show prospective tenants round, run credit checks, ask for references, arrange a standing order and do an inventory check on the property. I would recommend this if you work or live far away from the property.

The Bradford and Bingley VarsityLets Scheme

The most prominent and latest initiative in student letting services is the Bradford and Bingley Marketplace, which has introduced the VarsityLets Scheme. The new scheme is specifically aimed at buy-to-lets for the student market. Launched in April 2004, it aims to assist would-be landlords in their quest to penetrate this healthy market.

VarsityLets is a specialist lettings agency operating a management service to look after all the needs of a landlord. It claims that rental yields are on average 2% higher than the usual letting market and offers a unique rent guarantee insurance product.

Part of the product, Varsity SecureLet, covers landlords on legal expenses and provides free rent guarantee. It will cover the landlord for 365 days a year and will retrieve unpaid rent.

Right student tenants? No student tenants!

Drop-out rates

Before you think you've found that perfect house with potential for great returns, a factor that is amazingly overlooked by naïve landlords is the drop-out rate for the university. If you have a university where a large number of the students don't finish their course, then you may suffer the headache of being left with an empty property for half of the year. Despite the fact that student rental yields are quite stable and prices do not vary much across the UK, you might find it impossible to find a tenant. With council tax, service charges and maintenance bills, you would end up with a negative return on your investment.

Middlesborough, for example, has been in the headlines due to it being a property hotspot. Terraced housing in the centre of town has gained considerable value over the past few years, with buy-to-let investors capitalising on this for refurbishment and letting out to students. On the plus side, Middlesborough has seen accelerated house prices and there are a great number of students there who are potential tenants. However, the university is in the process of building new multi-million-pound halls of residence to accommodate the projected number of students. Taking this into consideration, and accounting for the fact that Teesside University suffers from a 12% drop-out rate[1], the shiny prospect of student lets in Middlesborough loses some of its gloss.

Figures show that a considerable number of London universities experience a high drop-out rate, with the University of North London witnessing 29% of its students dropping out of their courses. In contrast, Imperial College has a low drop-out rate of 4%. In the North West, 23% did not finish their course at the Bolton Institute of Higher Education. In Wales, the University of Wales Lampeter has a high drop-out rate of 19%. In Scotland the University of Abertay Dundee also sees a 19% drop-out rate[1].

Can't find a tenant!

If things do turn sour and the area you have purchased in does see a significant increase of unforeseen drop-outs or other negative factors, then the following suggestions are some ways to tackle this.

---

[1] Higher Education Funding Council statistics for 2001, www.hefce.ac.uk

Action	Why?
Reduce the rent	If you're having problems renting it out, then maybe you're asking for too much for the student area. Look at rental prices offered by other student landlords and then review your rental demands. Think about reducing the rent; or if you are asking for a full year's rent, consider only charging a deposit for the summer weeks when the students aren't there.
Promote and advertise your property	If you haven't already done so, consider registering your property with a letting agent who may have better access to students and will take up a lot of the work for a fee. Advertise your property through the student newspapers if possible and post your property details around campus if permissible!
Widen the target group	If you are having problems letting to students due to a downturn of student applications/numbers, increased accommodation offered by the university or other related factors, then consider renting it out to professionals, families and other possible tenants[2].
Furnish the property	If you haven't already done this, then maybe a few basic additions will increase the marketability of your property. Maybe look into installing hi-speed internet access to the property as this is a huge pull to the student market.
Sell the property	This should be a last resort, as any decent property should be possible to let to students. Your property will probably be in demand as it is a student area, so you should find it quite easy to sell.

Void periods

As we are probably all aware, tenants come in all shapes and sizes regardless of the 'student' tag. You should try to make your property as widely appealing as possible in order to avoid it being rejected because of the pink and green striped wallpaper you took a fancy to.

The best advice is to follow the usual guidelines:

- go for neutral decoration
- minimise junk
- invest in high demand student areas
- and fully promote your property by using all advertising means possible.

For information on covering the void period during the summer break, i.e. between the academic timetables, see Chapter 1.

---

[2] See *The Buy-to-Let Bible* by Ajay Ahuja for more information on these types of lettings.

Should I credit-check the student tenants?

Let's assume everything's going well and you find yourself inundated with potential student tenants wanting to rent your property (!). You will naturally ask yourself whether they can keep up with rent payments and you're not going to end up tenantless halfway through the academic year.

You can check the credit of your tenant like a lender credit-checks a borrower. This costs between £17.50–£94 depending on what service you require. But we're going to have face some facts here. First, it is not very likely that university students will have much work history, so credit referencing them will be a waste of time and money.

Also, it is well documented that students are experiencing some tough times these days. With the ongoing debate on additional tuition fees, and uncertainty about the amount of money they or their parents will invest, there are not many viable ways to guarantee rent payment.

The best option is to get the student tenants to sign one tenancy agreement, whereby if one of the student tenants leaves, they will all be responsible for the full payment of the shortfall or for finding a new flatmate. You may also wish to ensure they provide a guarantor, someone who will be responsible for their deposit and potential dilapidations to your property.

The relationship between landlord and tenant

We've all heard of those horror stories where the student tenants have had an all night party, trashed the place and done some serious fire-damage to the property due to their inability to make toast. Then on the flipside, we've also been exposed to stories from student tenants on how a crazed landlord has refused to fix the front door despite several burglaries within a week!

These extreme cases should be taken with caution and the point is to not assume too much. Your tenant is not your friend, but nor is he or she out to make life hell for you! Well, here's hoping not.

Remember that you are in business with each other and that is the only reason why you know each other. For the relationship to last, the following simple contract needs to hold:

- you are supplying a safe property for the tenant to live in and the tenant is paying you the rent on time.

University accredited lettings

You should consider using the university lettings system if you are finding it tough to channel your energies into finding tenants. They will have better access to the students and with full respect to other landlords, they will be trusted a lot more. However, it is often tough getting your property registered with the university lettings system, as there is much demand to be on it. They also have strict controls and measures on what type of property they want, so this will make it tougher.

Chapter 4
Tax

Types of tax

For those who want to get into the detail then here's an 'everything you wanted to know about tax but were too afraid to ask' guide.

There are three types of tax that property is subject to:

1. **Income tax.** This tax is applied to the profit generated from the renting out of the property. It has to be paid every year in half-yearly instalments on 31 January and 31 July. Taxable profit is deemed to be:

   taxable rental income – allowable expenditure = taxable profit

   Taxable rental income and, more importantly, allowable expenditure will be defined in detail so that you can easily calculate and reduce your taxable profit by claiming all allowable expenditure.

2. **Capital gains tax.** This tax is only applied once the property has been sold. It is essentially the tax applied to the profit you have made from selling the property.

   Detailed below are certain reliefs that you can claim to minimise your capital gains tax bill to zero!

3. **Council tax.** If your property is to be rented by full-time students, they will be exempt from paying council tax. The students should obtain a certificate from the university to prove that they are full-time students, which can be used in correspondence with the local council. In addition to full-time students, foreign language assistants who have registered with the Central Bureau for Educational Visits and Exchanges are exempt. Also take note that if one or more of the dwellers is not a student, then the property becomes taxable.

   You should contact the local council for up-to-date information concerning this, as there are always some operational differences between councils.

Income tax

You will have to pay tax to the Inland Revenue on any income from letting out the property. You may include expenses such as fuel, insurance and maintenance costs required in letting the property to offset the rent income.

Also on offer, if you decide to live in the property you purchase (and this will have knock-on effects on issues such as council tax, student tenant rights, etc.), then under a government scheme, you do not have to pay tax on rent from a lodger in your home if the gross annual amount of rent is no higher than a specified amount. Please access the Inland Revenue website at www.inlandrevenue.gov.uk if you wish to find out what this current value is and for the latest information available. Information is also available at any post office or the university housing office.

You will only ever pay tax on your taxable profits, that is to say you have to make money before you pay tax. Income has to exceed expenditure – if you have not achieved this then you should not even be interested in this chapter. If you are in the position where income does exceed expenditure then read on.

The equation

The simple equation for calculating your income tax bill is:

taxable rental income – allowable expenditure = taxable profit

So in order for your taxable profit to be the lowest possible the **taxable rental income** must be minimised and the **allowable expenditure** must be maximised.

Minimising 'taxable rental income'

This is very difficult to do. Taxable rental income is deemed to be any rental income earned in the period, the period usually being the tax year 6 April XX to 5 April XY. 'Earned' means not only what the tenant has paid but also what the tenant owes even if it has not been paid yet.

Basically there are no tricks in reducing taxable rental income, apart from one – if a tenant is 14 days in arrears then you can consider that debt as a bad debt and not include this as taxable rental income. The reason you can do this is because you can file for eviction of your tenant if they fall 14 days behind. If the tenant does end up paying then you can include the income in the following accounting period. Fourteen days' outstanding rent is in real terms not that much and you'll have to pay tax on the income in the following year anyway. The only real benefit is cashflow. This is because you save slightly on your tax bill and defer payment on this omitted rental income until your next tax return the following year.

Maximising 'allowable expenditure'

This is easier to do than minimising rental income. This is because the Inland Revenue grants certain allowances based on certain definitions as well as allowable expenditure. This means expenditure and allowances can be deducted from the taxable rental income to derive the taxable profit. The two pure definitions that you need to remember for allowable expenditure and taxable allowances, as stated by the Inland Revenue, are:

1. Any costs you incur for the sole purposes of earning business profits.

2. Capital allowances on the cost of buying a capital asset, or a wear and tear allowance for furnished lettings.

1. Any costs you incur for the sole purposes of earning business profits

Any expense you incur 'wholly, necessarily and exclusively' for the business is fully deductible from your rental income. Any personal expenditure that you make that relates to the business is partly tax deductible from your income. To make sure you include all expenses that are allowable against your rental income, refer to the following checklist of expenses for inclusion in your tax return.

	Expense	Description
Fully tax deductible	Repairs and maintenance	All repairs and maintenance costs are fully tax deductible. Where the property has been altered so extensively that it is deemed to have been reconstructed, the property is then considered to be modified rather than repaired, hence no amount of the expense is allowed. The only amount allowed would be the estimated cost of maintenance or repair made unnecessary by the modification. Examples of repairs and maintenance expenditure that are fully tax deductible are: • painting and decoration • damp treatment • roof repairs • repairs to goods supplied with the property, e.g. washing machine.
	Finance charges	Any interest you pay on a loan that you took out to acquire a property is fully tax deductible. It is only the interest and not the capital repayment part that is tax deductible. If any of the finance raised (the loan) is used for personal use, such as a holiday, then the interest paid on the cost of the holiday is not tax deductible.

Expense	Description
Finance charges	The typical interest payments that are allowed are: • Interest on the mortgage taken out to get the property. • Interest on any secured or unsecured loans taken out to get the property. Arrangement fees charged by a lender are also tax deductible. Interest paid on the car you use to run the property business is partly tax deductible – see below.
Legal and professional fees	Allowable expenditures are: • Letting agent's fees for the collection of rent including the VAT (unless you are VAT registered). • Legal fees for evicting tenants. • Accountancy fees for preparing your accounts. Disallowable expenditures are: • Surveyor's fees initially paid out to value the property (unless the survey was unsuccessful and you never acquired the property, in which case it is a fully deductible expense). • Legal fees incurred due to the purchase of the property. These expenses are added to the purchase price. When it comes to calculating the capital gain when you sell the property: gain = selling price – purchase price This results in the purchase price being higher than the actual price paid due to the addition of initial professional fees. So the taxable gain is lower. These fees are subject to full indexation, as is the purchase price, to allow for price inflation (see capital gains section below). So you do get some tax relief but only further down the line, when you sell the property.
Council tax, electricity, water and gas	If you are renting out all the rooms then all the usual running costs involved with a property are fully tax deductible. This assumes that none of the tenants make a contribution to the bills. If you let out your property inclusive of all the bills then you can fully charge all the bills you include with the rent. If you let out your property exclusive of all bills (which is the usual way) then you cannot claim. Remember, you can only claim the expense if you actually paid it!
Insurances	• Buildings insurance • contents insurance • rental guarantee insurance are fully tax deductible. Life assurance premiums are not as this is personal expenditure. Car insurance is, but only partly – see below.
Advertising	Any advertising costs in connection with finding a tenant or selling your property are fully tax deductible. This includes: • newspaper adverts • agent's commission.
Ground rent	This is the rent you pay if you own a leasehold flat, typically a nominal amount of £50 per annum.

	Expense	Description
	Service charges	Service charges are incurred if you own a leasehold flat. If you pay these charges then they are fully tax deductible.
	Letting agent's fees	Any fee that is charged by a letting agent is fully tax deductible, apart from any fees charged for leases created for longer than a year. If a fee is charged for creating a five-year lease then only one-fifth of the fee can be charged for each year.
	Stationery	Any stationery costs incurred in connection with running your property business are fully tax deductible. This will include items such as: • all paper and envelopes • postage • all printing expenditure.
Partly tax deductible	Motor expenses	Motor costs are allowable but only when your car is used in connection with the property business. It is up to you to decide how much time you think you spend using your car for private use and business use. It has to be reasonable. Once you have decided on the split of personal to business, say 70% personal 30% business, then you can charge the business percentage against your taxable rental income, in this case 30%. Typical motor expenses are: • car insurance • petrol • servicing and repairs • interest paid on the loan taken out to acquire the car. A fraction of the purchase price of the car can also be taken into account as an allowance – see below. I charge 80% of my motor expenses to the business. This is because I have 43 properties to maintain around the country and I spend 80% of my driving time on business engagements.
	Telephone calls	Again this is like motor expenses. If you spend 30% of your time on the phone in connection with your business then charge 30% of: • total landline call charges • total line rental for your landline • total mobile call charges • total line rental for your mobile. If there are obvious large private calls (say in excess of £5) then exclude these from the total call expense when calculating the 30% charge. If you have a fax line then charge 100% of fax expenses as it is difficult to convince the Inland Revenue that you own a fax machine for personal use!

Again this is not an exhaustive list. To make sure you legally maximise your allowable taxable expenditure you have to remember the following two principles:

- Include expenditure if it is 'wholly, necessarily and exclusively' needed for the business. If it is, include it. If it is not, exclude it or partly include it.
- Include a proportional amount of expenditure that is split between business and personal such as motor expenses and telephone calls.

2. Capital allowances on the cost of buying a capital asset, or a wear and tear allowance for furnished lettings

This basically means that you can either charge:

- 25% of the cost of any asset used to furnish the property, or
- 10% of the rent

as a tax-deductible expense. You cannot do both. I would always recommend doing the latter, charging 10% of the rent, because once you opt to do one or the other, you cannot change for the duration of your business. The reason I recommend 10% of the rent is because it is likely to be greater than 25% of the cost of the asset. If this is not the case now it will probably be in the future. It is better to suffer the lower deductible expense now for the benefit in the future.

You can still claim capital allowances for any asset that you use in the business, such as motor vehicles, but they will be restricted to the business element only. So in the example above of the motor vehicle with 30% business use, a car used in the business costing £5,000 would attract the following relief:

$$30\% \times 25\% \times £5,000 = £375$$

You can never charge the cost of an item that you intend to use for longer than one year against your rental income. Anything purchased for the use of longer than one year is deemed to be an asset and only 25% of the cost can be charged each year.

Capital gains tax

This tax only arises when you sell the property. The capital gain is worked out as:

$$\text{sale price} - \text{purchase price} = \text{capital gain}$$

The sale price is deemed to be the price achieved after deducting estate agents' costs, solicitors' fees and any other expenses that were incurred wholly, necessarily and exclusively in the sale of the property.

The purchase price is the cost of the property plus all survey and legal costs.

How to reduce your capital gain

The calculation

The way to reduce your capital gain is to understand the **capital gain calculation**. If you dispose of a property the following calculation will be made to work out your capital gain:

	Sale price		£125,000
Minus	Allowable costs		£100,000
	Purchase price	£80,000	
	(a) Incidental costs of purchase	£2,000	
	(b) Home improvements	£15,000	
	(c) Costs of establishing or defending title	£1,000	
	(d) Selling costs	£2,000	
Equals	Chargeable gain		£25,000

The sale price and the purchase price are fixed. You cannot change what you sold the property for or what you paid for it.

Allowable costs

To reduce your capital gain you have to maximise the other allowable costs. Let's look at the other allowable costs and what you can include. The following is adapted from the Inland Revenue.

Allowable costs	What you can include
(a) Incidental costs of purchase	• Fees, commission or remuneration paid for professional advice • the costs of transferring the property • stamp duty • the costs of advertising to find a seller • the costs of any valuations needed to work out your chargeable gain (but not the costs of resolving any disagreement with the Inland Revenue about your valuations).
(b) Home improvements	These are costs which: • you incurred for the purpose of enhancing the value of the property, and • are still reflected in the state or nature of the property at the date of its disposal. You may not claim the cost of normal maintenance and repairs.
(c) Costs of establishing or defending title	• Fees, commission or remuneration paid for professional advice.
(d) Selling costs	• Fees, commission or remuneration paid for professional advice • the costs of transferring the property • the costs of advertising to find a buyer • the costs of any valuations needed to work out your chargeable gain (but not the costs of resolving any disagreement with the Inland Revenue about your valuations).

So in a nutshell you can include:

- solicitors' costs
- accountancy fees
- mortgage brokers' fees
- redemption penalties on cleared mortgages
- stamp duty
- advertising
- estate agents' fees
- valuations needed to calculate your gain
- any improvements that still remain in the property
- legal costs in defending your title to the property.

So the first part of reducing your capital gain is to include *all* costs involved with the purchase, ownership period and sale of the property that fall within the definitions stated by the Inland Revenue. But it doesn't stop here! You can gain further relief on the gain. Read on.

Taper relief

You can reduce your calculated gain by up to 40%. Look at this table:

Number of whole years the property has been owned	Gain remaining chargeable (%)
Less than 1	100
1	100
2	100
3	95
4	90
5	85
6	80
7	75
8	70
9	65
10 or more	60

The longer you have owned the property the less gain you have to pay. So as the table above shows, after three complete years of ownership you start to attract taper relief. After ten years or more you attract the maximum amount of relief where only 60% of the gain is chargeable or, in other words, a 40% discount on the gain chargeable.

Please note that it has to be complete years. So another way to reduce your capital gain is, if possible, to stall your purchase to capture another year. Look at this example.

Harry has found a buyer for his investment property which he has owned for five years 11 months. The capital gain on the sale is £100,000. If he sells straightaway, then (see table above) 85% of the gain is chargeable, as he is deemed to have owned the asset for five complete years, equating to £85,000. However, if he stalls the sale for one month then he is deemed to have owned the asset for six complete years, so looking at the table only 80% of the gain is chargeable equating to £80,000. This method only works for assets being sold that have been owned for two to nine years. Otherwise it makes no difference.

Personal allowance

You can still reduce your gain further. Everybody gets a capital gains tax allowance of £7,900 per tax year, rising year on year with inflation. So if you have a gain of £10,000 then it is reduced by £7,900 to £2,100.

If you are selling a couple of properties, if you can, straddle the sales either side of the 5 April end of the tax year. This way you can apply your capital gains allowance for the tax year prior to 5 April on one of the properties and your capital gains allowance for the tax year after 5 April for the other property. This way you can make full use of your yearly allowances.

Principal place of residence (PPR)
There is one final trick – **principal place of residence.**

Your own personal residence is not liable for capital gains tax so any gain you make is all yours. If part of your strategy is to let out your home and move into another home, and you sell it within three years of leaving your home, then there is no tax to pay! If you sell after the three years then you still get relief for three years. Let's look at this example.

Roger lives in a house that has been his personal place of residence for eight years, when he bought it, but decides to move out and rent it out. If he sells two years after he rented it out there is no tax to pay. If he sells it five years later then only:

$$(5-3)/13 \text{ of the gain is chargeable.}$$

The equation being:

$$(\text{amount of years rented} - 3 \text{ years})/\text{period of ownership}$$

Parents buying property

More and more parents are realising that buying property for their sons or daughters whilst at university has become a shrewd investment. The obvious benefit is their offspring not having to pay rent for the property, as their housemates will most probably cover the mortgage payments with their rent. If the offspring has to make a contribution, then it isn't seen as 'dead money' as it will be helping to pay off the mortgage whereby the property will end up in the hands of the parent landlord, or even with the offspring themselves. Alternatively, once the university days are over, the parents anticipate selling off the property at a healthy profit and their kids will leave university with a smaller debt hanging over their heads.

If as a parent you are considering making the purchase, then make sure you put the property deeds into your offspring's name and not yours. This perfectly legal trick means that you will not be liable for capital gains tax. This is assuming you have a good relationship with your kids and the other student tenants won't cause problems with overdue rent, property damage, etc. To keep on the safe side, it would be best if you kept a proper tenancy agreement.

SIPP and FURBS

You may have heard of these terms in connection with properties and pensions. Let me explain their relevance to this subject.

SIPP

This stands for **self invested personal pension**. The reason why it is mentioned is that you can buy *commercial* property within this pension and enjoy all the tax breaks a normal pension has. The reason why a SIPP is not applicable in this situation is because we are investing in *residential* property. Residential property is not allowed under the SIPP scheme.

Commercial property is not as attractive as residential property, the reasons being:

- The yields are lower.
- Borrowing is restricted to 70% loan to value.
- Business risk is doubled – your are reliant on your tenant's business to trade well out of your property as well as the normal risks associated with owning the commercial property itself.

This is my own personal opinion. You may think that commercial property is for you. If you do get into this game I would seriously consider investing in commercial property under this umbrella of a SIPP as the shelter to tax is quite significant.

FURBS

This stands for a **funded unapproved retirement benefit scheme**. Its main beneficiaries are the higher rate tax payers only. So if you're not a higher rate tax payer and don't expect to be one then ignore this bit.

If you buy a residential property under this umbrella then:

- Profits from the scheme are taxed at 22% rather than 40% if you are a higher rate tax payer.
- Capital gains tax is 34% in comparison to 40%. A FURBS also attracts the normal taper relief explained above.

- You can pass a FURBS down to your family. There is no inheritance tax to pay when passed on after death as opposed to being subject to the normal inheritance tax limits (currently £259,000). A traditional pension fund is not passable down.
- There is no limit on the contributions to a FURBS but you do not get any tax relief on your contributions.
- The whole of the fund can be withdrawn tax free compared to a traditional pension fund being restricted to 25%.
- Retirement can be even after the age of 75. Traditional pension funds are restricted to age 75.

The two key things you need to consider when deciding whether to invest in property using a FURBS are:

1. You can only access the money at retirement. If you want to retire prior to normal retirement age it's not possible under this scheme. FURBS restricts your freedom. Once you invest your money in a FURBS you can't get at it till retirement.
2. There are administration costs. You have to use an accountant and the accounting for such a scheme has to be spot on.

Personally I like the freedom that I have. Maybe when I'm over 45 and FURBS are still about then I will consider one. I think if your target earning is more than £50,000 p.a. profit from property, you don't require any of this £50,000+ p.a. to live on today and you're aged over 45, then a FURBS may be for you. Seek professional advice.

Chapter 5
Security and Legal Issues

As a student let landlord, you have responsibilities and legal requirements to adhere to. This chapter deals with general guidelines and legal aspects that you should be aware of. Like any dealings with tenants, be they student or professionals, landlords face three broad categories:

- **contractual**
- **regulatory**
- **all-encompassing**[1].

Contractual requirements

This refers to the legal contracts that you must sign and adhere to if you wish to do business. You are expected to fulfil your legal obligations as outlined by the terms of the contract. Breach of terms could ultimately result in legal proceedings against you. As a landlord, you will enter into legal contracts with your lender, the tenant, the insurers and, possibly, the lettings agents.

Contracts with the lender

Prior to entering into a contract with a lender they have to know about you. The lender asks you a number of questions and expects the truth. If they find that you have misled then by any of your answers to their questions, they can demand repayment of the loan in full plus all recovery costs. They can also inform the police and charge you with obtaining finance by deception. This is fraud and you can go to prison.

Once the lender has established that you are a person worth lending to, you will have to sign their contract. As the lender has lent money to you it is their right to set the terms of the contract. Unless you are borrowing a large sum of money then you can never include any clauses in the contract based on your terms – that's just the way it is. The key terms of the contract are:

---

[1] Please review *Lawpacks Residential Lettings Guide* for more in-depth discussion.

- **Payment.** You have to pay the mortgage repayments on the dates the lender dictates. If you fail to do so the lender can repossess the property.
- **Maintenance.** You must keep the property in a good state of repair fit to be habitable.
- **Occupation.** You must not leave the property vacant for more than 30 days.

Contracts with the tenant

Several legal documents may be created in relation to your tenant:

1. An **inventory**.
2. An **Assured Shorthold Tenancy Agreement**.
3. An **eviction order**.

1. An inventory

An inventory is a list of all items that are in the property – it includes descriptions of items, quantities and condition. This list should be signed by both the tenant and the landlord. When the tenant decides to leave the property you can check the list to find out what is left in the property. If there are any omissions from the list you can charge the tenant to replace them. So, for example, if there were four dining chairs when the tenant moved in and now there are only three, you can deduct the cost of replacing the dining chair from the tenant's deposit.

If you get an inventory done it will ensure that the tenant thinks that you care about the place you are letting and they will be less likely to damage the property. If the condition of the carpet is recorded then they are more likely to remove any stains made by them as they will fear that you will deduct cleaning costs from their deposit.

Professional inventory services can be found in the *Yellow Pages* or by visiting www.yell.com.

2. An Assured Shorthold Tenancy (AST) Agreement

An Assured Shorthold Tenancy Agreement is the most common type of contract with a tenant. These can be made for a specific period of time, such as one academic year, but they are not usually made for a period of less than six months.

You should ask the students who are sharing the house to sign a **joint tenancy** or a **separate tenancy**. If they sign a joint tenancy they will all be responsible for each other's debts and damages. If they have their own contract and there are any discrepancies, the argument is between yourself and the individual student and should not involve the other students.

This AST agreement between the landlord and tenant binds both parties to certain duties and obligations. The main features of a tenancy agreement are:

- **Rent**. How much rent to be paid and the frequency of payment.
- **Duration**. An AST is for a minimum of six months and maximum of 12 months.
- **Running expenses**. It sets out who is liable for the running expenses of the property.
- **Tenant's obligations**. It details the tenant's obligations to the property and the landlord, such as maintenance, not to sublet, informing the landlord of problems in good time, and reporting damage.
- **Landlord's obligations**. It details the landlord's obligations to the property and the tenant, such as privacy and timeliness of repairs.

Both the tenant and the landlord have to sign, with both signatures witnessed by an independent third party.

Visit www.lawpack.co.uk for further information and links to obtain a ready-drafted AST. You can also obtain more information on legal matters and obligations by visiting www.landlordlaw.co.uk, run by specialist solicitor and Lawpack author Tessa Sanderson.

3. An eviction order

If you want to evict the student tenant(s) from your house then a legal process must be complied with before they can be evicted. This will include written notice and applying to the court for a possession order. If you evict the tenants without following the correct procedures you will be committing a criminal offence.

It would be advisable to try to get one tenancy agreement, whereby if one student leaves they will all be responsible for the full payment of the shortfall or finding a new flatmate.

A landlord must have a 'ground' for eviction and serve the proper notice on the tenant before any court action is started.

A landlord can evict a tenant and serve a Notice of Intention to Seek Possession (Section 8). A landlord can serve this notice and give a minimum of two weeks' notice to the tenant for the following main reasons:

1. The tenant is 14 days in arrears.
2. Repeatedly late rent payment (even if the tenant is not in arrears at the time the notice is served).
3. Any breach of the AST.
4. Annoyance to neighbours.
5. It is found that the tenant has given false information to obtain the tenancy.

A landlord can serve this notice and give a minimum of two months' notice to the tenant for the following main reasons:

1. You wish to reside in the property.
2. Mortgagees wish to repossess.

You can download eviction notices from our download section at www.propertyhotspots.net.

If the tenant doesn't leave then:

1. File copies of the notices sent to the tenant with the court. Sue for all rent arrears, legal costs and court fees.
2. Wait for 14 days' for the tenant to reply.
3. If no response is made (which is likely) then a possession order is made giving 14 days' notice.
4. If the tenant doesn't leave then call the police to evict them as they are now in your property unlawfully.

We have to face a reality here though. This procedure will take a long time, give you stress and you can potentially lose up to six months' rent. If you include court fees, solicitors' costs and the threat of damage to your property the whole eviction process could cost you in excess of £3,000. If you want the tenant out of your property and they have ignored all your notices then offer to pay them to leave. This option could be cheaper. I would suggest one month's rent as fair. This will pay the deposit for their next property.

Try to initiate a friendly separation. Do not add fuel to an already fiery situation by losing your temper and threatening immediate court action. Statistically only 2% of tenants tend to be bad ones – bad tenants being those who have no *intention* of paying the rent, not tenants who lose their job and can't pay their rent. If a tenant loses their job they are more than likely going to get another. If they have been relatively good payers of the rent then be patient with them.

In my experience I would say that the 2% statistic is right. The majority of people wish to settle in a home and feel secure. The best way for them to feel secure is to pay their rent on time.

Contracts with an insurer

You will have to enter legal contracts with insurance companies to cover you against certain risks. Your insurance will only ever be valid if you have originally told the truth on your proposal form when obtaining the insurance. The main insurances you will take out when investing in property will be:

- **Buildings insurance**. The insurance you pay to cover the property against fire, vandalism, water damage or weather damage.
- **Contents insurance**. This is insurance for items such as carpets, furniture and other fittings that you have provided for the property.
- **Rental guarantee**. Insurance against your tenant defaulting on the rental payments.
- **Emergency assistance**. This insurance will cover the costs of any emergency repairs that have to be carried out, including all call out charges.

When filling out the form they will ask you about previous claims. If you have any previous claims then reveal them. If you do have to make a claim and you have not told them about a previous claim then they do not have to pay out. It is very easy for them to find out if you have had a claim as they have a central register of all claims paid out.

If you do lie and they catch you out you will find it difficult to get insurance in the future, as you may be put on a blacklist which is accessible to all insurers.

Contracts with letting agents

If you do decide to use a letting agent then you have to read their terms and conditions very carefully. Watch for:

- **Timeliness of payment**. Check to see how soon the letting agent has to hand over the money once it has been received from the tenant. I would not accept any period longer than three days.
- **Get-out clauses**. Check to see how easy it is to get out if you decide to no longer use the letting agent One agent tried to sue me for all the lost commission he would have earned even though I was now collecting the rent! If you have an idea of using a letting agent at first and then taking over in six months then inform the letting agent of this intention. You may be able to strike a deal where you have a realistically priced option to get out of the contract.

Regulatory requirements

I may have rattled on about how to best negotiate business with student tenants, but you should take note of the fact that there are, and rightly should be, stringent measures which will help to protect them.

Houses in multiple occupation (HMOs)

If you live in a shared house and you are not related to the each other, your home is likely to be termed as a **house in multiple occupation** or **HMO**. Because of the extra demands of sharing a house, HMOs are subject to additional controlling features.

The much talked about Housing Bill, which at the time of writing is in the House of Lords, will go some way to make things a bit more rigorous for a would-be landlord. New measures will make sure that landlords become registered and aim to clean up the market by weeding out the rogue landlords who are giving some students an unpleasant experience.

As part of the new bill, landlords with properties of three or more storeys and five or more people will have to be properly licensed. Despite this being welcomed by student union representatives throughout the country, it is fair to say that they are disappointed that the definition of an HMO does not include or cover all student properties. The National Union of Students (NUS) claims that:

> *More than half of students living in privately rented accommodation do not live in properties of three or more storeys and five or more people. This means that hundreds of thousands of students will not be covered by the new legislation and will remain at risk.*

The key points of managing a HMO, which haven't been addressed elsewhere, are these.

- **Property management**. The repair, maintenance and cleanliness needed for the wellbeing of the tenants and clearing any fire hazards before the students move in. A means of water supply and drainage and other hygiene factors such as provision of waste disposal arrangements. Also, the name of the landlord or the manager should be clearly displayed within the house.
- **Fire safety**. Using all means necessary to reduce the risk of a fire hazard. Fitting fire detectors and smoke alarms is a good move. You may also wish to provide a fire extinguisher, but should contact the

university welfare office or the council before doing so for advice on what types are best. The council have a duty in helping you with fire safety, so you should get into contact with them for further advice. For more issues on fire safety, see below.

- **Furniture**. This is mainly to do with getting a written inventory and fire safety issues.
- **Provision of amenities**. Cookers, sinks, washbasins, toilets. The government is to publish a leaflet on a national code of guidance, which will be available at some point in 2004/2005.
- **Size of bedrooms**. The standard is an old one and is unlikely to be of much concern today; a room of only 70 sq ft, for example, is deemed large enough for one adult occupant and 110 sq ft for two.
- **Gas and electrical safety**. These are looked at below.
- **Registration scheme**. As outlined earlier.

Other points that are considered and should not be treated lightly by potential landlords are nuisances (e.g. damp) and vermin (rats, mice, cockroaches, etc).

To seek further detailed information, please access the NUS website at www.nusonline.co.uk.

Besides the HMO regulations, there are three main regulations governing the general renting of properties:

1. Gas safety.
2. Electrical safety.
3. Fire resistance.

1. Gas safety

By law, you will be regulated and responsible for making sure gas appliances (boilers, cookers, heaters) and pipe work are maintained in good order. You are required to carry out annual gas safety inspections using a CORGI registered engineer. The engineer will inspect:

- the central heating boiler
- oven and hob
- gas fire
- gas meters.

It cannot be stated strongly enough that such a simple task as ensuring safety for your tenants is in the best interests of everyone.

2. Electrical safety

All electrical appliances should be tested and have either a label on each piece of equipment or a certificate listing all the appliances that have been tested. Many landlords hold a NICEIC certificate, which proves that the property has had an electrical check within the last five years. Although this is recommended, it is not a legal requirement.

So it's quite obvious – keep the number of electrical items to a minimum! The fewer electrical items you supply the less is likely to go wrong. This limits the reasons why your tenant can ring you up telling you about a problem. You don't need your tenant ringing you up at 6am complaining about the kettle not working. An inspection will cover you against being sued if any electrical appliance were to harm your tenants or their guests.

3. Fire resistance

Fire issues should be one of the most important considerations for you as a landlord. The law is strict in this area and the old adage of it's better to be safe than sorry certainly applies here. You must install smoke alarms and only use fire-retardant mattresses and furniture.

Furnishings

In January 1997 the final phase of the Furniture and Furnishings (Fire Safety) Regulations 1988 came into force. All upholstered furniture supplied as part of the tenancy must comply with the fire and safety regulations. Broadly, this means that both coverings and fillings should pass ignition resistance tests. Telling whether or not items of furniture meet the standards is not easy but check any labels in the cushioning. It is now standard that any furniture purchased after 1990 will automatically comply with all fire regulations. Carpets, curtains and duvets are not covered by the regulations.

All-encompassing requirements

You will also be legally bound by the normal all-encompassing laws of the land. These include:

1. The law of tort: negligence and personal injury.
2. Criminal law.

Everyone is bound by the above two laws, not only property investors.

1. The law of tort

Even though you may have all the safety records in place you still owe a duty of care to your tenant and anyone who enters your property. If it can be shown that you were negligent in any way then you could be sued and ordered to pay damages. As a landlord you are liable for any damages if all of these conditions are satisfied:

i) your tenant or anyone entering your investment property suffers an injury and

ii) you owed a duty of care to the person entering your investment property who suffered the personal injury and

iii) you breached that duty of care.

So for example if Zak, the landlord, failed to fix the cooker socket in the kitchen and the tenant's guest, Liz, suffered an electric shock burn then Zak would be liable to compensate Liz for her injury. This is because:

i) Liz suffered injury.

ii) Zak owed a duty of care as it is realistically to be expected that a tenant would invite a guest into their property.

iii) Zak breached that duty of care as he did not fix the socket when asked to by the tenant.

2. Criminal law

Threatening your tenant or being violent to them because they haven't paid you any rent have no justification in the eyes of the law and are deemed criminal offences.

If the landlord interferes with the tenant's peace or comfort with unannounced visits, does not fulfil his or her responsibilities for basic repairs, or disconnects utility supplies, etc. this may amount to harassment – which is also a criminal offence.

Also, you should give prior warning of at least 24 hours to the tenant if you wish to enter the property to carry out legitimate maintenance checks and repairs.

Investing in property can sometimes challenge your ability to remain calm and situations can become quite heated. You have to be a responsible person and realise that if you want to take investing in property seriously then you have to act lawfully in every way.

TV licences

Just so it's clear, if the tenants bring a television into the rented property, then *they* are wholly responsible for paying the TV licence. However, if you supply a TV with the property, then you *share* responsibility with the tenant for ensuring that there is a TV licence. So in order to avoid a hefty fine, either:

- Don't provide a television.
- Do provide one and on the lease agreement make it clear that the tenant is responsible for the TV licence.
- Buy an annual licence and add the cost to the rent or service charges, but make sure that they are aware of this.

I usually opt for the second choice and let them sort out the TV licence.

The house requires only one licence as long as the tenants have a joint tenancy agreement. However, if the tenants have separate agreements with you, then they will need separate licences.

Deposits and holdings

You should ask for a deposit as security in case any of your tenants damage the property or furnishings. It can also be used to cover unpaid bills, rent or missing items. Most landlords will ask for a sum equivalent to four weeks' or a calendar month's rent but the maximum a landlord can charge by law is two months of the annual rent payable. The deposit should be refunded normally within 28 days after the student has left the property, assuming there are no problems with the condition of the house or its furnishings. This is another good reason why it's good to complete a full inventory prior to the signing of any agreement. Remember that as part of the AST agreement the tenant must take due care of the property and its furnishings and this should give you confidence when exchanging documents.

As with most deposits, the tenant may lose any holding deposit (forming part of the normal deposit) and may not be refunded if they decide to withdraw before the contract begins.

Tenancy deposit scheme (TDS)

The government has in principle agreed to put forward a **tenancy deposit scheme (TDS)** to be brought in to ensure that students and landlords are properly protected. Students pay the money they owe for any necessary reparations and landlords release deposit money that students paid when they moved in.

The scheme looks set to act to protect deposits through the housing bill. When and if it comes into effect is another matter.

Retainers

If you are to hold the property for the student tenants until the beginning of the academic year, then a retainer could form part of the contract. This means that the prospective tenant is assured that the property will not be leased out to anyone prior to his or her arrival. You may wish to use the time to redecorate or undertake maintenance work. The normal retainer figure is half-rent charged as per normal for the duration.

A retainer counts as rent, and confers certain rights and obligations. If you charge a summer retainer, the property must be habitable and it is important to stress that you may not let the rooms to other people, as it is illegal to charge rent twice. It is normal to allow students certain rights to the property if a retainer has been paid, such as occasional use (by prior arrangement) and storage facilities.

Checklist

Ask around	You've read this book so far – great! Now you have a good knowledge of how to go about purchasing a student buy-to-let property. However, you should do other important research in that particular student area you intend to invest in (see next chapter). Ask the lettings agents what the demand is like; speak to the students' union or university accommodation office and see what they say; read around the local and university press to see what the latest reports are.
Check property dimensions	With the Housing Bill set to affect thousands of student homes, make sure your property is habitable. There's no point in buying a house that states three bedrooms but with one being the size of a cupboard. The best properties are those with lots of rooms of fairly equal size because nobody wants the box room. Also, two reception rooms are considerably better than one long reception room as you can convert it to a bedroom and improve yields.
Do your sums	If the going rate around the area is £50 per week, and you have to charge £65 a week to make any profit, you should ask yourself if it's worth it. Assess your sums both short-term and long-term. You cannot always be assured of a full 12 months rent, so take that into account.
Find the best buy-to-let mortgage	The best way to do this is to speak to a broker. Feel free to contact my broker on 01708 443334. Mention my name to get a discount on the fees.

Furnishings	It's good to furnish the place, but remember not to fill your house with junk or old items from a charity shop that could be a potential fire hazard, e.g. old cushioning that isn't fire resistant. The higher the quality of the products, the more desirable they are, the more you can justifiably charge for rent.
Safety checks	Follow the guidelines as outlined in the legal section and get more in-depth information from the local council if you are unsure of anything.
Timing	Students tend to look for their new homes just after the Christmas holidays, so make sure the property you are to buy is let-worthy around this period.

Chapter 6
Lenders in the Student Rental Market

Most lenders do not like the properties they lend on to be let to students. However, the following lenders understand the student rental market and are happy to lend:

Bradford & Bingley
www.bradford-bingley.co.uk

Chelsea Building Society
www.chelseabs.com

Paragon
www.paragon-mortgages.co.uk

Shepshed
www.theshepshed.co.uk

Harpenden
www.harpenden-bs.co.uk

1st Buy-to-Let Mortgages
www.1st-buy-to-let-mortgages.co.uk

Bank of Scotland
www.bankofscotland.co.uk

Mortgage Express
www.mortgage-express.co.uk

Mortgage Trust
www.mortgagetrust.co.uk

Promise Finance
www.promisefinance.co.uk

The Money Centre
www.themoneycentre.net

Dunfermline Building Society
www.dunfermline-bs.co.uk

Chapter 7
University Cities and Towns

This reference section is divided into two parts:

1. University cities and towns in the UK
2. Universities in the London area.

Key to the guide

Note 1
★ Average yield A (full year's rent) = (52 weeks × room rate × number of bedrooms)/entry price.

Average yield B (42 weeks + summer rent e.g. half-rent or retainer) = (42 weeks × room rate × number of bedrooms) + (10 weeks × (room rate/2) × number of bedrooms)/entry price

Average yield C (42 weeks' full rent only) = (42 weeks × room rate × number of bedrooms)/entry price

Note 2
★★ This includes a weekly rent for catered, non-catered, en-suite, full en-suite, flatlets, on-campus and university owned accommodation near campus. Please note, prices should be taken as a rough guide.

Note 3
★★★ The entry price for property is given for areas where there is a large concentration of students or student communities already present. Lower/higher-valued property may be available in other areas not related to existing student areas.

Yield and profit

The yield and profit given are considered as a calculated minimum/calculated average and should be weighted roughly + 1% if the landlord decides to charge full rent for 52 weeks.

For example, for Bristol, the average expected yield range is between 6.2–6.7%, but could be as high as 7.5% if 52 weeks' full rent is charged:

Bristol

Campus room rental**	Minimum £40			Maximum £90
Yield range	6.2–6.7%			
Type of property	3 bed house (i.e. 2 bed upstairs + 1 converted other)	4 bed house	5 bed house	6 or more bed house
Entry price	£120,000	£145,000	£200,000	£230,000
Median room rate	£53	£52	£53	£55
Average yield B*	6.2%	6.7%	6.2%	6.7%
B – Estimated annual profit	£579	£1,296	£964	£2,058
Financial scores	Capital growth (out of 5) 3		Yield (out of 5) 2.5	Total (out of 10) 5.5

Note 4

After accessing websites and information sources, I have decided not to gather information for these colleges:

Cumbria Institute of the Arts, Dartington College of Arts, Falmouth College of Arts, Ravensbourne College, Rose Bruford College and Writtle College.

In each case this is for at least one of the following reasons:

- Not enough student numbers in the locality of the area/town to consider it as a student community.
- House prices too high compared to low ratio of student numbers to even consider the area.
- Most students live at home/are from student area/no information on renting.

Main sources used

Student Accommodation UK: www.accommodationforstudents.com

Geohive United Kingdom: www.geohive.com

HESA Institution Tables: www.hesa.ac.uk

UK Student Campus Accommodation: www.bunk.com

The National Directory of Estate Agents: www.ukpropertyshop.co.uk

UpMyStreet Classifieds: www.upmystreet.com

Unofficial-guides.com: www.unofficial-guides.com

Universities in Britain and Ireland: www.student-accom.com

Estate agents in the UK: www.estateangels.co.uk

Student Accommodation UK: www.student-accommodation-uk.co.uk

Association of Residential Letting Agents: www.arla.co.uk

University Cities and
Towns in the UK

Aberdeen

Universities	University of Aberdeen, Robert Gordon University
Population	226,940

	Student population	Undergraduate	Postgraduate	Total
	University of Aberdeen	10260	3405	13665
	Robert Gordon University	8840	3010	11850
	Total	19100	6415	25515
	Campus capacity	3300	700	4000
	Size of market	15800	5715	21515

Drop-out rates	University of Aberdeen	14%
	Robert Gordon University	13%

Student areas	Bridge of Don, City centre, Old Aberdeen, Woodside

Accommodation officer contacts

University	Tel	Address	Web	Landlord accreditation scheme?
University of Aberdeen	01224 273502	Accommodation Office, Central Refectory, Elphinstone Road, Aberdeen AB24 2TU	www.abdn.ac.uk	No
Robert Gordon University	01224 262140	Student Accommodation Service, Robert Gordon University, Schoolhill, Aberdeen AB10 1FR	www.rgu.ac.uk	No

Planned development for city	Aberdeen council has initiated work for the city's new £120m bypass, but locals opposed the construction. As part of a £90m city growth fund, outlined in 2003, to provide assistance for economic and social development over the next three years, £11.5m of government money will be going to Aberdeen.
Planned development for universities	University of Aberdeen Ranking among the premiership of the top 20 universities in the UK, it is also an active participant in the economic, industrial and cultural life of north east Scotland. In partnership with local research institutes, and through developing specialist centres, Aberdeen is acknowledged to be at the leading edge of research in many fields. Teacher training initiatives at the University are set to be revolutionised thanks to a £1.8m cash award from the Scottish Executive and The Hunter Foundation (THF).
	Robert Gordon University Late summer 2003 saw the start of building work on a new sports centre for The Robert Gordon University at its Garthdee campus in

	Aberdeen. The facilities, costing £10 million, will be a major asset for the University, local community and the north east of Scotland. Facilities include a 25-metre swimming pool, a dramatic climbing wall that will traverse through three floors, a main hall for indoor hockey, badminton, tennis, five-a-side football, basketball, cricket and volleyball, and an activity hall for fencing, judo, karate, aerobics, dance, yoga and table-tennis.			
Campus room rental**	Minimum £45		Maximum £90	
Yield range	10.9–13.3%			
Type of property	3 bed house (i.e. 2 bed upstairs + 1 converted other)	4 bed house	5 bed house	6 or more bed house
Entry price Median room rate Average yield B* B – Estimated annual profit	£55,000 £52 13.3% £3,389	£80,000 £55 13% £4,672	£100,000 £54 12.7% £5,652	£135,000 £52 10.9% £5,657
Financial scores	Capital growth (out of 5) 3	Yield (out of 5) 5	Total (out of 10) 8	
Description	Aberdeen is 103 miles from Edinburgh and 410 miles from London. It has plenty to offer in terms of pubs, clubs and shopping. There are two cinemas and several theatres. The beautiful sandy beaches close to the city are very popular for student beach parties during the summer. There are also the joys of Seaton Park, in which there is ample room to undertake sporting activities.			
Websites to advertise on	Local and national student listings: www.student-accom.com City information for students: www.accommodationforstudents.com Easy roommate: http://uk.easyroommate.com Link to Aberdeen listings online: www.letting-in-scotland.co.uk Letting agents: www.ledingham-chalmers.co.uk Student listings: www.studentpad.co.uk			

Estate agents	Address	Tel	Web
Burnside Kemp Fraser	48, Queens Rd, Aberdeen, Aberdeenshire AB15 4YE	01224 327500	www.burnside-kemp-fraser.co.uk
Clark and Wallace	33 Holburn Street, Aberdeen, Aberdeenshire AB10 6BS	01224 571704	www.clark-wallace.co.uk

Estate agents	Address	Tel	Web
Esslemont and Cameron	16 Holburn Street, Aberdeen, Aberdeenshire AB10 6BT	01224 212142	www.esslemont andcameron.com
Gray and Connochie	6 Alford Place, Aberdeen, Aberdeeenshire AB10 1YD	01224 649101	www.gray connochie.co.uk

Letting agents	Address	Tel	Web
Cohen and Co	1 St Swithin Row, Aberdeen, Aberdeenshire AB10 6DL	01224 582266	www.cohen-co.com
Iain Smith and Company	18–20 Queens Road, Aberdeen, Aberdeenshire AB15 4ZT	01224 645454	www.iainsmith.com
James and George Collie	12 Holburn Street, Aberdeen, Aberdeenshire AB10 1TL	01224 572777	www.jgcollie.co.uk
Kay and Co	9 Queens Gardens, Aberdeen, Aberdeenshire AB15 4YD	01224 561165	www.kayandco.com
Ledingham Chalmers	220 Union Street, Aberdeen, Aberdeenshire AB10 1TL	01224 632500	www.ledingham chalmers.com

Bangor

University	University of Wales, Bangor			
Population	20,000			
	Student population	Undergraduate 7430	Postgraduate 1825	Total 9255
	Campus capacity	2200	300	2500
	Size of market	5230	1525	6755
Drop-out rates	10%			
Student areas	Centre, Hyrail			

University	Accommodation officer contacts			
	Tel	Address	Web	Landlord accreditation scheme?
University of Wales, Bangor	01248 382032	Residential Services, University of Wales, Bangor, Bryn Haul, Victoria Drive, Bangor LL57 2EN	www.bangor.ac.uk	Yes

Planned development for city	Marks & Spencer is to open in Bangor and will, according to the developers, bring more shoppers into the region. It will also create around 50 new jobs when the new store opens in spring 2005. M&S are building the store in the proposed new Wellfield shopping centre. Developers Cathco said this move by a major high street retailer and the size of the Wellfield scheme would have a marked impact on retailing in north west Wales. The new store will occupy the first phase of the £25m redevelopment of the city's main shopping area.

Planned development for university	A major new cancer research laboratory, financed by £3.5 million of private and public funding, has been officially opened at the University of Wales, Bangor. The North West Cancer Research Fund Institute at the University's School of Biological Sciences will conduct fundamental research into the causes of cancer, and will make a significant contribution to cancer research in the UK.
	
	    A £10m world-class management centre is to be set up by Bangor University. The university's business school hopes the new centre will make a major contribution to the economy of north Wales by providing management courses to local business people.
	
	    A European Objective One grant of more than £5m will contribute to the development.

Campus room rental**	Minimum £40	Maximum £65
Yield range	6.6–7%	

Type of property	3 bed house (i.e. 2 bed upstairs + 1 converted other)	4 bed house	5 bed house	6 or more bed house
Entry price	£89,000	£120,000	£135,000	£170,000
Median room rate	£42	£42	£40	£41
Average yield B*	6.7%	6.6%	7%	6.8%
B – Estimated annual profit	£733	£917	£1,445	£1,600

Financial scores	Capital growth (out of 5)	Yield (out of 5)	Total (out of 10)
	2.5	3	5.5

Description	The city of Bangor lies just between the Menai Straits and the foot of the Snowdonia National Park. It has easy access from the A55 expressway, which makes it just 45 minutes from the major motorway networks. Bangor depends heavily on the University, which was founded in 1884, and during college term the city has a population of around 20,000. The city has two shopping centres and a good mix of local and national chain stores.
	Bangor is in a beautiful area, sandwiched between the sea and the mountains. The city itself is small. For places with more to offer, Chester and Liverpool are also quite close and many students head this way at the weekends. There are a couple of clubs in town and some good pubs.

Websites to advertise on	Local and national student listings: www.student-accom.com City information for students: www.accommodationforstudents.com Easy roommate: http://uk.easyroommate.com Student room lets: www.letalife.com Professionals and student lettings: www.professionalaccommodation.com/Bangor.asp

Estate agents	Address	Tel	Web
Dafydd Hardy Estate Agents	21 Bangor Street, Caernarfon, Gwynedd LL55 1AR	01286 677774	www.dafyddhardy.com
Reeds Rains	Stevenson House Wellfield, Bangor, Gwynedd LL57 1EF	01248 352323	
Carter Jonas North Wales	The Estate Office, Port Penrhyn, Bangor, Gwynedd LL57 4HN	01248 362536	www.carterjonas.co.uk
Bob Parry and Co Ltd	116 High Street, Bangor, Gwynedd LL57 1NS	01248 351475	www.bobparry.co.uk

Letting agents	Address	Tel	Web
W Owen	314 High Street, Bangor, Gwynedd LL57 1YA	01248 353357	
Warriners	372 High Street, Bangor, Gwynedd LL57 1YE	01248 354002	www.warriners.co.uk
Swetenhams	204 High Street, Bangor, Gwynedd LL57 1YA	01248 355333	www.sequence home.co.uk
Jones Peckover	129 High Street, Bangor, Gwynedd LL57 1NT	01248 362524	www.jonespeckover.com
Dafydd Hardy Estate Agents	18 Garth Road, Bangor, Gwynedd LL57 1ED	01248 371212	www.dafyddhardy.com

Bath

Universities	University of Bath, Bath Spa University College
Population	169,045

	Student population	Undergraduate	Postgraduate	Total
	University of Bath	9575	4180	13755
	Bath Spa University College	3490	1215	4705
	Total	13065	5395	18460
	Campus capacity	3150	600	3750
	Size of market	9915	4795	14710

Drop-out rates	University of Bath 5%
	Bath Spa University College 17%

Student areas	Engliscombe, Larkhall, Newbridge, Odd Down, Oldfield Park, Twerton, Victoria Park, Weston, Widcombe Hill

	Accommodation officer contacts			
University	**Tel**	**Address**	**Web**	**Landlord accreditation scheme?**
University of Bath	01225 383111	Accommodation Office, University of Bath, Bath BA2 7AY	www.bath.ac.uk/ accommodation	Yes
Bath Spa University College	01225 875843	Accommodation Office, Bath Spa University College, Newton Park Campus, Newton St Loe, Bath BA2 9BN	www.bathspa.ac.uk	Yes

Planned development for city	The ongoing development of Bath Spa has been the local talk for the last few years, but continuous hitches have delayed the original opening date of the £19m project, now estimated to cost £35m.
	The completion date – originally set for Autumn 2002 – has been put back several times. The spa project is funded in part by an £8m Millennium Commission grant. There remains no projected opening date.

Planned development for universities	University of Bath
	The University has been getting some mention in the national press for its footballing achievements over the past few years and intends becoming a Regional Centre for Sporting Excellence. Some new off-campus accommodation was recently built to accommodate students.
	An award of £13m has been given to the partnership between the Universities of Bath and Bristol to encourage enterprise and work with industry. It is the largest award the DTI's Higher Education Innovation Fund (HEIF) has ever made.
	The University's Department of Pharmacy and Pharmacology has been awarded a £4.16m grant to develop new drugs to tackle illnesses including cancer and diabetes.

| | A new £2m physics laboratory will place the University at the centre of nanotechnology research according to the university. Also, the University of Bath's Maths Department has been awarded a £1m grant to fund studies. |
| | Bath Spa University College
A new auditorium, music venue and a new set of halls of residence are planned. These will be between Bath and the Newton Park site and will probably be single room type corridor halls rather than flats.
    Bath Spa University College is celebrating after the award of substantial funds from the HEIF to support its work with business and the wider community. The multi-million pound award to Bath Spa University College will enable it to develop its work with creative industries. |

Campus room rental**	Minimum		Maximum	
	£42		£75	

Yield range				

Type of property	3 bed house (i.e. 2 bed upstairs + 1 converted other)	4 bed house	5 bed house	6 or more bed house
Entry price***	£110,000	£150,000	£200,000	£210,000
Median room rate	£64	£62	£65	£62
Average yield B*	8.2%	7.8%	7.6%	8.3%
B – Estimated annual profit	£2,270	£2,575	£3,220	£4,538

Financial scores	Capital growth (out of 5)	Yield (out of 5)	Total (out of 10)
	3	3	6

Description	Bath is a beautiful place to live, but it is also a lively student city with plenty of places to go and things to do. There is an excellent range of shops, music and culture to suit all tastes. There is a range of student accommodation available in Bath. Students can choose from halls of residence, self-catering flats and apartments, lodgings, house shares, and renting houses and flats. Bath is one of the most beautiful cities in England with some stunning architecture. There are a number of museums and cultural spots to discover. The town has all the shops you need and a fair selection of decent bars and restaurants.
Websites to advertise on	Local and national student listings: www.student-accom.com City information for students: www.accommodationforstudents.com Easy roommate: http://uk.easyroommate.com Link to student lets: www.letalife.com Bath classifieds: www.bathfocus.com

Estate agents	Address	Tel	Web
Allen and Harris	Bath Office, Bath, Avon BA1 2ED	01225 425111	www.sequence home.co.uk
Andrews Estate Agents	43 Newbridge Road, Bath, Avon BA1 3HF	01225 339622	www.andrewsonline. co.uk
Savills	Edgar House, 17 George Street, Bath, Avon BA1 2EN	01225 474500	www.savills.co.uk
Cobb Farr	35 Brock Street Circus, Bath, Avon BA1 2LN	01225 333332	www.cobbfarr.com
Letting agents	Address	Tel	Web
Connells Estate Agents	1 Wood Street, Queen Square, Bath, Avon BA1 2JQ	01225 336522	www.connells.co.uk
County Properties	4 The Street, Radstock, Bath, Avon BA3 3PL	01761 433566	www.teamprop.co.uk
Bradford & Bingley Marketplace Ltd	4 Princes Buildings, George Street, Bath, Avon BA1 2ED	01225 447966	www.bbg.co.uk
Palmer Snell	5 Fairfield Road, Fairfield Park, Bath, Avon BA1 6EP	01225 335566	www.palmersnell.co.uk
Halifax Property Services	8 Bridge Street, Bath, Avon BA2 4AS	01225 465805	www.halifax.co.uk

Belfast

Universities	Queen's University Belfast, St Mary's University College, Stranmillis University College, University of Ulster
Population	277,170

Student population	Undergraduate	Postgraduate	Total
Queen's University Belfast	17755	5215	22975
St Mary's University College	960	175	1135
Stranmillis University College	1200	190	1390
University of Ulster	19020	6035	25055
Total	38935	11615	50555
Campus capacity	4165	735	4900
Size of market	34770	10880	45655

Drop-out rates		
Queen's University Belfast		8%
St Mary's University College		4%
Stranmillis University College		6%
University of Ulster		12%

Student areas	Bostock, Botanic, Cregagh, Off Lisburn Road, Stranmillis, Ormeau

Accommodation officer contacts

University	Tel	Address	Web	Landlord accreditation scheme?
Queen's University Belfast	028 9027 3077	Student Accommodation, Queen's University, Belfast, Northern Ireland BT7 1NN	www.qub.ac.uk/	No
St Mary's University College	028 9032 7678	191 Falls Road, Belfast, Northern Ireland BT12 6FE	www.stmarys-belfast.ac.uk	No
Stranmillis University College	028 9038 4350	Refectory Building, Belfast, Northern Ireland BT9 5DY	www.stran-ni. ac.uk/	No
University of Ulster	028 7032 4665	Accommodation Office, University of Ulster, Cromore Road, Coleraine BT52 1SA	www.ulst.ac.uk	No

Planned development for city	A shopping centre in the heart of Belfast is in the process of being turned into one of Europe's biggest shopping developments. The £300m Victoria Square complex will consist of 500,000 sq ft of retail space with a hotel, health club and restaurant.

	A north Belfast housing action group is launching plans for an urban village in the city's dockland area. The St Patrick's and St Joseph's Housing Committee wants to inject new life into the Sailortown area, with a mix of social housing, schools and businesses. It wants to reflect the highly commended developments of the Liverpool Docklands. A new £30m hotel and apartment complex is also being planned for south Belfast. The new complex will offer a hotel with 144 bedrooms, more than 100 apartments and will include shops, restaurants, a gym and car parking.
Planned development for universities	Queen's University Belfast Queen's University Belfast was recently given a donation from Sir Anthony O'Reilly of £4m that will ensure a new world-class library project can proceed. The construction of a new state-of-the art library will be completed in 2008, the 100th anniversary of Queen's establishment as a university in its own right. The library will ensure that Queen's will have world-class facilities to continue to provide the highest standard of education to its 24,000 students and maintain its position as one of the leading civic universities in the United Kingdom. The new library will become a central hub of the University and, as more and more people engage in lifelong learning, it will take into account the needs of an increasingly diverse range of users, providing research and teaching facilities for part-time and full-time students, the local community and businesses. The total cost of the project is over £40m. The fund-raising campaign has been spearheaded by the Queen's University Foundation, and all the money has come from private funding.
	St Mary's University College In the mid to late 1990s, a major of programme of building and refurbishment was undertaken. The College now has a new library, Learning Resource Centre, Science Department, Technology and Design Department and Physical Education Centre. In addition, the existing buildings have been refurbished to the highest standard.
	Stranmillis University College No more than a 20-minute walk from the city centre, Stranmillis College was founded in 1922 to provide state-funded teacher training in Northern Ireland. Today the College is a multi-professional institution, no longer engaged solely in the education of teachers. It offers pre-service and in-service courses, for undergraduates and postgraduates.
	University of Ulster The University of Ulster has joined forces with Dundalk Institute of Technology and Dream Ireland to drive forward the Midas Project, a new £1.4m initiative aimed at developing a 'digital corridor' for Ireland's eastern seaboard. The project hopes to create the necessary infrastructure and supports to allow for the growth of small and medium creative and digital media enterprises in the region. The University yesterday recently opened a Nanotechnology Research Institute at its Jordanstown campus. The £8m research institute will

	position Northern Ireland at the forefront of nanotechnology research in the UK, and will be a catalyst for the future growth in the bio technology, medical devices and textile industrial sectors. In 2003 the University of Ulster opened a new £8m student housing development at Duncreggan, Londonderry. Built on land acquired from Foyle and Londonderry College, the 398 bedspaces provided at Duncreggan will bring the University's total student bedspace provision in the city to 630.			
Campus room rental**	Minimum £41		Maximum £70	
Yield range	8.7–14.4%			
Type of property	3 bed house (i.e. 2 bed upstairs + 1 converted other)	4 bed house	5 bed house	6 or more bed house
Entry price Median room rate Average yield B* B – Estimated annual profit	£45,000 £43 13.5% £2,826	£55,000 £42 14.4% £3,842	£85,000 £38 10.5% £3,319	£130,000 £40 8.7% £3,174
Financial scores	Capital growth (out of 5) 5	Yield (out of 5) 4	Total (out of 10) 9	
Description	Belfast is gradually shedding its troubled image and embracing the future. Its 300,000 residents are described as honest, cheerful, friendly and well mannered. The famous 'Golden Mile' is home to pubs, clubs, restaurants and entertainment venues, where you can find something to suit every student's pocket and tastes! The surrounding countryside is within easy reach, offering the chance to climb mountains, visit the ancient Lakeland and admire the Atlantic surf. Students can choose from halls of residence, self-catering flats and apartments, lodgings, rooms in private houses, and house or flat shares.			
Websites to advertise on	Local and national student listings: www.student-accom.com City information for students: www.accommodationforstudents.com Letting agents listings: www.pastures-new.co.uk University of Ulster Accommodation Services: www.ulst.ac.uk/accommodation Queens Student Accommodation links: www.qub.ac.uk/sacc			

Estate agents	Address	Tel	Web
Allen and Harris	326 Upper Newtownards Road, Belfast, County Antrim BT4 3EX	028 90471516	www.allenand harris.co.uk

▶

Estate agents	Address	Tel	Web
Eric Cairns	151 Stranmills Road, Belfast, County Antrim BT9 5AJ	028 90668888	www.ericcairns.co.uk
Wylie Property – Belfast	149–151 Victoria Street, Belfast, County Antrim BT1 4PE	028 90324465	www.wylie-property.co.uk
Steve Hewlett Associates	461 Ormeau Road, Belfast, County Antrim BT7 3GR	028 90222003	www.stevehewlett.com

Letting agents	Address	Tel	Web
Halifax Property Services	41 Arthur Street, Belfast, County Antrim BT1 4GB	028 90230211	www.halifax.co.uk
Morrow and Co	1 Clarence Street, Belfast, County Antrim BT2 8DY	028 90238993	www.morrowandco.co.uk
Nexus Property Rentals	7, Stranmillis Rd, Belfast County Antrim BT9 5AF	028 9066 4199	www.nexusproperty rentals.com
Philip Johnston and Co	54 Belmont Road, Belfast, County Antrim BT4 2AN	028 90655555	www.philipjohnston.co.uk
Ulster Property Sales – Lisburn Rd	589 Lisburn Road, Belfast, County Antrim BT9 7GS	028 90661929	www.propertynews.com

Birmingham

Universities	Aston University, University of Birmingham, University of Central England, Newman College of Higher Education
Population	977,091

	Student population	Undergraduate	Postgraduate	Total
	Aston University	5420	2165	7590
	University of Birmingham	20255	11300	31550
	University of Central England	18575	3955	22530
	Newman College of Higher Education	1855	225	2080
	Total	46105	17645	63750
	Campus capacity	8739	1397	10136
	Size of market	37366	16248	53614

Drop-out rates	Aston University	9%
	University of Birmingham	8%
	University of Central England	12%
	Newman College of Higher Education	8%

Student areas	Acocks Green, Aston, Balsall Heath, Bearwood, Bournville, City centre, Edgbaston, Erdington, Hall Green, Handsworth, Handsworth Wood, Harborne, Kings Heath, Kingstanding, Ladywood Moseley, Selly Oak, Weoley Castle, West Bromwich

Accommodation officer contacts

University	Tel	Address	Web	Landlord accreditation scheme?
Aston University	0121 359 3611	Accommodation Office, Aston University, Aston Triangle, Birmingham B4 7ET	d.lacey@aston.ac.uk www.aston.ac.uk/ accommodation	No
University of Birmingham	0121 414 6237	Housing Services, Birmingham University, Edgbaston, Birmingham B15 2TT	ugradaccom@ bham.ac.uk www.housing. bham.ac.uk	No
University of Central England	0121 331 5191	Accommodation Office, Franchise Street, Perry Barr, Birmingham B42 2SU	accommodation@ uce.ac.uk www.uce.ac.uk/ accommodation	No
Newman College of Higher Education	0121 476 1181	Newman College, Genners Lane, Bartley Green, Birmingham B32 3NT	c.reid@newman. ac.uk www.newman. ac.uk	No

Planned development for city	The £500m Bullring shopping complex finally re-opened in 2003 after some years of refurbishment and construction. It boasts more than 140 shops and kiosks and is expected to attract tens of millions of visitors over the next year. Despite losing out to Liverpool for the Culture Capital 2008, the city has done well to improve its image and will make further improvements in order to attract more visitors and investment.
Planned development for universities	Aston University Spring 2003 saw building work beginning on Aston University's new £10m Aston Academy of Life Sciences (AALS). The Aston Academy of Life Sciences will be a unique facility for biomedical research, which will build on Aston's excellently rated Neurosciences Research Institute (NRI). The project is funded by HEFCE's Science Research Investment Fund (SRIF).
	University of Birmingham £100 million has been committed to a master plan for the development and improvement of student accommodation. In addition, the programme of capital and infrastructure developments on campus will continue to gather pace, with £41m allocated in the financial year 2004/05. These include new buildings for the Schools of Sports and Exercise Studies; the Medical School's Nuclear Magnetic Resonance Spectrometer building; and new lecture theatres and IT clusters. £4.5m will be invested in new posts in academic schools at the University, building on the current financial year's spend of £3.4 million on the largest recruitment drive ever undertaken. The University of Birmingham announced has also secured over £6.2m of new funding under the second round of the Higher Education Infrastructure Funding (HEIF2) awards. The money will expand the University's considerable existing track record in successfully transferring academic knowledge into real business and industry.
	University of Central England UCE has been awarded £3m by the government HEFCE in recognition of the excellent work it is doing in supporting businesses based in the West Midlands.
	Newman College of Higher Education As a small higher education institution Newman provides a friendly community. Class sizes are small and lecturers are able to give students greater individual support. Newman's history and reputation for teacher training also mean that graduates leave with a degree from the University of Leicester.
Campus room rental:	Minimum Maximum £43 £100
Yield range	4.7–8.7%

Type of property	3 bed house (i.e. 2 bed upstairs + 1 converted other)	4 bed house	5 bed house	6 or more bed house
Entry price****	£90,000	£115,000	£200,000	£270,000
Median room rate	£50	£53	£50	£45
Average yield B*	7.8%	8.7%	5.9%	4.7%
B – Estimated annual profit	£1,590	£2,797	£400	-£1,998

Financial scores	Capital growth (out of 5)	Yield (out of 5)	Total (out of 10)
	2.5	4	6.5

Description	Famous for its curry houses, the city has been consistently criticised over the years but massive funding into the arts and the developments in the city centre are helping. Thankfully, the redevelopment is now paying off and some of the concrete monstrosities have been replaced by new, modern, glass structures.
	The University of Birmingham campus is so vast that it has its own ring road. Its centre is the Chamberlain clock tower, nicknamed Old Joe, which honours Joseph Chamberlain.
	Aston University is situated in the centre of Birmingham city centre so there's no need to want for anything socially. Birmingham is known for its multicultural appeal and there is plenty for everyone to do.
	Shops, cinemas, theatres and music venues abound in the city, in addition to the wide array of pubs. There is also no shortage of top quality day trips nearby, including the exciting Cadburys World! The National Exhibition Centre is not far away.

Websites to advertise on	Birmingham quality rentals: www.campbellproperty.co.uk Local and national student listings: www.student-accom.com City information for students: www.accommodationforstudents.com Private rented accommodation in the Midlands: www.midlandslandlords.co.uk Student lettings for the Birmingham area: www.studenthomes.net

Estate agents	Address	Tel	Web
Burchell Edwards	1 York Road, Erdington, Birmingham B23 6TE	0121 373 6320	www.burchell edwards.com
Savills	Caxton House, 1 Fore Street, Birmingham B2 5ER	0121 633 3733	www.savills.co.uk
Halifax Property Services	156 High Street, Harborne, Birmingham B17 9PN	0121 4262740	www.halifax.co.uk

Estate agents	Address	Tel	Web
Rice Estates	9 Oak Tree Lane, Selly Oak, Birmingham B29 6JE	0121 415 5213	www.riceestates.com

Letting agents	Address	Tel	Web
Quality Lettings	505 Bristol Road, Selly Oak, Birmingham B29 6AU	0121 472 1728	http://quality-lettings.co.uk
Accord Sales & Lettings	4 Brindley Place, Birmingham B1 2JB	0121 643 9505	www.accord-lets.co.uk
Birmingham Property Letting	Harborne, Birmingham B17	0121 458 7512	www.birmingham propertyletting.co.uk
Nicholas George Property	22 St Agnes Road, Moseley, Birmingham B13 9PW	0121 442 2049	www.nicholas george.co.uk
Britannia Property Services	521 Bristol Road, Selly Oak, Birmingham B29 6AU	0121 472 2200	www.britannia propertyservices.com

Bolton

University	Bolton Institute
Population	261,035

	Student population	Undergraduate	Postgraduate	Total
		5820	1340	7160
	Campus capacity	700	–	700
	Size of market	5120	1340	6460

Drop-out rates	23%
Student areas	Great Lever, Haulgh

Accommodation officer contacts

University	Tel	Address	Web	Landlord accreditation scheme?
Bolton Institute	01204 903484	Residential Services, BIHE, Deane Road, Bolton BL3 5AB	www.bolton.ac.uk	Yes

Planned development for city	A key strategy launched in December 2002 by Bolton Council is the community focused 'Clear Vison. Bright Future' programme, which aims to regenerate the local communities and to improve the quality of life of the citizens. This is defined as the plan for the Borough of Bolton from 2003 to 2012. To view the key aims and priorities in more detail, please access the Council website on www.bolton.gov.uk.
Planned development for university	Although its roots date from 1824, Bolton Institute was founded in its present form in 1982. It felt it had narrowly missed gaining university status in 1992 along with the polytechnics. However, in January 2005 it became the University of Bolton. It is expected that the university status will strengthen its reputation in research and development and support plans to expand enterprise activity. It should support and improve upon the Institute's international standing and forge new partnerships around the world.

Campus room rental:	Minimum		Maximum	
	£53		£53	

Yield range	6.9–8.4%			
Type of property	3 bed house (i.e. 2 bed upstairs + 1 converted other)	4 bed house	5 bed house	6 or more bed house
Entry price****	£55,000	£65,000	£90,000	£135,000
Median room rate	£35	£35	£39	£38
Average yield B*	9%	10.1%	10.2%	7.9%
B – Estimated annual profit	£1,473	£2,339	£3,465	£2,496

Financial scores	Capital growth (out of 5) 3.5	Yield (out of 5) 4	Total (out of 10) 7.5
Description	Bolton is a friendly, lively town with enough shops, sights and amenities to suit any student's tastes and needs. It has excellent motorway and rail links to the beautiful surrounding countryside and to Manchester and Liverpool – ideal for a night out. It has a proud industrial and economic heritage but looks to the future with a new lease of life.		
Websites to advertise on	Local and national student listings: www.student-accom.com City information for students: www.accommodationforstudents.com Easy roommate: http://uk.easyroommate.com Bolton Evening News, Bolton Classifieds: www.thisisbolton.co.uk National search engine: www.upmystreet.com Lancashire property links: www.thisislancashire.co.uk		

Estate agents	Address	Tel	Web
Weale & Hitchen	6 The Hillock, Harwood, Bolton BL2 3HP	01204 302150	www.weale-hitchen.co.uk
Rayson Wilshaw	9 Blackburn Road, Edgeworth, Bolton BL7 0BA	01204 883636	www.rayson wilshaw.co.uk
Bradford & Bingley	85 Bradshawgate, Bolton Lancashire BL1 1QQ	01204 523038	www.bbg.co.uk
JG Independent	211 Darwen Road, Bromley Cross, Bolton BL7 9BS	01204 598888	www.jgindependent. co.uk

Letting agents	Address	Tel	Web
Whitegates Estate Agency	24 Market Street, Westhoughton, Bolton BL5 3AN	01204 399388	www.white gates.co.uk
Regency Estates	34 Lee Lane, Horwich, Bolton BL6 7AE	01204 695919	www.regency estates.co.uk
Aston Estates	356 Chorley Old Road, Heaton, Bolton BL1 6AG	01204 491216	www.astonestates.com
T & S Crowley	13 Lee Lane, Horwich, Bolton BL6 7BP	01204 699077	www.tandscrowley estates.co.uk
Halifax Property Services	47 Bradshawgate, Bolton, Lancashire BL1 1DR	01204 531761	www.halifax.co.uk

Bournemouth

University	Bournemouth University
Population	153,441

	Student population	Undergraduate	Postgraduate	Total
		12500	2415	14915
	Campus capacity	1800	250	2050
	Size of market	10700	2165	12865

Drop-out rates	11%
Student areas	Charminster, Ensbury Park, near centre, Springbourne, Winton

Accommodation officer contacts

University	Tel	Address	Web	Landlord accreditation scheme?
Bournemouth University	01202 5953 85/8/9	Accommodation Office, Talbot House, Fern Barrow, Poole BH12 5BB	www. bournemouth.ac.uk	No

Planned development for city	There are plans to expand the Bournemouth International Centre (BIC). The council hope the multi-million pound plan will mean the centre can attract more high-profile entertainment artists. The intention is to create more than 1,000 jobs and attract an extra 250,000 people to the resort.
Planned development for university	The completed £5.3m campus Library and Learning Centre (LLC) opened its doors in January 2003 and is intended to meet the current and future needs of the University's academic community. It is designed to allow Academic Services to provide a broad integrated spectrum of services including computing, learning support, disability support, library, video editing suite, learning design studio and staff development.

Campus room rental**	Minimum	Maximum
	£60	£74

Yield range	7.5–8.7%

Type of property	3 bed house (i.e. 2 bed upstairs + 1 converted other)	4 bed house	5 bed house	6 or more bed house
Entry price	£100,000	£130,000	£170,000	£245,000
Median room rate	£60	£60	£59	£65
Average yield B*	8.6%	8.7%	8.2%	7.5%
B – Estimated annual profit	£2,340	£3,174	£3,442	£3,639

Financial scores	Capital growth (out of 5)	Yield (out of 5)	Total (out of 10)
	3	3	6
Description	Bournemouth is a modern, cosmopolitan and vibrant town. The university site is roughly five minutes' bus ride from the town centre. There are cinemas, the Pavilion Theatre and many excellent bars and clubs. On the whole the atmosphere is friendly and the town heaves with tourists in the summer. There are stacks of good bars and pubs with regular licences within striking distance of the town centre so take the time to check them all out.		
Websites to advertise on	Local and national student listings: www.student-accom.com City information for students: www.accommodationforstudents.com UNILET: www.bournemouth.ac.uk/accommodation/unilet.html		

Estate agents	Address	Tel	Web
Austin & Wyatt	113 Old Christchurch Road, Bournemouth, Dorset BH1 1EP	01202 296688	www.austinwyatt.co.uk
Bradford & Bingley Marketplace Ltd	116 Poole Road Westbourne, Bournemouth, Dorset BH4 9EF	01202 761221	www.bbg.co.uk
Chappell & Matthews	27 Castle Lane West, Bournemouth, Dorset BH9 3LH	01202 533959	www.palmersnell.co.uk
Fox & Sons	119 Old Christchurch Road, Bournemouth, Dorset BH1 1EP	01202 554242	www.sequence home.com

Letting agents	Address	Tel	Web
Allan & Bath	Hereford House, 4 Hinton Road, Bournemouth Dorset BH1 2EE	01202 292000	www.allanandbath.co.uk
Burns	144 Holdenhurst Road, Bournemouth Dorset BH9 2DS	01202 310277 01202 310299	www.burnslettings.com
Coulson Management	860 Wimborne Road, Bournemouth Dorset BH9 2DS	01202 533191	www.coulson management.co.uk

Letting agents	Address	Tel	Web
Ellis & Partners	Old Library House, 4 Dean Park Crescent, Bournemouth Dorset BH1 1LY	01202 552236	www.ellis-partners. co.uk
Jordan Property Letting & Management	99 Rushcombe Way, Corfe Mullen, Bournemouth Dorset BH21 3QU	01202 691415	

Bradford

University	University of Bradford			
Population	467,668			
	Student population	**Undergraduate**	**Postgraduate**	**Total**
	University of Bradford	8380	3575	11950
	Campus capacity	1549	451	2000
	Size of market	6831	3124	9950
Drop-out rates	13%			
Student areas	East Bowling, Frizinghall, Great Horton, Heaton, Keighley, Little Horton, Low Moor, Manningham, Moorfield estates, Scholemor, Wyke			

University	Accommodation officer contacts			
	Tel	**Address**	**Web**	**Landlord accreditation scheme?**
University of Bradford	01274 234890	Residence Department, University of Bradford, Bradford, West Yorkshire BD7 1DP	www.brad.ac.uk	Yes

Planned development for city	A £20m programme is underway to pave the way for the Broadway shopping development. Connecting The City includes the demolition of several 1960s buildings, drainage works and environmental improvements. It will make way for one of the city's biggest developments featuring shops, offices, apartments, a hotel and car parking.
Planned development for university	The University has won a £2.4m grant from the Higher Education Innovation Fund (HEIF) to help the region's businesses and communities benefit from its expertise. The University already has extensive links to industry by helping to develop new products, conduct research and provide training. In addition to the solo bid, it has also been successful in collaborative bids with other universities. Bradford University is hoping to attract prospective students by selling the city as the cheapest place to study in England. In previous research during summer 2002, the University came top of a poll of the cheapest places to study, with the cost of living estimated to be £3,200 for an academic a year.

Campus room rental:	Minimum £46	Maximum £72
Yield range	7.8–9.8%	

Type of property	3 bed house (i.e. 2 bed upstairs + 1 converted other)	4 bed house	5 bed house	6 or more bed house
Entry price	£55,000	£69,000	£85,000	£105,000
Median room rate	£30	£32	£35	£35
Average yield	7.8%%	8.9%	9.8%	9.6%
B – Estimated annual profit	£981	£1,811	£2,895	£3,339

Financial scores	Capital growth (out of 5)	Yield (out of 5)	Total (out of 10)
	3	3	6

Description	The local area is busy and vibrant. The city has plenty to offer in terms of shopping and nightlife. The relationship with the local community is not too bad. Bradford is also known for its large ethnic community, which adds a great flavour to the city. This brings with it hundreds of international restaurants, many of them Indian and within walking distance of the campus and most populated areas.

Websites to advertise on	Local and national student listings: www.student-accom.com City information for students: www.accommodationforstudents.com Student listings link: www.spot-property.co.uk Bradford letting: www.bradfordletting.co.uk

Estate agents	Address	Tel	Web
Bradford & Bingley	50 Towngate Wyke, Bradford, West Yorkshire BD12 9JA	01274 606838	www.bbg.co.uk
Halifax Property Services	48 Godwin Street, Bradford, West Yorkshire BD1 2SD	01274 733644	www.halifax.co.uk
James Ickringill and Co	12 New John Street, Bradford, West Yorkshire BD1 2RA	01274 734300	www.jiandco.com
Dunlop Heywood	8 Hall Ings, Bradford, West Yorkshire BD1 1DU	01274 390490	

Letting agents	Address	Tel	Web
Aps Estate Agents	55, Darley St, Bradford, West Yorkshire BD1 3HN	01274 737555	www.askaps.co.uk

Letting agents	Address	Tel	Web
Paul S Withey	73 Godwin Street, Bradford, West Yorkshire BD1 2SH	01274 739198	www.paulswithey.co.uk
Whitneys	City Center Head Office, #11 Mannor Row, Bradford, West Yorkshire BD1 4PB	01274 725953	www.whitneys.co.uk
William H Brown	25–27 Westgate, Bradford, West Yorkshire BD1 2QL	01274 309795	www.sequencehome.co.uk
Whitegates	65 Darley Street, Bradford, West Yorkshire BD1 3HN	01274 306611	www.whitegates.co.uk

Brighton

Universities	University of Brighton, University of Sussex
Population	247,820

	Student population	Undergraduate	Postgraduate	Total
	University of Brighton	15165	3640	18810
	University of Sussex	9375	2970	12350
	Total	24540	6610	31160
	Campus capacity	4500	600	5100
	Size of market	20040	6010	26060

Drop-out rates	University of Brighton	12%
	University of Sussex	9%

Student areas	Bevendean, Central Brighton, Coombe Road area, Elm Grove, Falmer Higher Bevendean, Lewes Road, Moulscoombe, Poynings

University	Accommodation officer contacts			
	Tel	Address	Web	Landlord accreditation scheme?
University of Brighton	01273 600900	Accommodation Service, The Manor House, Lewes Road, Brighton BN2 4GA	www.brighton. ac.uk	Yes
University of Sussex	01273 678220	Housing Office, Bramber House, Falmer, Brighton BN1 9QU	www.sussex.ac.uk	Yes

Planned development for city	City developers plan to build a £10m monorail in Brighton, designed to cut down on the congestion in the city centre. The first stage of the construction is to start from the marina and Brighton Pier. However, the motion is yet to be passed as the City Council has a preference for a rapid bus service.
	The £175m development project planned for the marina will take six to eight years to complete and could see 300 jobs created. Also proposed are 1,000 new apartments in the area with 400 allocated to affordable housing, in addition to restaurants and bars on the front.
Planned development for universities	University of Brighton
	Brighton and Sussex started a new Medical School in 2002–03. The Medical School has recently announced that it has received a £1 million donation from pharmaceutical company Pfizer.
	The University of Brighton has been awarded over £4m by the government to work with local business and the community. Brighton has been given the maximum allowed under the Higher Education Innovation Fund (HEIF) to enhance its ability to offer services to business.

	University of Sussex			
	The University of Sussex aims to create an innovative partnership between business and higher education with its proposals to develop a new research-led campus in West Sussex, which will complement the University's existing campus at Falmer. The plans, which are still at the evaluation stage, also identify a 150-acre site that would accommodate up to 4,000 students and 800 members of staff, drawn from both the region and internationally. Research and business facilities would also be accommodated on the site.			
Campus room rental:	Minimum £45		Maximum £85	
Yield range	7.3–8.8%			
Type of property	3 bed house (i.e. 2 bed upstairs + 1 converted other)	4 bed house	5 bed house	6 or more bed house
Entry price***	£120,000	£150,000	£210,000	£250,000
Median room rate	£68	£70	£65	£70
Average yield B*	8%	8.8%	7.3%	7.9%
B – Estimated annual profit	£2,271	£3,778	£2,770	£4,542
Financial scores	Capital growth (out of 5) 3	Yield (out of 5) 4		Total (out of 10) 7
Description	The city is vibrant with many bars and pubs. It is an expensive place to drink but you have to take the rough with the smooth. The city has one of the largest gay communities in England and some excellent clubs and bars. Two things make Brighton different to nearby towns and cities. The first is the vast array of antiques shops, mostly in the maze of lanes in the city centre. The second is the surfy atmosphere. Brighton is a hotspot along the south coast and the presence of a fair amount of surfers is reflected in the number of excellent surf shops. The 200-acre University of Sussex campus is based about three miles inland from Brighton, near the village of Falmer. The buildings, many designed by Basil Spence, are mostly modern, redbrick structures surrounding numerous quads. The campus is quite remote and as a result fully self-sufficient. It would be possible for a student to come here and never need to leave... but invariably they do, attracted by the temptations of Brighton. There are trains from Falmer station to Brighton and London.			
Websites to advertise on	Local and national student listings: www.student-accom.com City information for students: www.accommodationforstudents.com Easy roommate: http://uk.easyroommate.com University of Brighton official letting website: www.netletbrighton.co.uk Head leasing scheme through the University of Brighton: www.brighton.ac.uk/hubs/ss/p22.htm Homelets: www3.mistral.co.uk/mailorder/homelets			

Estate agents	Address	Tel	Web
Bradford & Bingley – Geering & Colyer	43 High Street, Rottingdean, Brighton, East Sussex BN2 7HE	01273 301066	www.bbg.co.uk
Wyatt & Son Estate Agents	156 Lewes Road, Brighton, East Sussex BN2 3LG	01273 604377	www.arunestates.co.uk
Bonett's Estate Agents	89 St Georges Road, Brighton, East Sussex BN2 1EE	01273 677365	www.bonetts-property.co.uk
Graves Jenkins	1 North Road, Brighton, East Sussex BN1 1YA	01273 601060	www.graves-jenkins.co.uk
Letting agents	**Address**	**Tel**	**Web**
Halls Estate Agents	27 New Road, Brighton, East Sussex BN1 1UG	01273 571955	www.halls-estate.com
Tanat-Jones & Co	49 Norfolk Square, (Western Road), Brighton, East Sussex BN1 2PA	01273–207207	www.tanat-jones.com
Parks Residential Letting	107 Queens Road, Brighton, East Sussex BN1 3XF	01273 202089	www.parksletting.co.uk
Tingleys Hove	46 Church Road, Hove, East Sussex BN3 2FN	01273 778844	www.tingleys.co.uk
Massey Property	109/110 Western Road, Brighton, East Sussex BN1 2AA	01273 747473	www.masseyproperty.com

Bristol

Universities	University of Bristol, University of the West of England
Population	380,615

Student population	Undergraduate	Postgraduate	Total
University of Bristol	14475	7715	22190
University of the West of England	20935	4370	25310
Total	35410	12085	47500
Campus capacity	7227	1000	8227
Size of market	28183	11085	39273

Drop-out rates	University of Bristol 4% University of the West of England 12%
Student areas	Ashley Down, Bedminster, Clifton, Eastville, Horfield, Redland, St George's, Upper Eastville, Westbury Park

Accommodation officer contacts

University	Tel	Address	Web	Landlord accreditation scheme?
University of Bristol	0117 954 5740	4th Floor, Union Building, Queen's Road, Clifton, Bristol BS8 1LN	www.bris.ac.uk/ accom	Yes
University of the West of England	0870 901 0773	Student Accommodation Services, University of the West of England, Frenchay Campus, Coldharbour Lane, Bristol BS16 1QY	www.uwe.ac.uk/ accommodation	Yes

Planned development for city	After losing out to Liverpool for the coveted Culture Capital 2008, Bristol has been working hard to attract attention and investment into the city. On the back of this work, it received an award of £1,550,000 for its work on culture in urban areas in July 2004. The grant will go towards a two-year programme of festivals, displays, exhibitions, arts and heritage events. The grant received is one of the highest of its kind from the Arts Council England and the Millennium Commission. In 2005 there will be a celebration of the city's creativity, and events in 2006 will mark the life and work of engineer Isambard Kingdom Brunel. In other areas, Bristol International Airport is the fastest growing major regional airport in the UK, providing flights to all major UK destinations, Europe and the USA. The South West region is to become home to a major £300m science park thanks to a new investment by the South West Regional Development Agency. The science park will make the South West an

	even more attractive place for investment and create around 6,000 highly skilled, high value jobs when completed over the next decade.			
Planned development for universities	University of Bristol Selling off halls and raising tuition fees are the plans that have been floating around. However, the University has entered into an agreement with Unite to provide student accommodation close to the University precinct for 2004. Unite House offers 392 rooms arranged as flats for up to seven students and will be available for undergraduate and postgraduate students. As part of the new investment in the region in the form of a science park as described earlier, an innovation centre will be developed on the site which will be operated partly in collaboration with the University of Bristol.			
	University of the West of England UWE is renowned for its links to industry and accommodating research partners with major companies including, Hewlett Packard, Motorola and British Aerospace. In 2004 UWE won major government funding likely to total £4.3m over five years to build on its successful track record in collaborating with business and industry in the region.			
Campus room rental**	**Minimum** £40		**Maximum** £90	
Yield range	6.2–6.7%			
Type of property	3 bed house (i.e. 2 bed upstairs + 1 converted other)	4 bed house	5 bed house	6 or more bed house
Entry price **Median room rate** **Average yield B*** **B – Estimated** **annual profit**	£120,000 £53 6.2% £579	£145,000 £52 6.7% £1,296	£200,000 £53 6.2% £964	£230,000 £55 6.7% £2,058
Financial scores	Capital growth (out of 5) 3	Yield (out of 5) 2.5	Total (out of 10) 5.5	
Description	Bristol has a lot to offer socially, and as a result attracts a lot of the Students' Union's custom with the bars, clubs and eateries around the city. The relationship between locals and students is generally healthy and improving. Notorious tension between the Bristol University and UWE students is limited. Bristol transport links are generally very good. Wales is only a few miles away. London is 111 miles east down the M4, and the M5 is good for getting to the north.			
Websites to advertise on	Flatline: www.flatlineuk.co.uk Accommodation Unlimited: http://aul.org.uk/landlords Rents Direct Bristol: www.rentsdirect.com Local and national student listings: www.student-accom.com City information for students: www.accommodationforstudents.com			

Estate agents	Address	Tel	Web
Chappell & Matthews	46 College Green, Bristol BS1 5SH	0117 930 9900	www.chappelland matthews.co.uk
Connells Clifton	195–197, Whiteladies Road, Clifton, Bristol BS8 2SB	0117 970 6379	www.connells.co.uk
Savills	Bull Wharf, 135–137 Redcliff Street, Bristol BS1 6QR	01179 100 300	www.savills.co.uk
Bradford & Bingley	104 Whiteladies Road, Bristol BS8 2QQ	0117 974 1703	www.bbg.co.uk
Letting agents	Address	Tel	Web
Countrywide Residential Lettings	108 Whiteladies Road, Clifton, Bristol BS8 2RP	0117 923 8868	www.crldirect.co.uk
Holbrook Moran	283 Church Road, Redfield, Bristol BS5 9HT	01179 540033	www.hmestateagents. co.uk
Mayfair Residential Lettings	64 Alma Road, Clifton, Bristol BS8 2DJ	0117 923 7123	www.mayfair-bristol.co.uk
Kingsley Thomas	1 & 3 Whiteladies Rd, Clifton, Bristol BS8 2PH	0117 9466767	www.kingsley thomas.co.uk
Anthony James & Co	The Coach House, 38 Cotham Hill, Bristol BS6 6LA	0117 9237316	www.anthony james.uk.com

Cambridge

Universities	Anglia Polytechnic University, University of Cambridge
Population	108,879

	Student population	Undergraduate	Postgraduate	Total
	Anglia Polytechnic University	21740	3675	25420
	University of Cambridge	16550	8885	25435
	Total	38290	12560	50855
	Campus capacity	12,495	3,100	15595
	Size of market	25795	9460	35260

Drop-out rates	Anglia Polytechnic University	12%
	University of Cambridge	2%

Student areas	Chesterton, Girton, Romsey

	Accommodation officer contacts			
University	Tel	Address	Web	Landlord accreditation scheme?
Anglia Polytechnic University	01223 363271	Room 15, Ruskin Building, APU, East Road, Cambridge CB1 1PT	www.anglia.ac.uk/ housing/	No
University of Cambridge	01223 353518	Accommodation Service, 18 Silver Street, Cambridge CB3 9EL	www.cam.ac.uk	No

Planned development for city	The city has laid out plans to build homes near a famous Cambridge beauty spot. The government has recommended building 2,000 homes near Grantchester Meadows, by the River Cam.
	However, there is some discontent from the local people concerning the plans. The proposal is part of the local structure plan to cope with demand for affordable homes.

Planned development for universities	Anglia Polytechnic University
	Tax exile and graduate Michael Ashcroft donated £5m to the development of a new management centre at Chelmsford. Plans for more student accommodation are also in the pipeline.
	The first phase of development on the Cambridge campus, Opus 1, is now being used for accommodation and teaching.
	University of Cambridge
	A multi-million pound plan could see a major expansion of Cambridge University, which could include three new colleges. They will be the first since Robinson was founded in 1979.
	Much of the proposed 57-hectare site, which is owned by the University, is designated green belt land.

	Cambridge City Council has now agreed to put the proposal into the draft local plan which is set to be debated over the next year.			
Campus room rental**	Minimum £50		Maximum £120	
Yield range	6.4–8.5%			
Type of property	3 bed house (i.e. 2 bed upstairs + 1 converted other)	4 bed house	5 bed house	6 or more bed house
Entry price	£145,000	£160,000	£240,000	£310,000
Median room rate	£70	£72	£75	£70
Average yield B*	6.8%	8.5%	7.3%	6.4%
B – Estimated annual profit	£1,371	£3,629	£3,300	£1,842
Financial scores	Capital growth (out of 5) 2.5	Yield (out of 5) 3	Total (out of 10) 5.5	
Description	It is hard to imagine Cambridge without the University. It would be a small village, with no tourists and a quiet river, different from what it is now. The University really is the focal point of the city, with its light golden stone buildings spanning eight centuries of English architecture. Cambridge has many many good pubs – arguably some of the country's best during the summer. There is a wide variety of student housing available in Cambridge but demand for this accommodation is very high. Student accommodation ranges from university halls of residence, self-catering flats to bedsits and house shares in private rented accommodation.			
Websites to advertise on	Local and national student listings: www.student-accom.com City information for students: www.accommodationforstudents.com Cambridge letting: www.cambridgeletting.co.uk Online search: www.brettward.co.uk Cambridge Classifieds: www.cambridge-news.co.uk Advertise through the University: www-accommodation.admin.cam.ac.uk			

Estate agents	Address	Tel	Web
Bradford & Bingley Marketplace Ltd	January House, 7/8 Downing Street, Cambridge, Cambridgeshire CV2 3DR	01223 363291	www.bbg.co.uk
Savills	Bridge Place, 132–134 Hills Road, Cambridge, Cambridgeshire CB22PA	01223 347000	www.savills.co.uk

Estate agents	Address	Tel	Web
Halifax Property Services	65 Regent Street, Cambridge, Cambridgeshire CB2 1A	01223 358285	www.halifax.co.uk
Spicer Mccoll – Cambridge	64 Regent Street, Cambridge, Cambridgeshire CB2 1DP	01223 351351	www.spicermccoll.co.uk

Letting agents	Address	Tel	Web
Pocock & Shaw – Cherry Hinton	26 High Street, Cherry Hinton, Cambridge, Cambridgeshire CB1 9HZ	01223 516174	www.pocock.co.uk
Hockeys	81 Regent Street, Cambridge, Cambridgeshire CB2 1AW	01223 356054	www.hockeys.co.uk
The Tucker Partnership	85 Regent Street, Cambridge, Cambridgeshire CB2 1AW	01223 508508	www.tucker-partnership.co.uk
Tylers	19 High Street Histon, Cambridge, Cambridgeshire CB4 9JD	01223 235111	www.tylers.net
W H Brown Estate Agents	65 Regent Street, Cambridge, Cambridgeshire CB2 1AB	01223 358285	www.sequencehome.co.uk

Canterbury

Universities	Canterbury Christ Church University College, The University of Kent at Canterbury
Population	135,287

	Student population	Undergraduate	Postgraduate	Total
	Canterbury Christ Church University College	9880	3680	13725
	The University of Kent at Canterbury	11535	2485	14025
	Total	21415	6165	27750
	Campus capacity	3540	630	4170
	Size of market	17875	5535	23580

Drop-out rates	Canterbury Christ Church University College 12% The University of Kent at Canterbury 11%
Student areas	Brymore, Hales Place, Longport, St Martins, St Stephens, Sturry Road, Wincheap

Accommodation officer contacts

University	Tel	Address	Web	Landlord accreditation scheme?
Canterbury Christ Church University College	01227 782286	Accommodation Office, Canterbury Christ Church College, North Holmes Road, Canterbury CT1 1QU	www.cant.ac.uk	No
The University of Kent at Canterbury	01227 766660	Accommodation Office, UKC Hospitality, Tanglewood, Canterbury CT2 7LR	www.kent.ac.uk	No

Planned development for city	There are many economic regeneration initiatives and projects being lined up, to improve the infrastructure developments and local area improvements, amongst other plans. A key project for the next few years is the £100m Whitefriars shopping development in the centre of Canterbury. It is due to open in 2006 and will maintain Canterbury's strong position as a leading retail business, leisure and tourism destination. The developers claim that this will ensure Canterbury City is the premier employment centre in East Kent.

Planned development for universities	Canterbury Christ Church University College
	In 2003 the University completed new halls of residence on one of its campus areas.
	    The £3m Northwood Halls complex will give students from across the country the opportunity to study at Thanet campus. The building provides residential accommodation for 84 full time students.
	    In 2004 the university was awarded £1.2m from the Higher

	Education Innovation Fund (HEIF) for business development. The grant is part of the government's drive to boost the UK's innovation performance and productivity.		
	The University of Kent at Canterbury In a similar fashion to Christ Church College, the University of Kent will receive £2.2m as part of the government's largest funding awards yet given to support knowledge transfer from universities to business and the wider community. Also in the news is the £50m Medway initiative, which is to be at the heart of the strategy to bring economic prosperity to Medway. It is a partnership led by the University of Kent and the University of Greenwich, together with Mid-Kent College and Canterbury Christ Church University College and multiple initiative groups support the scheme. The Universities at Medway initiative is a key project in the North Kent section of the Thames Gateway regeneration programme and will see student numbers rise to 6,000 by 2010. It will have a major impact on the region's economy, adding £10m of additional expenditure and creating more than 600 direct and indirect jobs. As for student developments, the main plans are to regenerate the Students' Union and increase the amount and quality of activity and the profile of the Union.		

Campus room rental**	Minimum £51		Maximum £110	
Yield range	7.9–8.2%			
Type of property	3 bed house (i.e. 2 bed upstairs + 1 converted other)	4 bed house	5 bed house	6 or more bed house
Entry price	£120,000	£150,000	£180,000	£210,000
Median room rate	£66	£62	£60	£60
Average yield B*	7.9%	7.9%	8%	8.2%
B – Estimated annual profit	£2,204	£2,774	£3,420	£4,374

Financial scores	Capital growth (out of 5) 3	Yield (out of 5) 4	Total (out of 10) 7
Description	Canterbury is one of Britain's most famous cathedral towns, attracting huge numbers of tourists and visitors annually. The cosmopolitan feel of the city is enhanced by Canterbury's huge population of foreign students. On a social level however, the range of late night and new bars is very limited, as there are strict noise controls imposed by the city council.		
Websites to advertise on	Local and national student listings: www.student-accom.com City information for students: www.accommodationforstudents.com Lettings portal: www.upmystreet.com Jon Gauld student lets: www.student-let-kent.com Student lets: www.letalife.com		

Estate agents	Address	Tel	Web
Regal Estates Elliott & Goddard	57 Castle Street Canterbury, Kent CT1 2PY	01227 763888	www.regal-estates.co.uk
Bradford & Bingley – Geering and Coyler	81 Castle Street, Canterbury, Kent CT1 2QD	01227 457253	www.bbg.co.uk
Strut and Parker	2 St. Margaret's Street, Canterbury, Kent CT1 2SL	01227 451123	www.struttandparker.co.uk
Cluttons	3 Beer Cart Lane Canterbury, Kent CT1 2NJ	01227 457441	www.cluttons.com

Letting agents	Address	Tel	Web
Berrys Canterbury	70 Castle Street, Canterbury, Kent CT1 2QD	01227 765268	www.berryscanterbury.fsnet.co.uk
GW Finn	Brooklands, Fordwich, Canterbury, Kent CT2 0BS	01227 710200	www.gwfinn.co.uk
Caxtons Residential Ltd	1 Castle Street, Canterbury, Kent CT1 2QF	01227 788088	www.caxtonscanterbury.co.uk
The Letting Shop	76 Castle Street, Canterbury, Kent CT1 2QD	01227 784 784	www.thelettingshop.com
Countrywide Residential Lettings	79 Castle Street, Canterbury, Kent CT1 2QD	01227 763393	www.crldirect.co.uk

Cardiff

Universities	Cardiff University, University of Wales College of Medicine, University of Wales Institute Cardiff, Royal Welsh College of Music and Drama
Population	305,340

Student population	Undergraduate	Postgraduate	Total
Cardiff University	17040	5710	22750
University of Wales College of Medicine	2420	1330	3750
University of Wales Institute, Cardiff	7500	1590	9090
Royal Welsh College of Music and Drama	450	140	590
Total	27320	8770	36180
Campus capacity	5100	900	6000
Size of market	22220	7870	30180

Drop-out rates	Cardiff University 8% University of Wales College of Medicine 8% University of Wales Institute, Cardiff 13% Royal Welsh College of Music and Drama 11%
Student areas	Cathays, Gabalfa, Heath, Roath

Accommodation officer contacts

University	Tel	Address	Web	Landlord accreditation scheme?
Cardiff University	029 2087 4849	P.O. Box 533, Southgate House, Bevan Place, Cardiff CF14 3XZ	www.cardiff.ac.uk	No
University of Wales College of Medicine	029 2074 2141	Accommodation Office, Neuadd Merionnydd, Heath Park, Cardiff CF14 4YS	www.uwcm.ac.uk	Yes
University of Wales Institute, Cardiff	029 2041 6188/89	Accommodation Office, Llandaff Campus, Western Avenue, Cardiff CF5 2YB	www.uwic.ac.uk	No
Royal Welsh College of Music and Drama	029 2034 2854	Student Services, Royal Welsh College of Music and Drama, Castle Grounds, Cathays Park, Cardiff CF10 3ER	weirba@rwcmd.ac.uk	No

Planned development for city	Cardiff was a major competitor for the coveted Culture Capital 2008 title, which eventually went to Liverpool. However, the City was recognised as a centre of cultural excellence. In 2004 Cardiff was awarded £1.3m of National Lottery funding from the Millennium Commission to support its cultural programme for 2005. The city also aims to continue and build upon South Glamorgan County Council's 2020 Vision, which was launched in 1993 to map out an ambitious 30-year agenda for Cardiff.
Planned development for universities	Cardiff University Roughly £40m has been spent on University accommodation in the last six years and it has done wonders for the general state of accommodation services offered by Cardiff University. In August 2004 the University of Wales College of Medicine and Cardiff University will merge to create a new, dynamic and internationally competitive university.
	University of Wales College of Medicine As part of the forecasted merger, new developments and projects have already been proposed. A £10m centre of excellence for research into the human brain is being set up in Cardiff. Scientists from Cardiff University and UWCM will soon be able to use state of the art technology to unravel the mysteries of the human brain after a multi-million pound grant was awarded by the Department of Trade and Industry (DTI).
	University of Wales Institute, Cardiff Plans to merge the University of Glamorgan and the University of Wales Institute Cardiff to create a super college for 30,000 students were discarded in December 2003. However, this did not stop the delight of UWIC being ranked as the top 'new university' in the UK by the Times Good University Guide.
	Royal Welsh College of Music and Drama The Higher Education Funding Council for Wales (HEFCW) has announced that, for the first time, RRWCMD is to be funded on a par with similar conservatoires in England and Scotland and, from September 2000, the College received an additional £1.75m a year to bring its annual grant to £4.5m. The College, which incorporates a music conservatoire and drama school, is of only 12 recognised conservatoires in the UK and one of only two that incorporates a drama school.
Campus room rental**	Minimum Maximum £45 £70
Yield range	6.6–10%

Type of property	3 bed house (i.e. 2 bed upstairs + 1 converted other)	4 bed house	5 bed house	6 or more bed house
Entry price	£72,000	£100,000	£135,000	£210,000
Median room rate	£50	£50	£48	£48
Average yield B*	10%	9.6%	8.5%	6.6%
B – Estimated annual profit	£2,520	£3,180	£3,141	£1,610

Financial scores	Capital growth (out of 5)	Yield (out of 5)	Total (out of 10)
	3	4	7

Description	Cardiff is a vibrant city, with plenty to do in the way of shopping and museums. The buildings tend to be in a Victorian or Georgian style with some more newly developed areas such as the Docklands and Cardiff Bay. The north of the city is industrial and grew up around the famous Welsh coal mines.
	The Welsh capital is well situated for travel. The airport has both domestic and international flights, the M4 takes you direct to London and there are train links throughout the UK most notably the easy journey (30 minutes) across the water to Bristol.
	Unusually for a city university, Cardiff has its own unofficial student village situated in the Cathays area. It's private accommodation, but might as well be a campus as it's all students. This means there's a campus-like atmosphere in the very centre of the city.
	On a general note, Cardiff claims to be Europe's fastest growing city and describes itself as a capital bursting with things to do and places to go, but is, amazingly, one of the cheapest places to study in the UK.

Websites to advertise on	Local and national student listings: www.student-accom.com
	City information for students: www.accommodationforstudents.com
	Recommendations from UWIC: www.uwicsu.co.uk/main/advice/housing
	Local agent for residential lettings: www.porters-uk.com
	Specialists on student housing: www.taffhousing.co.uk
	Online portal: www.rentdirect.biz

Estate agents	Address	Tel	Web
Barbara Rees	144 Crwys Road, Cathays, Cardiff CF24 4NR	02920 371917 & 371795	www.barbararees.net
Peter Alan	798 Newport Road, Cardiff CF3 4FH	029 2079 2888	www.peteralan.co.uk
Allen & Harris	183 Cowbridge Road East, Canton, Cardiff CF1 9AJ	029 2022 2344	www.sequence home.co.uk

Estate agents	Address	Tel	Web
Moginie James	90 Albany Road, Roath, Cardiff CF24 3RS	029 20 484 898	www.moginie james.co.uk

Letting agents	Address	Tel	Web
Chris John & Partners	95 Pontcanna Street, Pontcanna, Cardiff CF11 9HS	029 2039 7152	www.chrisjohn.co.uk
Yeoman Edwards	108 Bute Street, Cardiff Bay CF10 5AD	029 2045 4433	www.yeoman edwards.co.uk
Hern and Crabtree	8 Waungron Road, Llandaff, Cardiff CF5 2JJ	029 2055 5198	www.hern-crabtree.co.uk
Glenn Abraham	76 Crwys Road, Cathays, Cardiff CF24 4NP	029 2037 7226	www.glenn-abraham.co.uk
Thomas George	32 Churchill, Cardiff CF10 2DZ	029 2039 5563	www.thomas-george-lettings.co.uk

Cheltenham

University	University of Gloucestershire
Population	110,025

	Student population	Undergraduate	Postgraduate	Total
		1535	7680	9215
	Campus capacity	800	–	800
	Size of market	735	7680	8415

Drop-out rates	14%
Student areas	Battledown area, Leckhampton, Pittville, St Pauls

University	Accommodation officer contacts			
	Tel	Address	Web	Landlord accreditation scheme?
University of Gloucestershire	01242 532773	Accommodation Office, Francis Close Hall, Swindon Road, Cheltenham GL50 4AZ	www.glos.ac.uk	No
Planned development for city	Owners of derelict homes in Cheltenham are being offered renovation grants to make their properties habitable again. The borough council will provide up to £15,000 to cover the cost of building works and professional fees. Landlords will be encouraged to let their improved homes to help cut the housing waiting list. More than 500 private properties are currently lying empty in the Gloucestershire town. The government has asked for an increase in housing in Gloucestershire's development plans for the next 12 years. The county has had to submit an outline of its transport, housing and economic plans until 2016. The government suggested a review of land between Cheltenham and Gloucester to relieve pressure on the Cotswolds.			
Planned development for universities	The University of Gloucestershire only came into existence in 2001, when the Cheltenham and Gloucester College of Higher Education was granted university status – the first institute for ten years to receive approval from the privy council. Although based on three campuses in Cheltenham, the university has plans to open new buildings in Gloucester over the next couple of years.			

Campus room rental**	Minimum	Maximum
	£59	£73
Yield range	7–8.6%	

Type of property	3 bed house (i.e. 2 bed upstairs + 1 converted other)	4 bed house	5 bed house	6 or more bed house
Entry price	£95,000	£120,000	£150,000	£210,000
Median room rate	£52	£50	£55	£52
Average yield B*	7.7%	7.8%	8.6%	7%
B – Estimated annual profit	£1,591	£2,120	£3,590	£2,282

Financial scores	Capital growth (out of 5)	Yield (out of 5)	Total (out of 10)
	3	3	6

Description	Cheltenham became a spa town in 1716. According to tradition, the first medicinal waters were discovered when locals saw pigeons pecking at salty deposits which had formed around a spring. The town received Royal patronage in 1788 when King George III came to drink the waters. This led to the rapid development of Cheltenham as a fashionable spa between 1790 and 1840. Cheltenham is one of the few English towns in which traditional and contemporary architecture complement each other. The student community is vibrant, friendly and progressive, offering a wide range of academic programmes but retaining the qualities of an institution small enough to be able to take an individual interest in each student.

Websites to advertise on	Local and national student listings: www.student-accom.com City information for students: www.accommodationforstudents.com Management specialists: www.yandgpropertymanagement.co.uk Letting specialists Cheltenham: www.hmt.co.uk

Estate agents	Address	Tel	Web
Adams Estate Agents	23 Bath Street, Cheltenham, Gloucestershire GL50	01242 260088	www.adamsestate agents.co.uk
Bensons	10 High Street Prestbury, Cheltenham, Gloucestershire GL523AS	01242 529600/1	www.por928.team.co.uk
Halifax Property Services	3 Cambray Place, Cheltenham, Gloucestershire GL50 1JS	01242 583128	
Peter Ball and Co	29–30 Bath Street, Cheltenham, Gloucestershire GL50 7YA	01242 255288	www.peterball.co.uk

Letting agents	Address	Tel	Web
R A Bennett	Leckhampton, Cheltenham, Gloucestershire GL53 7NA	01242 570570	www.rabennett.co.uk
Young and Gilling	3 Crescent Terrace, Cheltenham, Gloucestershire GL50 3PE	01242 521129	www.youngand gilling.com
The Cherringtons Group	14 Rodney Road, Cheltenham, Gloucestershire GL50 1JJ	01242 523075	www.cherringtons estateagents.co.uk
Philip Pugh	25 Bath Street, Cheltenham, Gloucestershire GL50 1YA	01242 261222	www.philip-pugh.co.uk
Jigsaw Estate Agents	36 Suffolk Parade, Cheltenham, Gloucestershire GL50 2AD	01242 222770	www.jigsawestate agents.co.uk

Chester

University	University College Chester
Population	118,207

	Student population	Undergraduate	Postgraduate	Total
		8540	1150	9690
	Campus capacity	850	150	1000
	Size of market	7690	1000	8690

Drop-out rates	16%
Student areas	Chrisleton, Chester

University	Accommodation officer contacts			
	Tel	Address	Web	Landlord accreditation scheme?
University College Chester	01244 392700	Accommodation Office, Chester College, Parkgate Road, Chester CH1 4BJ	www.chester.ac.uk	Yes

Planned development for city	Projects geared towards improving the quality of life in Chester have accumulated to nearly £6m. Between 2003 and 2004 the council successfully bid for £5.6m towards council and partnership projects.
Planned development for university	Chester is waiting to hear whether it will be officially recognised as a university. University College Chester has just completed a stringent three-year long examination of the quality of its academic programmes and procedures. Its students numbers grew to 8,800 undergraduates and postgraduates in in the 2003–04 academic year and it is turning over £40m. Chester's Campus is still one of the fastest growing of the HE institutions in the UK over the last five years.

Campus room rental**	Minimum	Maximum
	£46	£97

Yield range	7.1–8.5%

Type of property	3 bed house (i.e. 2 bed upstairs + 1 converted other)	4 bed house	5 bed house	6 or more bed house
Entry price	£120,000	£150,000	£180,000	£250,000
Median room rate	£60	£58	£65	£65
Average yield B*	7.1%	7.3	8.5%	7.3%
B – Estimated annual profit	£1,368	£1,974	£4,120	£3,414

Financial scores	Capital growth (out of 5) 3	Yield (out of 5) 2.5	Total (out of 10) 5.5
Description	Chester has a rich and fascinating history and enjoys an international reputation for its wealth of architecture and archaeological features, as well as for its quantity and quality of leisure and relaxation facilities. It is packed with nightlife, sports, arts and cultural activities as well as restaurants and pubs. There is a wide choice of shopping at the heart of the city, from specialist shops, mediaeval rows, a covered gallery and indoor market, to modern indoor shopping precincts. It is also considered as the gateway to North Wales with the Snowdonia National Park, seaside resorts and ancient castles, and is only a short drive from the lively cities of Liverpool and Manchester. The University of Liverpool awards the degrees.		
Websites to advertise on	Local and national student listings: www.student-accom.com City information for students: www.accommodationforstudents.com Campus accommodation: www.bunk.com Property letting: www.letalife.com Flat share portal: www.flatshare-house-share.co.uk		

Estate agents	Address	Tel	Web
Beresford Adams Commercial	7 Grosvenor Street, Chester, Cheshire CH1 2DD	01244 351212	www.beresfordadams. co.uk
Dodds Property World	17 Grovesnor Street, Chester, Cheshire CH1	01244 348737	www.door-key.com
Halifax Property Services	41 Hoole Road Hoole, Chester, Cheshire CH2 3NH	01244 345661	www.halifax.co.uk
Swetenhams	28, Lower Bridge St, Chester, Cheshire CH1 2DY	01244 321321	www.sequencehome. co.uk

Letting agents	Address	Tel	Web
Reeds Rains	29 Watergate Street, Chester, Cheshire CH1 2LB	01244 328257	www.reedsrains.co.uk
Strutt & Parker	19 Grosvenor Street, Chester, Cheshire CH1 2DD	01244 320747	www.struttandparker. co.uk

Letting agents	Address	Tel	Web
Thomas C Adams	The Dutch House, 22 Bridge Street, Chester, Cheshire CH1 1NQ	01244 340340	www.thomascadams.com
Whitegates	52 Watergate Street, Chester, Cheshire CH1 2LA	01244 351789	www.whitegates.co.uk
Wright Manley	6–8 Watergate Street, Chester, Cheshire CH1 2LA	01244 317833	www.wrightmanley.co.uk

Colchester

University	University of Essex
Population	155,794

	Student population	Undergraduate	Postgraduate	Total
		7295	3690	10985
	Campus capacity	900	200	1100
	Size of market	6395	3490	9885

Drop-out rates	11%
Student areas	Brightlingsea, Dutch Quarter, Greenstead, town centre, Wivenhoe Park

University	Accommodation officer contacts			
	Tel	Address	Web	Landlord accreditation scheme?
University of Essex	01206 872355	Accommodation Office, University of Essex, Wivenhoe Park, Colchester CO4 3SQ	www.essex. ac.uk/ accommodation	Yes

Planned development for city	It is anticipated that thousands of jobs will be created in Essex after the biggest private finance initiative (PFI) scheme in the UK gathers pace over the next four years or so.
	The scheme to revamp and modernise the Army's Colchester Garrison is expected to cost £560m – part of a £2b private finance initiative to develop and operate the garrison for the next 35 years.
	Developers plan to move the town's soldiers to new accommodation and build an urban village of more than 2,000 homes on the garrison site. The scheme will transform the town centre with new houses, offices, workshops, stores and sports facilities.

Planned development for university	Summer 2002 saw the opening of a new £2.9m teaching and office building. There is also a major riverside student accommodation development consisting of 750 new study bedrooms located a short walk from campus.
	Future plans include extending the Biological Sciences building, adding a new research park and building a £6m network centre.
	In 2004 the University of Essex was awarded over £2m by the Higher Education Funding Council for England (HEFCE) to fund business development initiatives.
	The award was made from HEFCE's Higher Education Innovation Fund (HEIF), supporting higher education institutions in knowledge transfer to, and interactions with, business and the wider community.

Campus room rental**	Minimum	Maximum
	£45	£75

Yield range	7.3–8.4%

Type of property	3 bed house (i.e. 2 bed upstairs + 1 converted other)	4 bed house	5 bed house	6 or more bed house
Entry price	£95,000	£125,000	£140,000	£190,000
Median room rate	£52	£50	£50	£49
Average yield B*	7.7%	7.5%	8.4%	7.3%
B – Estimated annual profit	£1,591	£1,895	£3,100	£2,505

Financial scores	Capital growth (out of 5)	Yield (out of 5)		Total (out of 10)
	2.5	4		6.5

Description	The University has over 200 acres of attractive parkland, much of which was landscaped in the 18th century. It is a mile away from the village of Wivenhoe with its lively quayside and variety of pubs and restaurants.
	The Colchester Arts Centre is a good venue for live bands, comedy clubs, etc. The town also has a range of cinemas, cafes and good wine bars. The student hang-out in Colchester itself is the Hippodrome – though this is becoming less popular amongst the students. The students tend to steer away from the army hang-outs.
	The close knit Colchester campus has shops, banks and restaurants, and the University is able to offer accommodation to a high proportion of its students. It also boasts excellent sporting facilities.

Websites to advertise on	Local and national student listings: www.student-accom.com City information for students: www.accommodationforstudents.com Students and residential specialists: www.essexandsuffolk.co.uk Colchester lettings: www.thelettingshop.uk.com

Estate agents	Address	Tel	Web
Bradford & Bingley Marketplace	159 High Street, Colchester CO11PG	01206 561166	www.marketplace.co.uk
Bairstow Eves	50 Victoria Place, Brightlingsea, Colchester CO7 0AB	01206 304061	www.bairstoweves countrywide.co.uk
Ann Quarrie	61 High Street, Wivenhoe, Colchester CO7 9AB	01206 825403	www.rollo estates.co.uk
David Martin Estate Agents	27 Mile End Road, Colchester CO4 5BT	01206 851626	www.davidmartin.co.uk

Letting agents	Address	Tel	Web
Belvoir	43 Sir Isaacs Walk, Colchester CO1 1JJ	01206 364444	www.belvoir colchester.com
Martins & Co.	Suite 22, Colchester Business Centre, 1 George Williams Way, Colchester CO1 2JS	01206 760950	www.martinco.com
Boydens	Aston House, 57–59 Crouch Street, Colchester CO3 3EY	01206762276	www.boydens.co.uk
Rollo Estates	61 High Street, Wivenhoe, Colchester CO7 9AZ	01206 825403	www.kemc.co.uk
Lucas	16 Victoria Place, Brightlingsea CO7 0BX	01206 302639	www.lucasestates.com

Coventry	
Universities	Coventry University, University of Warwick
Population	300,844
	Student population Undergraduate Postgraduate Total Coventry University 15525 2835 18360 University of Warwick 18790 8565 27355 **Total** 34315 11400 45715 **Campus capacity** 9034 1100 10134 **Size of market** 25281 10300 35581
Drop-out rates	Coventry University 13% University of Warwick 6%
Student areas	Canley, Chapelfields, Cheylesmore, city centre, Coundon, Earlsdon, Far Gosford, Foleshill, Hillfields, Hollyhead, Lower Stoke, Radford, Stoke, Tile Hill, Wyken

Accommodation officer contacts

University	Tel	Address	Web	Landlord accreditation scheme?
Coventry University	0124 7688 7303/4	Accommodation Office, Priory Street, Coventry CV1 5FB	www.coventry .ac.uk	Yes
University of Warwick	0124 7652 3771	Accommodation Office, University of Warwick, Senate House, Coventry CV4 7AL	www.csv.warwick .ac.uk	Yes

Planned development for city	Coventry's council houses will be transferred to a private company, paving the way for £240m of repairs. In 2004 the council voted to allow the transfer of the 20,000 homes to the Whitefriars Housing Group. The government has agreed to pay off the 'over-hanging debt', which the council still owed for building the houses. Coventry's Hippodrome Theatre will be demolished early next year following the government's approval of its purchase for the Phoenix Initiative. The £25m development has been given the go-ahead following a public inquiry.
Planned development for universities	Coventry University The Students' Union recently carried out substantial new development. A new Union building will replace one of the two old ones, which will be sold off for £1.6m. The University itself is also building a new library and school of performing arts for £20m.
	University of Warwick A new hall of residence for postgraduates is to be built.

	The University was given almost £7.5m in funding as part of the HEIF government scheme designed to encourage enterprise, technological innovation and the development and support of high technology businesses. The award to Warwick is the highest made to any Midlands University in this round of the HEIF funding programme.

Campus room rental:	Minimum		Maximum	
	£51		£95	

Yield range	4.5–6.4%			

Type of property	3 bed house (i.e. 2 bed upstairs + 1 converted other)	4 bed house	5 bed house	6 or more bed house
Entry price	£100,000	£160,000	£220,000	£290,000
Median room rate	£46	£45	£45	£46
Average yield B*	6.4%	5.3%	4.8%	4.5%
B – Estimated annual profit	£689	–£432	–£1,440	–£2,672

Financial scores	Capital growth (out of 5)	Yield (out of 5)	Total (out of 10)
	2	2	4

Description	Coventry has been rebuilt in a variety of imaginative styles since it was bombed during the Second World War.
	The BMW Group British headquarters, together with Rolls Royce and Jaguar, are based here. It is recommended that students stick to the Universities and Student Union areas until they acclimatise to the street wisdom of the area.
	Warwick University is a little isolated being on the outskirts of Coventry, which has both advantages and disadvantages. It is green, quiet and beautiful in the summer. Most students are to be found outside when the weather gets warm. Buses are good and run late during term time but it can be difficult to get to places in a hurry.

Websites to advertise on	Accommodation to students: www.coventrystudenthomes.co.uk
	Student housing in Leamington Spa: www.leamingtonstudenthomes.co.uk
	Local and national student listings: www.student-accom.com
	City information for students: www.accommodationforstudents.com
	General classifieds Coventry www.coventryfocus.com
	Property portal in Coventry and Warwickshire: www.cwhomes.co.uk/home

Estate agents	Address	Tel	Web
Robin Jones Independent Estate Agents	115 New Union St, Coventry CV1 2NT	024 766 33355	www.robinjones.co.uk

▶

Estate agents	Address	Tel	Web
Whitegates	137–139 New Union Street, Coventry CV1 2NT	024 76 222656	www.whitegates.co.uk
Hawkins Estate Agents	24 Warwick Row, Coventry CV1 1EY	024 76 257281	www.hawkins-online.co.uk
Bradford & Bingley	149 New Union Street, Coventry CV1 2RP	024 76 226011	www.bbg.co.uk
Letting agents	Address	Tel	Web
Oakley Box	145 New Union St, Coventry CV1 2PH	024 76 555500	www.oakleybox.co.uk
Acorn Estates	245 Cross Road, Coventry CV6 5GP	024 76 667123	www.acorn estates.co.uk
Heart Property Services	36 New Union Street, Coventry CV1 2HN	024 76 630080	www.heart propertyservices.com
Bansal Estates	14 Warwick Row, City Centre, Coventry CV1 1EX	024 76 23132	http://home. btconnect.com/ Bansalestates/ index.htm
Loveitts	29 Warwick Row, Coventry CV1 1DY	024 76 228111	www.loveitts.co.uk

Derby

University	University of Derby
Population	221,716

	Student population	Undergraduate	Postgraduate	Total
		10865	2305	13170
	Campus capacity	1368	626	1994
	Size of market	9497	1679	11176

Drop-out rates	14%
Student areas	Allestree, Ashbourne, Ashbourne Rd, city centre, Five Lamps, Kedleston Road, Kegworth, Normanton, Rowditch, Spondon

	Accommodation officer contacts			
University	Tel	Address	Web	Landlord accreditation scheme?
University of Derby	01332 622222	Student Housing Centre, Ground floor, South Tower, Kedleston Road, Campus, Derby DE22 1GB	i.terry@derby.ac.uk www.derby.ac.uk/ residential	Yes

Planned development for city	The local council's plan for the next few years involves the continuing improvement and refocusing on services whilst maintaining their performance in other areas. They outline the main issues affecting Derby and the council up to March 2007 and the council describes its vision and objectives, setting out ten priorities for 2004–05, on www.derby.gov.uk.
	On a more political note, The UK Independence Party won a seat in Derby in 2004, which could have repercussions for the balance of political activity in Derby.
Planned development for university	In the last five years or so the University has spent £40m on new halls of residence. A new arts centre has also been established and the University focuses much attention on fashion and art displays. It has won grants to build a new health research centre, a new multi-cultural faith centre and a further £5m for much-needed accommodation projects.

Campus room rental:	Minimum	Maximum
	£40	£60
Yield range	5.8–7.4%	

Type of property	3 bed house (i.e. 2 bed upstairs + 1 converted other)	4 bed house	5 bed house	6 or more bed house
Entry price	£85,000	£130,000	£179,000	£205,000
Median room rate	£45	£40	£45	£45
Average yield B*	7.4%	5.8%	5.9%	6.2%
B – Estimated annual profit	£1,251	£170	£405	£927

Financial scores	Capital growth (out of 5)	Yield (out of 5)	Total (out of 10)
	2.5	2.5	5

Description	Derby is a good sized city with easy access to most places by foot. You can walk across the main shopping centre in 20 minutes. Most of the halls are roughly halfway between the centre and the Kedleston Road campus, so getting about is easy – especially as buses link all the main campuses and halls.
	Escape to the countryside and beyond is also an easy option. The Peak District National Park is just 30 minutes away by train, bus or car. It's the most visited National Park – after Mount Fuji – in the world. Derby's geographical location is an added bonus – London is just two hours away by train.

Websites to advertise on	Local and national student listings: www.student-accom.com
	City information for students: www.accommodationforstudents.com
	Derby property lettings and management: www.greenparkproperty.co.uk
	National listings: www.letalife.co.uk

Estate agents	Address	Tel	Web
Ashley Adams	3 Market Place, Derby DE1 3PW	01332 200020	www.mab.org.uk
Bairstow Eves	8 Market Place, Derby DE1 3QE	01332 341200	www.bairstoweves countrywide.co.uk
Bradford & Bingley Marketplace Ltd	18 St James Street, Derby DE1 1RJ	01332 331181	www.bbg.co.uk
Hall & Partners	19–21 James Street, Derby DE1 1RF	01332 203020	www.hallandbenson. com

Letting agents	Address	Tel	Web
Burchell Edwards	30 Market Place, Derby DE1 1HA	01332 345645	www.burchelledwards. com

Letting agents	Address	Tel	Web
Everington and Ruddle	7 Bridge Street, Belper, Derby DE6	01773 829942	www.everingtonruddle. co.uk
Halifax Property Services	5 Derby Road, Melbourne, Derby DE73 1FE	01332 864545	www.halifax.co.uk/ estateagency/home. shtml
Long and Partners	2B Chapel St, Spondon, Derby DE21 7JP	01332 544488	www.longandpartners. co.uk
Jonathan Fox	1 Risley Lane, Breaston, Derby DE72 3AU	01332 874489	www.jonathanfox.co.uk

Dundee

Universities	University of Abertay Dundee, University of Dundee
Population	145,460

	Student population	Undergraduate	Postgraduate	Total
	University of Abertay Dundee	3815	680	4495
	University of Dundee	12340	4125	16465
	Total	16155	4805	20960
	Campus capacity	2380	420	2800
	Size of market	13775	4385	18160

Drop-out rates	University of Abertay Dundee	19%
	University of Dundee	13%

Student areas	Central, Charleston, Clepington, Dens, West End

Accommodation officer contacts

University	Tel	Address	Web	Landlord accreditation scheme?
University of Abertay Dundee	01382 308059	Accommodation Office, University of Abertay Dundee, Bell Street, Dundee DD1 1HG	www.abertay .ac.uk	No
University of Dundee	01382 344040	Residences Office, University of Dundee, 3 Cross Row, Dundee DD1 4HN	www.dundee.ac.uk	No

Planned development for city	The city council's economic department has launched a new property website as part of the ongoing drive to market Dundee's economic opportunities. The online property search facility lists hundreds of commercial properties across the city. The website is designed to be easy to use and features properties from 25 agents. It is part of an ongoing city council campaign to attract investment into the city by highlighting the economic attractions of Dundee to as wide an audience as possible. To access, follow the link: www.locate-dundee.co.uk/property.
	A £20m Digital Media Park in Tayside has been given the green light and will form part of a major thrust to promote Scotland's creative industries internationally. Scottish Enterprise Tayside plans to transform a former railway goods yard in the city into 260,000 sq ft of tailored accommodation to serve digital media companies. The development will complement similar projects in the area. The media park will have the potential to create 1000 jobs and will support the start-up and existing digital media companies.
	Recent developments near the University include a revitalised cultural quarter and the Overgate Shopping Centre. Dundee isn't exactly a tourist magnet so prices (and wages) tend to be relatively low.

Planned development for universities	University of Abertay Dundee The new Abertay Psychology Centre will help play a key role in shaping thinking for the 21st century. The Centre is a state-of-the-art research complex comprising advanced laboratories, testing rooms and a language-recording suite. Funding for came from a grant from the Scottish Higher Education Funding Council's Science Research Investment Fund.			

	University of Dundee
	The Students' Union recently received an extensive overhaul. Belmont Hall is also due to be upgraded though details are not yet clear.
	    The University has developed a major reputation within the medical and biosciences sector and thus substantial funding for research has been obtained. For those following genetics, a Post Genome Research Centre is due to be established. Further plans are in place for the Queen Mother's Centenary Research Centre.
	    To complement the opening of the Centre for Legal Practice, Dundee is to be a centre for the Scottish Institute for Enterprise.			

Campus room rental**	Minimum £42		Maximum £75	
Yield range	9.9–10.9%			
Type of property	3 bed house (i.e. 2 bed upstairs + 1 converted other)	4 bed house	5 bed house	6 or more bed house
Entry price Median room rate Average yield B* B – Estimated annual profit	£58,000 £45 10.9% £2,466	£80,000 £42 9.9% £2,717	£100,000 £42 9.9% £3,396	£120,000 £45 10.6% £4,752
Financial scores	Capital growth (out of 5) 4	Yield (out of 5) 3.5	Total (out of 10) 7.5	

Description	The capital of Tayside Region and with a population of roughly 150,000, Dundee is large enough to support all the activities expected of a major city but small enough not to be overwhelming.
	    Dundee University's main campus is a short walk from the city centre. Architecturally, there is a mixture of old and new.
	    The city overlooks the beautiful River Tar. The local area is in the lowest insurance band rating, and this is just one reflection of the success of council-police community safety initiatives. The city itself is kept relatively clean and is generally calm.			

Websites to advertise on	Local and national student listings: www.student-accom.com City information for students: www.accommodationforstudents.com Student lettings: www.student-accommodation-uk.co.uk Student lets Dundee region: www.lets-stay.com			

Estate agents	Address	Tel	Web
Blackadders	40 Whitehall Street, Dundee DD1 4AF	01382 342222	www.blackadders.co.uk
Your Move	22 Whitehall Crescent, Dundee DD1 4AU	01382 224333	www.your-move.co.uk
Michael A Brown	17 South Tay Street, Dundee DD1 1NR	01382 204242	
Cowie Campbell	95 Fort Street, Broughty Ferry, Dundee DD5 2AA	01382 776200	www.cowiecampbell.co.uk
Letting agents	Address	Tel	Web
Miller Hendry	8 Whitehall Crescent, Dundee DD1 4AU	01382 200301	www.miller-hendry.com
Shield and Kyd	15 Whitehall Crescent, Dundee DD1 4AR	01382 202773	www.shieldandkyd.co.uk
Thorntons	3 Whitehall Crescent, Dundee DD1	01382 200099	www.thorntonsws.co.uk
Lawson Coull and Duncan	136–138 Nethergate, Dundee DD1 4PA	01382 227555	www.lawsoncoull.co.uk
Keir Moodie and Co	20 Whitehall Crescent, Dundee DD4 4AU	01382 204138	www.mge.uk.net

Durham

University	University of Durham
Population	87,725

	Student population	Undergraduate	Postgraduate	Total
		10765	4550	15315
	Campus capacity	4786	600	5386
	Size of market	5979	3950	9,929

Drop-out rates	5%
Student areas	Bowburn, Framwellgate Moor, Gilesgate Moor, Langley Moor, Meadowfield, Viaduct, Nevilles Cross, Claypath, Centre, West Cornforth

Accommodation officer contacts

University	Tel	Address	Web	Landlord accreditation scheme?
University of Durham	0191 374 3330	Students' Union, Dunelm House, New Elvert, Durham DH1 3AN	www.dur.ac.uk/ colleges.htm	Yes

Planned development for city	There are plans to radically transform the city.
	   The 20-year masterplan aims to put it on par with favoured tourist destinations like Cambridge, Bath, York and Chester.
	   Some of the strengths highlighted from a report in 2004 include the city's heritage, setting, people, learning and its authenticity. However, weaknesses requiring attention include a 'chronic' under-investment in marketing and communications, accessibility problems and 'mediocre' retail provision.
	   The parties involved in the proposed transformation include Durham City and Durham County councils, One NorthEast, Durham University and the Dean and Chapter. The popular travel writer Bill Bryson was awarded an honorary degree by Durham University after he praised the city of Durham, prompting readers 'If you have never been to Durham, go there at once.'

Planned development for university	Pencilled in over the forthcoming years is the construction of its long-planned 16th college, a new 600-bed college and refurbishments to two other colleges, that in total will add 1000 student rooms to the city. The overall £35.5m project is due for completion in 2006.
	   The University has expanded student numbers over the past 15 years in line with the policies of successive governments, and although it has already built about 1000 extra rooms during the same period, the number of students who live out of college in rented housing has increased.
	   A £20m science centre was also opened recently.

Campus room rental:	Minimum £55			Maximum £78	
Yield range	5.6–8.5%				
Type of property	3 bed house (i.e. 2 bed upstairs + 1 converted other)	4 bed house	5 bed house	6 or more bed house	
Entry price***	£80,000	£100,000	£145,000	£225,000	
Median room rate	£47	£45	£45	£45	
Average yield B*	8.3%	8.5%	7.3%	5.6%	
B – Estimated annual profit	£1,702	£2,268	£1,935	£27	

Financial scores	Capital growth (out of 5) 3	Yield (out of 5) 3	Total (out of 10) 6

Description	Durham is one of Britain's most beautiful cities and a pleasure to live in. The University is a very big part of town and supplies a decent chunk of the local population. The locals are friendly and most students really enjoy being there. It receives quite a lot of exposure internationally and is a tourist highlight for visitors nationally and from abroad.
Websites to advertise on	Local and national student listings: www.student-accom.com City information for students: www.accommodationforstudents.com Easy roommate: http://uk.easyroommate.com

Estate agents	Address	Tel	Web
Halifax Property Services	34 Saddler Street, Durham DH1 3NU	0191 3844722	www.halifax.co.uk
Reeds Rains	3a Old Elvet, Durham DH1 3HL	0191 384 1222	durham@ reedsrains.co.uk www.reedsrains.com
JW Wood Estate Agents	7 Old Elvet, Durham DH1 3HL	0191 3869921	durham@jww.co.uk www.jww.co.uk
Pattinson Estate Agents	25 Claypath, Durham DH1 1RH	0191 3832133	durham@ pattinson.co.uk www.pattinson.co.uk

Letting agents	Address	Tel	Web
Stuart Edwards Estate Agents	1 Blue Coat Building, Clay Path, Durham DH1 1RF		

Letting agents	Address	Tel	Web
Robinsons Chartered Surveyors	Residential Lettings & Management, 52 Old Elvet, Durham DH1 3HN	0191 386 2777	www.robinsons estateagents.co.uk
Emmatt Rundle	PO Box 371, Lanchester, Durham DH7 0WZ	01207 528037	emmatt.rundle@ btclick.com www.emmatt-rundle.co.uk
Bairstow Eves	23 Elvet Bridge, Durham DH1 3AA	0191 3862829	www.bairstoweves countrywide.co.uk
Bradley Hall	17 Old Elvet, Durham City, Durham DH13HL	0191 3839999	www.bradleyhall.co.uk

Dyfed (Wales) – Aberystwyth, Carmarthen, Lampeter

Universities	University of Wales Aberystwyth, Trinity College Carmarthen, University of Wales Lampeter
Population	173,635

Student population	Undergraduate	Postgraduate	Total
University of Wales Aberystwyth	8425	2395	10825
Trinity College Carmarthen	2325	285	2610
University of Wales Lampeter	6055	1050	7105
Total	16805	3730	20540
Campus capacity	3910	690	4600
Size of market	12895	3040	15940

Drop-out rates	University of Wales Aberystwyth	7%
	Trinity College Carmarthen	14%
	University of Wales Lampeter	19%

Student areas	Penglais, Carmarthen, Pentre Jane Morgan, Pen-y-Lan, Godre'r Glais, Lampeter

Accommodation officer contacts

University	Tel	Address	Web	Landlord accreditation scheme?
University of Wales Aberystwyth	01970 622772/3	Residential Services, Penbryn, Penglais, Aberystwyth SY23 3BY	www.aber.ac.uk	No
Trinity College Carmarthen	01267 676714	Accommodation Office, Trinity College, Carmarthen SA31 3EP	www.trinity-cm.ac.uk	No
University of Wales Lampeter	01570 424783	Lampeter, Ceredigion SA48 7ED	www.lamp.ac.uk	No

Planned development for city	A new £15m scheme shopping development, which could create up to 250 jobs, has been given the go-ahead by planning chiefs in mid Wales. The major town centre development in Aberystwyth will be built on the site of a livestock market. It is claimed that the shopping centre will attract more shoppers and increase spin-off trade for other town centre shops. Plans for a multi-screen cinema, bowling centre, department store and new shops on a former cattle mart site in Carmarthen were approved in 2004. Councillors have given unanimous backing in principle to the proposal – the seventh in two years. The chamber of trade believes it will bring more visitors to the town.

Planned development for universities	University of Wales Aberystwyth The University has recently completed a new Sports and Excercise Department. Another project, a new International Politics building, is planned. Over £6.5m has been put forward for investment with the refinancing of student accommodation of the student village Pentre Jane Morgan. The agreement grants a 25-year lease for Pentre Jane Morgan to Tai Cartrefi, and a subsidiary of Gwalia Housing Group, and a not-for-profit social landlord registered with The National Assembly for Wales.
	Trinity College Carmarthen The University of Wales has recommended that the University should be strengthened and expanded to include other university sector colleges in Wales. The recommendation would include Carmarthen's Trinity College as a full member of the University of Wales alongside such universities as Aberystwyth, Bangor, Cardiff, Lampeter and Swansea. At the moment the College is an Associate College that awards University of Wales degrees.
	University of Wales Lampeter In January 2004, the University broke with tradition by enrolling students to start courses in January. This is the first Welsh institution to offer admission to some degrees in January, as well as in the traditional month of September. This means that students starting their degree course this month can 'fast-track' their studies to graduate at the same time as students who began in the autumn, by taking extra modules during summer holidays.

Campus room rental**	Minimum £42		Maximum £95

Yield range	5.4–6.1%			

Type of property	3 bed house (i.e. 2 bed upstairs + 1 converted other)	4 bed house	5 bed house	6 or more bed house
Entry price	£100,000	£130,000	£180,000	£200,000
Median room rate	£43	£41	£41	£41
Average yield B*	6.1%	5.9%	5.4%	5.8%
B – Estimated annual profit	£351	£318	-£392	£250

Financial scores	Capital growth (out of 5)	Yield (out of 5)	Total (out of 10)
	2	3	5

Description	If you like pubs, Aberystwyth is the place to be. Some students complain about how far Aberystwyth is from any other large cities. In reality the situation isn't that bad. Aberystwyth is the terminus of the mainline railway from Birmingham, which makes rail travel fairly simple.

	Lampeter is set in the beautiful Teifi Valley. The scenery is absolutely stunning and this is what attracts many students. The town itself is pretty with a population of 3000 and a few small shops. The nearest big towns are Carmarthen and Aberystwth. This can be really important as Lampeter can get a bit claustrophobic at times. Carmarthen is the commercial centre for a large and thriving area. A busy market town, it has a good mix of traditional and modern shopping facilities, excellent leisure facilities and nightlife. It is served by major road and rail networks and is within easy reach of ferry services to and from Ireland.
Websites to advertise on	Local and national student listings: www.student-accom.com City information for students: www.accommodationforstudents.com

Estate agents	Address	Tel	Web
Aled Ellis and Co Ltd	16 Terrace Road, Aberystwyth, Dyfed SY23 1NP	01970 626160	www.aledellis.com
Gerald R Vaughan Estate Agents	27 Lammas Street, Carmarthen, Dyfed SA31 3AL	01267 220424	www.geraldvaughan.co.uk
Roderick Price	19–20 Lammas Street, Carmarthen, Dyfed SA31 3AL	01267 230571	www.roderickprice.co.uk

Letting agents	Address	Tel	Web
Halifax Property Services John Francis	18 Lammas Street, Carmarthen, Dyfed SA31 3AJ	01267 233111	www.johnfrancis.co.uk
Lloyd Herbert And Jones	10 Chalybeate Street, Aberystwyth, Dyfed SY23 1HS	01970 624328	www.lhj-property.co.uk
Morgan & Davies – Ceredigion	12 Harford Square, Lampeter, Dyfed SA48 7DT	01570 423623	www.morgananddavies.co.uk
Peter Evans and Co	24 Blue Street, Carmarthen, Dyfed SA31 3LY		www.petersonline.co.uk
Shearer And Morris	23 Terrace Road, Aberystwyth, Dyfed SY23 1NP	01970 625020	www.shearerandmorris.co.uk

Edinburgh

Universities	University of Edinburgh, Edinburgh College of Art, Heriot-Watt University, Napier University, Queen Margaret University College
Population	449,020

	Student population	Undergraduate	Postgraduate	Total
	University of Edinburgh	1295	5945	22095
	Edinburgh College of Art	16150	280	1575
	Heriot-Watt University	5130	3065	8195
	Napier University	10745	2590	13335
	Queen Margaret University College	3680	905	4585
	Total	37000	12785	49785
	Campus capacity	9200	1800	11000
	Size of market	27800	10985	38785

Drop-out rates	University of Edinburgh	7%
	Edinburgh College of Art	14%
	Heriot-Watt University	14%
	Napier University	18%
	Queen Margaret University College	15%

Student areas	Abbeyhill, Bruntsfield, city centre, Corstorphine, Fountainbridge, Leith, Marchmont, Morningside, New Town, Newington, Polwarth, Sighthill, West End

Accommodation officer contacts

University	Tel	Address	Web	Landlord accreditation scheme?
University of Edinburgh	0131 667 1971	Allocations Division, Pollock Halls of Residence, 18 Holyrood Park Road, Edinburgh EH16 5AY	www.ed.ac.uk	Yes
Edinburgh College of Art	0131 221 6023	Student Welfare Services, Lauriston Place, Edinburgh EH3 9DF	www.eca.ac.uk	No
Heriot-Watt University	0131 451 3386	Accommodation Office, Hugh Nisbet Building, Riccarton Campus, Edinburgh EH14 4AS	www.hw.ac.uk	Yes
Napier University	0131 455 4545/ 4211	Accommodation Service, Craiglockhart Campus, 219 Colinton Road, Edinburgh EH14 1DJ	www.napier.ac.uk	No

Queen Margaret University College	0131 317 3311	Accommodation Office, Corstorphine Campus, Clerwood Terrace, Edinburgh EH12 8TS	www.qmced.ac.uk Yes
Planned development for city	The redevelopment of one of Edinburgh New Town's most famous buildings is to cost £60m. The former post office site is being turned into the capital's biggest speculative office development. Waverley Gate is a flagship development in the heart of Edinburgh's historic New Town.		
	Recycling services in Edinburgh will receive an £83m boost from the Scottish Executive's strategic waste fund. The money will go towards initiatives aimed at recycling an extra one million tonnes of material by 2020. The funding is part of £138m awarded to four councils in Scotland.		
Planned development for universities	University of Edinburgh Plans for the £200m flagship facility for Scotland's biotechnology activities could create up to 6,000 jobs. The biomedical research park will be built at Little France, next to the new Edinburgh Royal Infirmary and Chancellor's Building, the University's Medical School.		
	Edinburgh College of Art Edinburgh College of Art has an international reputation as one of the most successful independent art colleges in the UK. The facilities are excellent and staff are practising artists, designers, architects, curators and writers, many with international reputations.		
	Heriot-Watt University The first Beer Academy in Scotland, set up by brewing companies with a view to lifelong learning among consumers as well as people in the trade, was launched in 2004.		
	It has a budget of £240,000 donated by Britain's brewers and industry organisations.		
	Napier University Napier University's redeveloped Craiglockhart campus will be home to the University's Business School and has undergone a £25m redevelopment. It features the iconic egg-shaped lecture theatre that has already become a landmark in the capital.		
	Queen Margaret University College The planning committee of East Lothian Council has backed recommendations to grant outline planning permission for Scotland's first university campus of the 21st century. Queen Margaret University College (QMUC), in association with architects Dyer Associates, will prepare detailed plans for the 35-acre site at Craighall. Over 4000 staff and students will relocate from existing campuses at Corstorphine and Leith in 2007. The multi-million pound development will largely be financed by a deal with property developers Persimmon, which will inherit the prime residential site at Corstorphine. Other cash will be raised from the sale of the Leith campus and development fundraising activities.		

Campus room rental**	Minimum £45		Maximum £100	
Yield range	4.7–8.5%			
Type of property	3 bed house (i.e. 2 bed upstairs + 1 converted other)	4 bed house	5 bed house	6 or more bed house
Entry price	£100,000	£155,000	£210,000	£350,000
Median room rate	£60	£61	£58	£58
Average yield B*	8.5%	7.4%	6.5%	4.7%
B – Estimated annual profit	£2,268	£2,200	£1,454	−£2,665
Financial scores	Capital growth (out of 5) 2.5	Yield (out of 5) 3.5	Total (out of 10) 6	
Description	Edinburgh is a vibrant and beautiful city, with the castle overlooking the Princes Street Gardens and Scotland's relaxed licensing laws. However, like all large cities, it is quite expensive though many pubs offer happy hours or student discount nights. Edinburgh has a variety of interesting museums, and numerous beautiful buildings, not to mention theatres. During the Edinburgh Festival the whole city comes alive.			
Websites to advertise on	Local and national student listings: www.student-accom.com City information for students: www.accommodationforstudents.com Student pad Edinburgh: www.studentpad.co.uk/index.htm Queen Mary private sector list: www.qmced.ac.uk/accommod/acclists.htm Information for students: www.studentnewspaper.org Residential lettings: www.drm-residential.fsnet.co.uk Edinburgh property rentals: www.charleswhite.propertysalesonline.com			

Estate agents	Address	Tel	Web
James Gibb	4 Atholl Place, Edinburgh EH3 8HT	0131 2293481	www.jamesgibb.co.uk
Grigor Hales	135 Gorgie Road, Edinburgh EH11 1TH	0131 3135556	www.grigorhales.com
Strutt and Parker	Edinburgh Office, Edinburgh EH3 7HR	0131 2262500	www.struttandparker.co.uk
The M G Partnership	43 Manor Place, Edinburgh EH3 7EB	0131 2400970	www.admit.co.uk

Letting agents	Address	Tel	Web
Savills	46 Charlotte Square, Edinburgh EH2 4HQ	0131 2473700	www.savills.co.uk
Bennett and Robertson	16 Walker Street, Edinburgh EH3 7NN	0131 2254001	www.benrob.co.uk
Shield and Kyd	100 Easter Road, Edinburgh EH7 5RH	0131 6618300	www.shieldandkyd.co.uk
Somerville and Russell	2a Coates Crescent, Edinburgh EH3 7AL	0131 2203503	www.somervilleand russell.co.uk
MacLachlan and MacKenzie	8 Walker Street, Edinburgh EH3 7LH	0131 2203336	www.macmac.com

Exeter	
University	University of Exeter
Population	111,078

	Student population	Undergraduate	Postgraduate	Total
		9370	3775	13150
	Campus capacity	3300	700	4000
	Size of market	6070	3075	9150

Drop-out rates	6%
Student areas	Newton, St James, Pennsylvania

Accommodation officer contacts

University	Tel	Address	Web	Landlord accreditation scheme?
University of Exeter	01392 262524	Accommodation Office, Northcote House, The Queen's Drive, Exeter EX4 4QJ	www.ex.ac.uk	Yes
Planned development for city	A £100m investment in schools in Exeter has been given the go-ahead by Devon County Council. The council has signed a 30-year contract with Mowlem and Innisfree as part of a private finance initiative. All five of Exeter's secondary schools will have new buildings. A £3.5m expansion scheme is being carried out at the airport, creating nearly 100 jobs. A new hangar will enable low cost airline Flybe to expand, creating 96 new full-time jobs in the next five years.
Planned development for university	The University has recently launched a Centre for Climate Change Impact Forecasting, in association with the University of Plymouth. It is also investing a further £35m in accommodation over the next five years. In the first phase this means a brand new hall (Holland Hall) and additional purpose-built rooms at Lopes Hall. About 100 new jobs are being created as part of the Combined Universities in Cornwall initiative. The University of Exeter is to move 500 students and all of its Cornwall-based operations to Tremough Campus at Penryn. They will join the 750 students of Falmouth College of Arts, which has owned and occupied the site since 1999. Falmouth College of Arts and the University of Exeter are to share new buildings, costing £50m, which have been funded mainly by Objective One as part of the Combined Universities in Cornwall (CUC) initiative. The final phase contains laboratories for the University of Exeter and shared facilities such as a library, restaurants and a fitness centre. The two institutions have also paid for a new £18m 500-bed student residence at Tremough.

Campus room rental**	Minimum	Maximum
	£61	£108

Yield range	6.8–7.4%			
Type of property	3 bed house (i.e. 2 bed upstairs + 1 converted other)	4 bed house	5 bed house	6 or more bed house
Entry price	£110,000	£140,000	£175,000	£220,000
Median room rate	£53	£55	£55	£56
Average yield B*	6.8%	7.4%	7.4%	7.2%
B – Estimated annual profit	£1,029	£1,972	£2,465	£2,734

Financial scores	Capital growth (out of 5)	Yield (out of 5)	Total (out of 10)
	2.5	3	5.5

Description	Exeter is in the heart of the West Country. It's not a big city but it is beautiful. According to the EU it has the highest quality of life of any English city and when you get there you can see why. Although not full of clubs, Exeter does have a few. As many potential students seem to suspect, mainstream and cheese rule but contrary to some reports the city does have a decent alternative scene.
Websites to advertise on	Local and national student listings: www.student-accom.com City information for students: www.accommodationforstudents.com Link from University: www.exeteruniversityaccommodation.co.uk Easy roommate: http://uk.easyroommate.com

Estate agents	Address	Tel	Web
Bower & Bower	25 Cowick Street, Exeter EX4 1AL	01392 270778	www.teamprop.co.uk
Bradford & Bingley Marketplace Ltd	12–13 South Street, Exeter EX1 1DZ	01392 274953	www.themarketplace.co.uk
Fulfords	21 Cowick Street, St Thomas, Exeter EX4 1AL	01392 411255	www.fulfords.co.uk
Your Move	79 Fore Street, Exeter EX4 3 HR	01392 491418	www.your-move.co.uk

Letting agents	Address	Tel	Web
Cardens	The Octagon, 54 New North Road, Exeter EX4 4EP	01392 433866	www.cardensestateagents.co.uk

Letting agents	Address	Tel	Web
Connell Estate Agents	8–9 South Street, Exeter EX1 1DZ	01392 221331	www.connells.co.uk
Savills	13 Southernhay West, Exeter EX1 1PJ	01392 253 344	www.savills.co.uk
Miller	19 Paris Street, Exeter EX1 2JB	01392 411917	www.millerco.co.uk
Whitton and Laing	20 Queen Street, Exeter EX4 3SN	01392 259395	www.whittonand laing.com

Glasgow

Universities	Glasgow Caledonian University, Glasgow School of Art, University of Glasgow, Royal Scottish Academy of Music and Drama, University of Strathclyde
Population	578,710

Student population	Undergraduate	Postgraduate	Total
Glasgow Caledonian University	12915	2270	15185
Glasgow School of Art	1205	230	1440
University of Glasgow	19380	5080	24465
Royal Scottish Academy of Music and Drama	555	120	675
University of Strathclyde	14035	8935	22975
Total	48090	16635	64740
Campus capacity	6375	1125	7500
Size of market	41715	15510	57240

Drop-out rates	
Glasgow Caledonian University	17%
Glasgow School of Art	8%
University of Glasgow	12%
Royal Scottish Academy of Music and Drama	6%
University of Strathclyde	12%

Student areas	Anniesland, Bridgeton, Broomhill, Charing Cross, Clydebank, Garnethill, Hillgrove Gardens, Hillpark, Maryhill, Queens Park, Shettleston, West End

Accommodation officer contacts

University	Tel	Address	Web	Landlord accreditation scheme?
Glasgow Caledonian University	0141 331 3980	Caledonian Court, 202/222 Dobbies, Loan, Glasgow G4 0JF	www.gcal.ac.uk	Yes
Glasgow School of Art	0141 332 7683	Accommodation Office, Margaret MacDonald House, 89 Buccleuch Street, Glasgow G3 6QT	www.gsa.ac.uk	No
University of Glasgow	0141 330 4743	Accommodation Office, University of Glasgow, 73 Great George Street, Glasgow G12 8RR	www.gla.ac.uk	Yes
Royal Scottish Academy of Music and Drama	0141 332 4101	100 Renfrew Street, Glasgow G2 3DB	www.rsamd.ac.uk	No

University of Strathclyde	0141 548 3454/ 3561	Residence and Catering Service, Graham Hills Building, 50 Richmond Street, Glasgow G1 1XP	www.strath.ac.uk Yes
Planned development for city	Scotland's first casino resort is set to be built in Glasgow as part of a £562m development on the banks of the River Clyde. The redevelopment will take place on the site of the Scottish Exhibition and Conference Centre (SECC) in the city. At the same time Glasgow-based developer Elphinstone will transform the western end of the SECC into a £350m sustainable urban village. Subject to planning consent, work on the village could be completed by 2011. The development will provide housing, a primary school, nursery and mini-supermarket, with a proposed new £50m, 12,500-seat arena also in the pipeline.		
Planned development for universities	**Glasgow Caledonian University** Glasgow Caledonian University and the University of Glasgow have initiated the evaluation of a new joint School of Nursing to develop new and innovative ways of delivering nurse education and research in Nursing and Midwifery in Glasgow. Initially, both institutions would continue to award their own degrees but would rapidly move to rationalise the provision.		
	Glasgow School of Art The Glasgow School of Art has appointed new staff with Roberta Doyle appointed as Governor. Her interests include the visual arts, theatre, dance, architecture and design.		
	University of Glasgow The University of Glasgow is to share in a £20m cross-research council investment in stem cell research. A major international collaborative project between the University of Glasgow and Motorola Ltd is set to develop the next generation of microchips, backed by £4.5 million funding. SHEFC (Scottish Higher Education Funding Council) has just announced that the University of Glasgow has been awarded £22.627m from the second round of the Science Research Investment Fund (SRIF). The University's Medical School is one of the largest in Europe with over 200 doctors graduating every year. In summer it opened a multi-million pound addition to the medical school.		
	Royal Scottish Academy of Music and Drama The RSAMD School of Music has been rated No. 1 in the UK for music education. The School of Drama is ranked No. 5 in the same league table for drama. The *Guardian* eduction university guide surveyed over 100 universities and colleges throughout the UK, and the RSAMD did particularly well.		

	University of Strathclyde
	The University of Strathclyde has been awarded over £4m to set up the UK's first Doctoral Training Centre in medical devices. The £4.3m award is part of a £25m investment being made by the Engineering and Physical Sciences Research Council (EPSRC) Life Sciences Interface programme, which aims to foster and strengthen collaboration between physical scientists, engineers and life scientists. Four similar centres will be established, at Imperial College London, University College London, the University of Strathclyde, the University of Warwick and a consortium made up of the Universities of Leeds and Sheffield.

Campus room rental**	Minimum	Maximum
	£47	£85

Yield range	11.9–14.4%			
Type of property	3 bed house (i.e. 2 bed upstairs + 1 converted other)	4 bed house	5 bed house	6 or more bed house
Entry price	£69,000	£79,000	£98,000	£124,000
Median room rate	£58	£59	£60	£58
Average yield B*	11.9%	14%	14.4%	13.2%
B – Estimated annual profit	£3,438	£5,319	£6,870	£7,505

Financial scores	Capital growth (out of 5)	Yield (out of 5)	Total (out of 10)
	5	4	9

Description	The city has been dogged with the closure of the steel and ship building industries. Throughout the late 1970s and 1980s, Glasgow fell into a depression, and images of dark buildings and poverty still rest in the minds of many. But in recent years Glasgow has flourished and a grand clean up programme has been part of the process. There are still rough areas with a serious drug and violence problem and it is best to stay clear of these.
	There is plenty to do in Glasgow, especially if you are interested in art. There are over 30 museums and art galleries, and Glasgow was awarded the 1999 City of Architecture and Design.
	Pubs are everywhere in the city centre from trendy bars like Bargo, Candy Bar, and the Buddha and Monkey, to established Irish theme pubs.

Websites to advertise on	Local and national student listings: www.student-accom.com
	City information for students: www.accommodationforstudents.com
	Student room finder: www.thestudentvillage.com
	Student information: www.studentlandlord.org.uk
	Flathunting and rooms to let: www.glasgowwestend.co.uk/flathunting

Estate agents	Address	Tel	Web
Allen and Harris	560 Alexandra Parade, Dennistoun, Glasgow G31 3BP	0141 5567661	www.allenand harris.co.uk
Barton and Hendry	8 Ettrick Walk, Cumbernauld, Glasgow G67 1NE	01236 731816	www.solicitors.gb.com
CKD Galbraith	1 Hillfoot Drive, Bearsden, Glasgow G61 3QL	0141 942 6460	www.ckdgalbraith .co.uk
Clyde Property	145 Byres Road, West End, Glasgow G12 9TT	0141 5761777	www.clydeproperty. co.uk

Letting agents	Address	Tel	Web
Countrywide Estate Agents	107–111 Byres Road, West End, Glasgow G11 5HW	0141 3341214	www.sequence homes.co.uk
Savills	163 West George Street, Glasgow G2 2JJ		www.savills.co.uk
G S Properties	West End, Glasgow G113 1NU	0141 9501919	http://S1homes.com
Seal Estate Agents	450 Paisley Road West, Glasgow G51 1PX	0141 4271112	www.sealestateagents. co.uk
Slater Hogg and Howison	3 Spey Walk, Cumbernaud, Glasgow G67 1DS	01236 458468	www.slaterhogg.co.uk

Guildford

Universities	Surrey Institute of Art and Design University College, University of Surrey
Population	129,717

Student population	Undergraduate	Postgraduate	Total
Surrey Inst of Art and Design			
University College	2890	75	2965
University of Surrey	9825	5845	15670
Total	12715	5920	18635
Campus capacity	3150	550	3700
Size of market	9565	5370	14935

Drop-out rates	Surrey Inst of Art and Design University College 17% University of Surrey 9%
Student areas	Central, near station, Park Barn, Stoughton

Accommodation officer contacts

University	Tel	Address	Web	Landlord accreditation scheme?
Surrey Inst of Art and Design University College	01252 722 441	Accommodation Office, Falkner Road, Farnham GU9 7DS	www.surrart.ac.uk	No
University of Surrey	01483 689092	Accommodation Office, University of Surrey, Guildford GU2 7XH	www.surrey.ac.uk	No

Planned development for city	Businesses in Guildford pump approximately £2 billion into the economy every year and forecasts suggest that the number of people working in the borough is set to rise from 71,300 to 85,100 by 2010. Unemployment is at 0.9 per cent. The services sector dominates the local economy, fuelled by the decision to locate the Regional Development Agency and the Government Office for the South East in Guildford. There is also a growing technology sector.
Planned development for universities	Surrey Inst of Art and Design University College The Surrey Institute of Art and Design University College is submitting an outline planning application for future long-term improvements to its campus in Falkner Road, Farnham, following a successful presentation of its proposals to local residents as part of a public consultation process. Aimed at upgrading facilities as it works towards attainment of university status, the proposed developments will be realised over several years.
	University of Surrey The Engineering and Physical Sciences Research Council (EPSRC) has recognised and rewarded the University's commitment to industrially

	focused research and training with an £8.8m grant. The 30% increase in revenue, the maximum increase allowed, will fund a new Collaborative Training Account (CTA) to continue it world-class research and training programmes.

Campus room rental**	Minimum £45		Maximum £100	
Yield range	6.6–7.8%			

Type of property	3 bed house (i.e. 2 bed upstairs + 1 converted other)	4 bed house	5 bed house	6 or more bed house
Entry price	£150,000	£180,000	£250,000	£285.000
Median room rate	£75	£75	£70	£70
Average yield B*	7.1%	7.8%	6.6%	6.9%
B – Estimated annual profit	£1,710	£3,180	£1,910	£2,967

Financial scores	Capital growth (out of 5) 2.5	Yield (out of 5) 3	Total (out of 10) 5.5

Description	Guildford is a pretty place for the most part. The town centre has some nice old buildings, and plenty of decent pubs. Heading into London is probably your best chance of finding some decent entertainment after 11 pm. This is relatively easy but trains don't run late so you will either have to drive or club till dawn. However, Guildford boasts over 25 pubs and bars and a variety of restaurants to suit every taste and budget.
Websites to advertise on	Local and national student listings: www.student-accom.com City information for students: www.accommodationforstudents.com Information provided by the University pf Surrey: www.surrey.ac.uk/Accommodation/buy.html National letting portal: www.letalife.com The letting office: www.naea.co.uk

Estate agents	Address	Tel	Web
Savills	8 Quarry St, Guildford GU1 3UY	01483 796 800	www.savills.co.uk
Curchods	4 London Road, Guildford GU1 2AF	01483 458800	www.curchods.co.uk
Callards Estate Agents	19 Epsom Road, Guildford GU1 3JT	01483 502626	www.callards.net

Estate agents	Address	Tel	Web
Bradford & Bingley	255 High Street, Guildford GU1 3BS	01483 533366	www.bbg.co.uk

Letting agents	Address	Tel	Web
Meldrum Salter Edgley	Pilgrim House, 254 High Street, Guildford GU1 3JG	01483 535533	www.mseproperty.co.uk
Wellers	70 Guildford Street, Chertsey KT16 9BB	01932 568678	www.wellers-auctions.co.uk
Principal	Principal House, 6 Chertsey Road, Woking GU21 5AB	01483 762626	www.principal.uk.com
Alliance Property Management	Matrix House, 2b Merrow Business Centre, Guildford GU4 7WA	01483 211 345	www.alliance-properties.co.uk
Howard Morley & Sons	276 High Street, Guildford GU1 3JL	01483 575304	www.hmorley.co.uk

Hatfield

University	University of Hertfordshire
Population	97,546

	Student population	Undergraduate	Postgraduate	Total
		17015	3885	20900
	Campus capacity	2600	400	3000
	Size of market	14615	3285	17900

Drop-out rates	13%
Student areas	Birchwood, Millwards, Potters Bar

University	Accommodation officer contacts			
	Tel	Address	Web	Landlord accreditation scheme?
University of Hertfordshire	01707 284063	Residential Services, Butler Hall, Bishops Rise, Hatfield AL10 9BT	www.herts.ac.uk	Yes

Planned development for city	The council considers its main objective to be continuous improvements in the quality of life by providing accessible, quality services in the areas of sport, leisure, culture and recreation.
Planned development for universities	A new campus was opened in 2003 and as a result the fabric and identity of the university will change greatly. The new de Havilland Campus in Hatfield will be the largest academic development in the UK (with a whopping £105m being spent). This means that there will be just two major campuses within walking distance of each other. The University of Hertfordshire will operate virtually as a single campus community giving it a far better chance of developing a strong, unified identity. New facilities are planned to include a main sports hall with 12 badminton courts, also available for volleyball, basketball and indoor hockey, a 25-metre eight-lane swimming pool, a large health and fitness suite, a four-lane indoor cricket centre, a 12-metre high climbing wall, as well as new grass and artificial pitches. A new Postgraduate Medical School opens in 2005.

Campus room rental**	Minimum	Maximum
	£46	£70

Yield range	5.2–7%

Type of property	3 bed house (i.e. 2 bed upstairs + 1 converted other)	4 bed house	5 bed house	6 or more bed house
Entry price	£150,000	£165,000	£210,000	£300,000
Median room rate	£62	£62	£55	£55
Average yield B*	5.8%	7%	6.2%	5.2%
B – Estimated annual profit	£244	£1,900	£890	−£1,092

Financial scores	Capital growth (out of 5)	Yield (out of 5)	Total (out of 10)
	2.5	3	5.5

Description	All the sites are in the same general area north of London. Getting into town is quite easy. Each of the sites has its charms. Apart from Hatfield they have some history and are pleasant. Amenities are good with supermarkets and leisure facilities that you would expect from any fair sized town.
Websites to advertise on	Local and national student listings: www.student-accom.com City information for students: www.accommodationforstudents.com National listings: www.upmystreet.com Link to local lettings: www.letalife.com National listings: www.torent.co.uk

Estate agents	Address	Tel	Web
Century 21 Estates	4 The Arcade, Hatfield AL10 0JY	01707 266885	www.century21uk.com
Wrights of Hatfield	26 Town Centre, Hatfield AL10 0LD	01707 273183	www.wrightshomes.co.uk
Holloway & Co Estate Agents	Fillingham Way, Salisbury Village, Hatfield AL4 0JJ	0845 4300404	www.hollowayandco.co.uk
Andrew Ward	35 Bradmore Green, Brookmans Park, Hatfield AL9 7QR	01707 649779	www.andrewward.co.uk

Letting agents	Address	Tel	Web
Statons	53 Bradmore Green, Brookmans Park, Hatfield AL9 7QS	01707 661144	www.statons.co.uk

Letting agents	Address	Tel	Web
Pikes Estate Agents	7 The Arcade, Hatfield AL10 0JY	01707 260707	www.pikesestate agents.co.uk
Mather Marshall – Hatfield	5 Town Centre, Hatfield AL10 0JZ	01707 270777	www.mathermarshall. com
Langleys Estate Agents	193 Hatfield Road, St Albans AL1 4LH	01727 891010	www.langleysestate-agents.co.uk/
J E Grubb	7 The Broadway, Hatfield AL9 5BG	01707 271450	www.jegrubb.co.uk

Huddersfield

University	University of Huddersfield
Population	388,576

	Student population	Undergraduate	Postgraduate	Total
		14750	3640	18395
	Campus capacity	1650	300	1950
	Size of market	13100	3340	16445

Drop-out rates	14%
Student areas	Birkby, Central, Fixby, Lockwood, Longroyd Bridge, Marsh, Milnsbridge, Moldgreen, Mountjoy, Newsome, Springwood

Accommodation officer contacts

University	Tel	Address	Web	Landlord accreditation scheme?
University of Huddersfield	01484 472738	Accommodation Services, Level 2, Great Hall, Queensgate Campus, Huddersfield HD1 3DH	www.hud.ac.uk/ accommodation	Yes

Planned development for city	A surprising property boom in Huddersfield hit the headlines in summer 2003. Potential buyers queued for their chance to buy one of the apartments in a £20m conversion of a former foundry and mill in the town. One estate agent sold 52 out of 57 homes in 1535 The Melting Pot in three hours – making it is the fastest selling development in the UK. More conversions are planned for nearby mill towns including Huddersfield and Dewsbury. As for the developments through the council, much inward investment is being sought. The focus seems to be on regenerating the town centres of Huddersfield and other major towns in the area. The Town Centre Strategy as outlined by the council sets out to assist the process of regeneration and help each town find appropriate catalysts for growth or investment.
Planned development for university	A planned merger between the University of Huddersfield and Doncaster College was abandoned in 2003. Despite early signs that they could work together to attract more students, funding and discussions indicating that 2006 would be the date, the talks slowly dwindled to a close after Huddersfield University backed out. Tacked onto the side of the Students' Union is Eden. This used to be a nightclub but is currently under redevelopment. No one is quite sure what will become of it but indications suggest that it won't be a nightclub any more.

Campus room rental**	Minimum £55	Maximum £82
Yield range	9.3–14.3%	

Type of property	3 bed house (i.e. 2 bed upstairs + 1 converted other)	4 bed house	5 bed house	6 or more bed house
Entry price	£54,000	£63,000	£95,000	£140,000
Median room rate	£50	£48	£46	£46
Average yield B*	13%	14.3%	11.4%	9.3%
B – Estimated annual profit	£3,210	£4,385	£4,373	£4,078

Financial scores	Capital growth (out of 5)	Yield (out of 5)	Total (out of 10)
	5	3.5	8.5

Description	The University of Huddersfield is a dynamic and expanding institution in a thriving West Yorkshire town. It has a friendly reputation, an excellent graduate employment record and high level of student support. Students come from all over the UK and over 60 countries.
	The University has strong links with industry, commerce and the arts and is among the UK's top five providers of 'sandwich courses' where students can take advantage of a paid work placement in industry or commerce. Over 4,000 undergraduates a year benefit from a year's work placement during their course.
	On the social scene, there are stacks of good pubs and bars in Huddersfield, many of which have a late licence.

Websites to advertise on	Local and national student listings: www.student-accom.com
	City information for students: www.accommodationforstudents.com
	Student housing: www.housinguk.net
	Huddersfield classifieds: www.huddersfieldontheweb.com
	Local listings: www.huddsonline.co.uk

Estate agents	Address	Tel	Web
Whitegates	30 Westgate, Huddersfield HD1 1NX	01484 548126	www.white gates.co.uk
William H Brown	8 Westgate, Huddersfield HD1 1NN	01484 542072	www.sequence home.co.uk
Bradford & Bingley	20 Cloth Hall Street, Huddersfield HD1 2EG	01484 422337	www.bbg.co.uk
Reeds Rains	23 Market Place, Huddersfield HD1 2AA	01484 517822	www.reedsrains.co.uk

Letting agents	Address	Tel	Web
Simon Blythe Estate Agents	11–13 Byram Arcade, Westgate, Huddersfield HD1 1ND	01484 424422	www.simonblyth.co.uk
Huddersfield Properties	16 Imperial Arcade, Huddersfield HD1 2BR	01484 543225	www.huddersfield properties.com
Whitworths	17 Cloth Hall Street, Huddersfield HD1 2DX	01484 427467	www.whitworths estateagents.co.uk
Lancasters Property	19 Railway Street, Huddersfield HD1 1JS	01484 532476	www.lancasters-property.co.uk
Dowling Kerr Estates	102 Huddersfield Road, Holmfirth, Huddersfield HD9 3AX	01484 680800	www.earnshawkay estates.co.uk

Hull	
University	University of Hull
Population	243,595

	Student population	Undergraduate	Postgraduate	Total
		17725	4215	21940
	Campus capacity	2580	0	2580
	Size of market	15145	4215	19360

Drop-out rates	10%
Student areas	Beverley Road, Cottingham, Central Hull, Newland Avenue, Princess Avenue

	Accommodation officer contacts			
University	Tel	Address	Web	Landlord accreditation scheme?
University of Hull	01482 305342	Accommodation Office, University of Hull, 11 Salmon Grove, Hull HU6 7RX	www.hull.ac.uk/ accom	Yes

Planned development for city	Designs for the biggest, most ambitious city centre redevelopment in Hull have been revealed. The £160m Ferensway development will generate over 2,500 permanent jobs and transform Hull city centre. The 40-acre Ferensway development comprises a new, state of the art integrated transport interchange; a shopping and leisure complex, including around 30 shops and stores; new homes for the Hull Truck Theatre and the Albemarle Music Centre; a hotel and a residential quarter.
Planned development for university	The University of Hull has secured more than £1 million of funding to help boost enterprise and innovation in the Yorkshire and Humber region. The award was made under the second round of funding for the Higher Education Innovation Fund (HEIF2). The University will use the cash to consolidate work already carried out in the field of knowledge transfer. The University also shares a total of £2.5m with other regional partner organisations to be used to deliver a range of activities aimed at boosting enterprise and with it the local economy.

Campus room rental**	Minimum	Maximum
	£61	£75

Yield range	10.8–11.6%

Type of property	3 bed house (i.e. 2 bed upstairs + 1 converted other)	4 bed house	5 bed house	6 or more bed house
Entry price***	£45,000	£65,000	£80,000	£99,000
Median room rate	£35	£40	£38	£38
Average yield B*	11%	11.6%	11.1%	10.8%
B – Estimated annual profit	£1,923	£3,091	£3,544	£4,118

Financial scores	Capital growth (out of 5)	Yield (out of 5)	Total (out of 10)
	4	4.5	8.5

Description	Kingston-upon-Hull is Britain's third largest port and is situated on the Humber estuary, into which the River Hull flows. The surrounding coastline is spectacular, but remains quite grey throughout the year.
	The University is situated two miles from the city centre in a leafy residential area, but the campus itself is ruined somewhat by the array of 1930s and 1960s architecture. However, there are plenty of grassy areas and trees.

Websites to advertise on	National Student website, focus on Hull: www.studentpad.co.uk
	Sister site to studentpad: www.studentlandlord.com
	Local and national student listings: www.student-accom.com
	City information for students: www.accommodationforstudents.com
	Easy roommate: http://uk.easyroommate.com

Estate agents	Address	Tel	Web
Beercock, Wiles & Wick	368 Holderness Road, Hull HU9 3DL	01482 320000	www.beercockwiles.co.uk
Halifax Property Services	Willerby Office, Hull HU1	01482 658822	www.halifax.co.uk
Larards	26 Princes Dock Street, Hull HU2 1JX	01482 223300	www.larards.co.uk
Reeds Rains	2 Kingston Road, The Square, Willerby, Hull HU10 6BN	01482 654464	www.reedsrains.co.uk

Letting agents	Address	Tel	Web
William H Brown – Hull	82 Newland Avenue, Hull HU5 3AB	01482 447748	www.sequencehomes.co.uk

Letting agents	Address	Tel	Web
Whitaker and Thompson	Holderness Road, Hull HU19 3DL	01482 790970	www.whitaker thompson.co.uk
Quick and Clarke	Willerby Office, Hull HU17 7UA	01482 651155	www.quickclarke.co.uk
Philip Bannister and Co	58 Hull Road, Hessle, HU13 0AN	01482 649777	www.philipbannister. co.uk
Garness Jones	732a Amlaby Road, Hull HU4 6BP	01482 564564	www.garness-jones. co.uk

Keele

University	Keele University
Population	122,040

	Student population	Undergraduate 9700	Postgraduate 3180	Total 12880
	Campus capacity	2,220	480	2700
	Size of market	7480	2700	10180

Drop-out rates	8%
Student areas	Dresden, Hanley, Shelton

University — Accommodation officer contacts

University	Tel	Address	Web	Landlord accreditation scheme?
Keele University	01782 583086	Accommodation Centre, University of Keele ST5 5BG	www.keele.ac.uk	Yes

Planned development for city	A £20m flagship regeneration project which could create nearly 5,000 jobs in north Staffordshire was submitted in spring 2004. Advantage West Midlands says the plan for the Chatterley Valley, near Tunstall, will see 288 acres of brownfield land become a hi-tech business park with an urban forest. Around two million square feet of the site will be cleared for development.
Planned development for university	A new £1.2m centre which aims to revolutionise the teaching of science in the West Midlands has been recently built in Staffordshire. The centre is a joint venture between Staffordshire County Council, Keele University, Stoke Education Authority, Staffordshire University and Serco. The facility will serve the entire region and a further £1.3m will be spent over five years to run the centre. Three new institutes have been opened at Keele University's Medical School: the Institute of Primary Care and Health Sciences, the Institute of Ageing and the Institute for Science and Technology in Medicine.

Campus room rental**	Minimum £46	Maximum £76

Yield range				
Type of property	3 bed house (i.e. 2 bed upstairs + 1 converted other)	4 bed house	5 bed house	6 or more bed house
Entry price	£70,000	£90,000	£130,000	£175,000
Median room rate	£40	£42	£42	£44
Average yield B*	8.1%	8.8%	7.6%	7.1%
B – Estimated annual profit	£1,362	£2,267	£2,046	£2,052

Financial scores	Capital growth (out of 5)	Yield (out of 5)	Total (out of 10)
	3	3.5	6.5
Description	Keele University is situated between the towns of Stoke-on-Trent and Newcastle-under-Lyme, on a staggering 617-acre campus, the largest university campus in the country. Many students feel as if they are in the middle of nowhere, and you can understand why. Their feelings, however, are more to do with the fact that there is no large city nearby (the largest, Manchester, being 35 miles away.) There is neither a train station nor a National Express bus stop in Keele, although both of these amenities are available in Stoke. Stoke boasts the Potteries Shopping Centre housing all the major national chains. There are also two cinemas, numerous pubs, a few cheesy clubs and an excellent live music scene.		
Websites to advertise on	Local and national student listings: www.student-accom.com City information for students: www.accommodationforstudents.com National and local listings: www.quality-lettings.co.uk		

Estate agents	Address	Tel	Web
Bradford & Bingley Marketplace Ltd	54 Merrial Street, Newcastle-under-Lyme, Staffordshire ST5 1PT	01782 626321	www.marketplace.co.uk
Brown and Corbishley	Queens Chambers 2–4 Queen Street, Newcastle-under-Lyme, Staffordshire ST5 1EE	01782 717222	www.brownand corbishley.co.uk
E M and F Staffordshire	113 Hassell Street, Newcastle-under-Lyme, Staffordshire ST5 1AX	01782 711022	
Reeds Rains	2a Hassell Street, Newcastle-under-Lyme, Staffordshire ST5 1AH	01782 717273	www.reedsrains.co.uk

Letting agents	Address	Tel	Web
Lowden Noall	71 High Street, Newcastle-under-Lyme, Staffordshire ST5 1PN	01782 618128	www.lowden-noall. co.uk
Property Ease	15 Willotts Hill Road, Newcastle-under-Lyme, Staffordshire ST5 7TF	08701 995 135	www.propertyease. co.uk

Letting agents	Address	Tel	Web
Reeds Rains	2a Hassell Street, Newcastle-under-Lyme, Staffordshire ST5 1AH	01782 717273	www.reedsrains.co.uk
Roger Follwell and Partner	35 Ironmarket, Newcastle-under-Lyme, Staffordshire ST5 1RP	01782 615530	www.follwells.co.uk
Town and Country Property Services	73 High Street, Newcastle-under-Lyme, Staffordshire ST5 1PN	01782 711488	

Lancaster

Universities	Lancaster University, St Martin's College
Population	133,914

	Student population	Undergraduate	Postgraduate	Total
	Lancaster	13515	3215	16730
	St Martin's College	7190	2860	10050
	Total	20705	6075	26780
	Campus capacity	3948	650	4598
	Size of market	16,757	5425	22,182

Drop-out rates	Lancaster University	6%
	St Martin's College	11%

Student areas	University, Greaves, Bowerham, Hala, Scotforth, Primrose, Moorlands, centre and central.

Accommodation officer contacts

University	Tel	Address	Web	Landlord accreditation scheme?
Lancaster University	01524 594910	College and Residence Office, University House, Lancaster University, Lancaster LA1 4YW	www.lancs.ac.uk/ users/cro	Yes
St Martin's College	01524 384336	Bowerham Road, Lancaster LA1 3JD	www.ucsm.ac.uk/ services	No

Planned development for city	The Economic Development Service in the local area was expanded in 2002 to improve the tourism services at Lancaster and Morecambe. The Service is designed to help existing local companies and also to attract investment and businesses. The North West of England was also awarded £175m of European funding to aid and regenrate the region and create Economic Development Zones (EDZs), with Lancaster being one of the 15 locations to receive a share. From this £175m, £8m was awarded to Lancaster to develop the business base and encourage new initatives, leading to 33,000 new jobs and attracting future investment.
Planned development for universities	Lancaster University InfoLab21 – based at Lancaster University – will be a major new ICT (Information and Communication Technologies) facility in the North West of England. The £15m building was made possible with funding from the Northwest Development Agency (NWDA). One of the largest environmental research centres in Europe was launched in spring 2004 at Lancaster University, providing a key facility in the quest to sustain the planet.

	The £25m Lancaster Environment Centre brings together around 300 researchers and lecturers, all working to find solutions to major environmental problems from tracking pollutants to generating sustainable energy. The University is also working extensively on upgrades to its campus accommodation.			
	St Martin's College St Martin's College has been awarded £700,000 by the Higher Education Innovation Fund (HEIF) – a major part of the government's strategy to increase prosperity and provide high quality job opportunities. It will support new and existing initiatives over the next two years to increase knowledge transfer to businesses and the wider community in Cumbria and Lancashire.			
Yield range	7.7–8.5%			
Type of property	3 bed house (i.e. 2 bed upstairs + 1 converted other)	4 bed house	5 bed house	6 or more bed house
Entry price Median room rate Average yield B* B – Estimated annual profit	£80,000 £45 7.9% £1,476	£95,000 £43 8.5% £2,193	£135,000 £44 7.7% £2,197	£155,000 £44 8% £2,952
Financial scores	Capital growth (out of 5) 3	Yield (out of 5) 4	Total (out of 10) 7	
Description	Lancaster is one of the largest towns in Lancashire, and has easy train access to both London and Edinburgh. An historic city, it is surrounded by countryside, but four or five miles to the west are the seaside towns of Morecambe and Heysham. Just to the north is the Lake District, famous for its beautiful landscape, rolling hills and bitter winds. 　　The city itself can only be described as charming. It is friendly (as only Lancashire can be), and yet it has all the amenities of a large city, including shopping at Marketgate and the St Nicholas Arcade. It rains quite a lot too in Lancaster, so be prepared. Lancaster is only 15 minutes train ride from Preston and has good access to Manchester.			
Websites to advertise on	Local and national student listings: www.student-accom.com City information for students: www.accommodationforstudents.com Student lettings: www.student-accommodation-uk.co.uk Lancaster student housing: www.studenthousinglancaster.co.uk Students' Union links: www.lusu.co.uk			
Estate agents	Address	Tel	Web	
Sue Bridges	43 China Street, Lancaster LA1 1EX	01524 68811	www.suebridges.co.uk suebridgesestate @aol.com	

Estate agents	Address	Tel	Web
Ratcliffe and Bibby Solicitors	69/71 Church Street, Lancaster LA1 1ET	01524 39039	lancaster@rblegal.co.uk www.ratcliffe-bibby.co.uk
Reeds Rains	48 Market Street, Lancaster LA1 1HS	01524 63494	lancaster@ reedsrains.co.uk www.reedsrains.com
Fisher Wrathall	The Old Warehouse, Castle Hill, Lancaster LA1 1YN	01524 68822	property@ fisherhwrathall.co.uk www.fisher wrathall.co.uk

Letting agents	Address	Tel	Web
Reeds Rains	48 Market Street, Lancaster LA1 1HS	01524 63494	lancaster@ reedsrains.co.uk www.reedsrains.com
Fisher Wrathall	The Old Warehouse, Castle Hill, Lancaster LA1 1YN	01524 68822	property@ fisherhwrathall.co.uk www.fisherwrathall .co.uk
Richard Turner & Son	Royal Oak Chambers, Main Street, Bentham, Lancaster LA2 7HF	015242 61444	property@rturner.co.uk www.rturner.co.uk
Farrell Hayworth	53a Market Street, Lancaster LA1 1JG	01524 842222	lancaster@farrell heyworth.co.uk www.farrell heyworth.co.uk
Countrywide Residential Lettings	12 New Street, Lancaster LA1 1EG	01524 68383	www.crldirect.co.uk

Leeds

Universities	University of Leeds, Leeds Metropolitan University, Trinity and All Saints, Northern School of Contemporary Dance
Population	715,404

Student population	Undergraduate	Postgraduate	Total
University of Leeds	25685	9880	35570
Leeds Metropolitan University	22460	4375	26830
Trinity and All Saints	2130	400	2530
Northern School of Contemporary Dance	160	0	160
Total	50435	14655	65090
Campus capacity	9227	1400	10527
Size of market	41208	13255	54563

Drop-out rates		
University of Leeds		8%
Leeds Metropolitan University		12%
Trinity and All Saints		13%
Northern School of Contemporary Dance		15%

Student areas	Beeston, Burley, Headingley, Hyde Park, Kirkstall, Meanwood, Woodhouse

Accommodation officer contacts

University	Tel	Address	Web	Landlord accreditation scheme?
University of Leeds	0113 343 7777	Accommodation Services, The University of Leeds, Leeds LS2 9JT	www.leeds.ac.uk/ accommodation/ costs.htm	Yes
Leeds Metropolitan University	0113 283 5972	Room D207, Leeds Metropolitan University, Calverley Street, Leeds LS1 3HE	www.leedsmet. ac.uk/services/ accom_types.htm	Yes
Trinity and All Saints	0113 283 7111	Accommodation Office, Brownberrie Lane, Horsforth, Leeds LS18 5HD	www.tasc.ac.uk	Yes
Northern School of Contemporary Dance	0113 219 3000	98 Chapeltown Road, Leeds LS7 4BH	www.nscd.ac.uk	No
Planned development for city	Plans for a Leeds supertram are to be revamped due to spiralling costs. The supertram is the largest single project of engineering ever undertaken in the city.			

	A plan for a £400m scheme to regenerate an undeveloped part of Leeds city centre is to be looked into further. The area is the Eastgate and Harewood quarter. The development will include shops, offices, houses and extra parking. It is hoped the project will attract more businesses to the area, especially national chains.

Planned development for universities	University of Leeds
	In 2001 Leeds University officially merged with Bretton Hall College. This has distinctly added to the University due to the highly respected reputation of Bretton Hall in the fine arts.
	    Leading cancer researchers and experts in genetics, pathology, immunology and molecular medicine from the University of Leeds are to join forces in a new £20m building to be based at St James' University Hospital in Leeds.
	    The University of Leeds has won £2.5m to boost the region as a target for inward investment, develop business in Yorkshire and aid regeneration in Leeds. The programmes result from a successful bid in the second round of the HEIF.

	Leeds Metropolitan University HEIF has also provided Leeds Met with a further £1.2m over two years to boost its incubator developments and business support activities to Yorkshire businesses.
	Trinity and All Saints A new student services centre, conference room, better disabled access and a new IT infrastructure are happening thanks to a capital allocation of nearly £1 million from the Higher Education Funding Council for England (HEFCE).
	Northern School of Contemporary Dance The Institution was founded in 1985 and is a specialist dance training college with less than 200 students. Before the turn of the millennium, it completed a £3.2m redevelopment, including 'state of the art', purpose-built dance training facilities.

Campus room rental:	Minimum		Maximum	
	£40		£90	

Yield range	8.6–9.8%			
Type of property	3 bed house (i.e. 2 bed upstairs + 1 converted other)	4 bed house	5 bed house	6 or more bed house
Entry price***	£85,000	£100,000	£135,000	£165,000
Median room rate	£52	£52	£54	£56
Average yield B*	8.6%	9.8%	9.4%	9.6%
B – Estimated annual profit	£2,041	£3,321	£4,077	£5,209

Financial scores	Capital growth (out of 5)	Yield (out of 5)	Total (out of 10)
	3.5	4	8.5

Description	A vibrant, affluent city which complements its economic success with a lively arts, sporting and entertainment scene. It is the second largest metropolitan district in the UK, extending 15 miles from east to west, and 13 miles from north to south. Leeds has transformed its once neglected Waterfront into a thriving visitor attraction and fashionable restaurant area. It is also Britain's most significant legal and financial centre outside London. This provides students with many opportunities for work experience.
	Leeds is a city that has a vibrant, youthful feel about it, and also has some of the best clubs in the country. Socially Leeds has much to offer. Thanks to the tolerant council, Leeds is an all-night town with many clubs and bars open until the early hours.
Websites to advertise on	Local and national student listings: www.student-accom.com City information for students: www.accommodationforstudents.com Easy roommate: http://uk.easyroommate.com Leeds student newspaper: www.healheadingley.org.uk Leeds lets: www.leedsstudenthomes.com Leeds property association: www.lpa.org.uk

Estate agents	Address	Tel	Web
Acorn Estates	71 High Street Yeadon, Leeds LS19 7SP	0113 2391193	www.acorn-leeds.co.uk
David Moor	129 Queen Street Morley, Leeds LS27 8HE	0113 2534151	www.property world.com/ davidmoor
Halifax Property Services	Leeds City Square, Leeds LS1 5NS	0113 2150735/7	www.halifax.co.uk
Jump	Beeston, Leeds, West Yorkshire	0113 3872500	www.homestarterplc. com

Letting agents	Address	Tel	Web
Manning Stainton	Oakwood, Leeds LS8 4BA	0113 2351361	www.manningstainton. co.uk
Morehouses	50 Austhorpe Road Crossgates, Leeds LS15 8DX	0113 2608484	www.morehouses.co.uk
Pickerings	16 St. Annes Road, Leeds LS6 3NX	0113 2744775	www.pickeringhomes. com
Morgans City Living	46 The Calls, Leeds LS2 7EY	0113 3980098	www.cityliving.co.uk
Morfitt Shaw Estate & Letting Agents	80 Street Lane, Leeds LS22 5AG	0113 393 0113	www.morfittshaw.co.uk

Leicester

Universities	De Montfort University, University of Leicester
Population	279,923

	Undergraduate	Postgraduate	Total
Student population			
De Montfort University	18190	3915	22105
University of Leicester	9215	6705	15920
Total	27405	10620	38025
Campus capacity	4407	780	5187
Size of market	22998	9840	32838

Drop-out rates	De Montfort University 13% University of Leicester 9%
Student areas	Aylestone, city centre, Clarendon Park, Evington Road, Narborough Road, off London Road, West End, Western Park

Accommodation officer contacts

University	Tel	Address	Web	Landlord accreditation scheme?
De Montfort University	0116 255 1551	The Accommodation Manager, Fletcher Building, The Gateway, Leicester LE1 9BH	www.dmu.ac.uk	No
The University of Leicester	0116 252 2428	Accomodation Office, University Road, Leicester LE1 7RH	www.le.ac.uk	No

Planned development for city	A new theatre development in Leicester has been awarded a £12m grant by Arts Council England. The new centre, which will replace the city's Haymarket and Phoenix venues, is scheduled to open in 2007. The development, which will cost £31m in total, is part of a £60m scheme for the city's St George's district. A new 3,000 home village is being planned for Leicester by the city council. The proposed 'eco-village' near Beaumont Leys is being called the most innovative in the city in 30 years. The Ashton Green development is planned to meet the growing demand for housing in the city area.
Planned development for universities	De Montfort University East Midlands Incubation Network (EMIN) has been awarded £2m to continue EMIN's core remit, which is to drive up rates of new start businesses in the region. DMU's institutional award is for £1.93m for a project which will see DMU continue capitalising on its own expertise, research and facilities, as well as the experience and infrastructure already developed. DMU has a few campuses located throughout the UK, but its main location is in Leicester.

	The University of Leicester The University is involved in a number of regional partnerships – including Nottingham, Loughborough and De Montfort universities – which have attracted over £9m from the Higher Education Funding Council. The funding direct to Leicester from these partnerships is a substantial £1.6m.			
Campus room rental**	Minimum £45		Maximum £100	
Yield range	6.9–8.8%			
Type of property	3 bed house (i.e. 2 bed upstairs + 1 converted other)	4 bed house	5 bed house	6 or more bed house
Entry price Median room rate Average yield B* B – Estimated annual profit	£78,000 £45 8.1% £1,566	£92,000 £43 8.8% £2,328	£140,000 £46 7.7% £2,348	£175,000 £43 6.9% £1,826
Financial scores	Capital growth (out of 5) 3	Yield (out of 5) 3.5	Total (out of 10) 6.5	
Description	Leicester is a decent sized city which has plenty going on. Quite a lot of the students are locals and with Leicester University also in the town there is plenty of provision. It is a city with a long and varied past, which looks to the future. Primarily it is a city of diversity, offering citizens and visitors alike the benefits of a cosmopolitan environment. It has long been a major commercial and manufacturing centre for the Midlands. There is easy access from London, East Midlands and Birmingham International airports. The city's strong Indian population is reflected in the number of good curry restaurants. For a cultural day out with bargains on the menu, head for the market, the largest of its kind in Europe.			
Websites to advertise on	Local and national student listings: www.student-accom.com City information for students: www.accommodationforstudents.com Leicester student homes: www.leicesterstudenthomes.co.uk Leicester classifieds: www.leicesterontheweb.com/classifieds Leicester flat share: www.flatshare-flatmate.co.uk/Leicester			

Estate agents	Address	Tel	Web
Bradford & Bingley Marketplace Ltd	48 Granby Street, Leicester LE1 1 DH	0116 2551518	www.bbg.co.uk
Connells Estate Agents	8/10 Leicester Road, Blaby, Leicester LE84GQ	0116 2477477	www.connells.co.uk

Estate agents	Address	Tel	Web
Haart	25 Halford Street, Leicester LE1 1JA	0116 2629913	www.spicer haart.co.uk
Spencers	22–30 Halford Street, Leicester LE7 2JT	0116 2538711	www.spencers.co.uk
Letting agents	Address	Tel	Web
Foxtons Estate Agents	19 Halford Street, Leicester LE1 1JA	0116 2512211	www.foxtons.com
Halifax Property Services	City Centre, Leicester LE1 1JA	0116 2539977	www.halifax.co.uk
James Sellicks	56 Granby Street, Leicester LE1 1DH	0116 2854554	www.jamessellicks.com
Moore & York	83 Narborough Road, Leicester LE3 0LF	0116 254 9555	www.moore-york.co.uk
Seths Estate Agents	173 Melton Road, Leicester LE4 6QT	0116 2668536	www.seths.co.uk

Lincoln

Universities	Bishop Grosseteste College, University of Lincoln
Population	85,616

Student population		Undergraduate	Postgraduate	Total	
	Bishop Grosseteste College	895	320	1215	
	University of Lincoln	13110	2205	15320	
	Total	14005	2525	16535	
	Campus capacity	1384	200	15824	
	Size of market	12621	2325	14951	

Drop-out rates	Bishop Grosseteste College 11%
	University of Lincoln 13%

Student areas	Central, High Street, Newlands, off Monks Road, Uphill, West End, West Parade

University	Accommodation officer contacts			
	Tel	Address	Web	Landlord accreditation scheme?
Bishop Grosseteste College	01522 527347	Accommodation Office, Lincoln LN1 3DY	www.bgc.ac.uk	No
University of Lincoln	01522 886225	Residential Services, University of Lincoln, Brayford Pool, Lincoln LN6 7TS	www.ulh.ac.uk	No

Planned development for city	A plan to tackle key issues in the heart of Lincoln, such as transport, the economy and the environment, has been given the go-ahead in a ten-year City Centre Masterplan. The project will provide a vision for the city centre, address key issues and provide a context for future public and private sector investment decisions. It will also contribute to the Local Development Framework, to be completed in 2006 through the commissioning of a Central Rail Corridor Action Plan.
Planned development for universities	**Bishop Grosseteste College** The University of Leicester formed a closer alliance with Bishop Grosseteste in 2003, validating their degrees and undertaking joint research projects. It was also announced in 2003 by the government and the Wellcome Trust that Bishop Grosseteste College, in partnership with the University of Nottingham and University of Leicester, would form one of England's first six science learning centres as part of a £51m project to improve science teaching.
	University of Lincoln There is an ambitious new five-storey building with fancy restaurant and studios. Probably most important however is the new Students'

	Union building in converted Victorian railway sheds, aiming to be the best SU in the UK. There are also plans for an arts centre.			
Campus room rental**	Minimum £54		Maximum £76	
Yield range	8.1–10.4%			
Type of property	3 bed house (i.e. 2 bed upstairs + 1 converted other)	4 bed house	5 bed house	6 or more bed house
Entry price Median room rate Average yield B* Annual profit	£78,000 £48 8.7% £1,905	£90,000 £50 10.4% £3,470	£130,000 £47 8.5% £2,986	£160,000 £46 8.1% £3,178
Financial scores	Capital growth (out of 5) 3.5	Yield (out of 5) 3	Total (out of 10) 6.5	
Description	Lincoln is a stunning city which has managed to keep its charm without being snobby. This means that there are stacks of good pubs and bars to drink in, many in the new Quayside development next to Brayford Pool. Trips to Nottingham and other big cities can be easily organised. There are still massive plans to make the city one of the top places in the UK but the lack of capital is a stumbling block. A great atmosphere.			
Websites to advertise on	Local and national student listings: www.student-accom.com City information for students: www.accommodationforstudents.com Student accommodation: www.lincolnstudentpad.co.uk Lincoln portal online: www.lincolnontheweb.com			

Estate agents	Address	Tel	Web
Brogden Bews Brown Estate Agents	38–39 Silver Street, Lincoln LN21 1EU	01522 531321	www.bewsbrown.com
Savills	21 Newland, Lincoln LN1 1XG	01522 551100	www.savills.co.uk
Halifax Property Services	42 Silver Street, Lincoln LN2	01522 513456	www.halifax.co.uk
Hodgson Elkington	343 High Street, Lincoln LN5 7DQ	01522 567645	www.hodgson elkington.co.uk

Letting agents	Address	Tel	Web
Kirk Superior Homes	2 Saltergate, Lincoln LN2 1DH	01522 542201	www.kirkhomes.co.uk

Letting agents	Address	Tel	Web
Robert Bell & Co	43, Silver St, Lincoln LN2 1EH	01522 538888	www.robert-bell.org
Stapleton and Co	21 Guildhall Street, Lincoln LN1 1TR	01522 532653	www.stapletonco.co.uk
Turner Evans Stevens	33 Silver Street, Lincoln LN2 1EW	01522 545111	www.ukonline.co.uk
William H Brown – Lincoln	35–36 Silver Street, Lincoln LN2 1EW	01522 534771	www.sequencehome.co.uk

Liverpool

Universities	Edge Hill College of Higher Education, University of Liverpool, Liverpool Hope University College, Liverpool John Moores University
Population	439,476

Student population	Undergraduate	Postgraduate	Total
Edge Hill College of HE	8415	2730	11145
University of Liverpool	16765	5390	22150
Liverpool Hope University College	5645	1685	7330
Liverpool John Moores University	17660	3060	20720
Total	48485	12865	61350
Campus capacity	8108	500	8608
Size of market	40377	12365	52742

Drop-out rates	Edge Hill College of HE 14% University of Liverpool 9% Liverpool Hope University College 17% Liverpool John Moores University 15%
Student areas	Aigburth, Allerton, Anfield, Bebington, city centre, Crosby, Edge Hill, Kensington, Kensington Fields, Mossley Hill, Old Swan, Seaforth, Sefton, Smithdown Rd, Tuebrook, Walton, Wavertree

Accommodation officer contacts

University	Tel	Address	Web	Landlord accreditation scheme?
Edge Hill College of HE	01695 584253	Accomodation Office, St Helens Road, Ormskirk, Lancashire L39 4QP	www.edgehill.ac.uk	No
Liverpool Hope University College	0151 291 3434	Accommodation Office, Liverpool Hope University, Hope Park, Liverpool L16 9JD	www.livhope.ac.uk	Yes
Liverpool John Moores University	0151 231 4166	Residential Services, JMU Tower, 24 Norton Tower, Liverpool L3 8PY	www.livjm.ac.uk	Yes
University of Liverpool	0151 794 5873/2	Student Services Centre, 150 Mount Pleasant, Liverpool L69 3GD	www.liv.ac.uk/ accommodation	Yes

Planned development for city	Liverpool will be the European Capital of Culture in 2008. The city is already renowned for its cultural features.

	It will be hosting themed years in the run up to 2008. The programme offers every Liverpool citizen an opportunity to realise their creative ambitions. Extensive city centre regeneration is planned over the coming years along with a new arena and exhibition venue.
	
	    Economists predict that Liverpool's success could generate 14,000 jobs and lever in an additional £200m in tourism in the run up to 2008. It is estimated that the Culture title could net Liverpool an extra 1.7m visitors to the city.
	
	    However, problems have already been encountered. The so-called 'Fourth Grace' was recently discarded due to its 'unworkability'. The council had hoped the £228m waterfront development would be the centrepiece for 2008.

Planned development for universities	Edge Hill College of HE The £4m CMIST building, Edge Hill's Centre for Media, Information Systems and Technology at the Ormskirk Campus, was opened in 2004. The building, which houses degree programmes in media production, journalism and computing, provides students and staff with the very latest in new media technology. CMIST is one of four new buildings forming the Western Campus development, where in the last six years building programmes have contributed to Edge Hill's continued investment in its learning infrastructure. .

	University of Liverpool
	The University of Liverpool has been awarded £2.4m by the government to expand its programme of research and business activities in the North West.
	    Business wise, the completion of the superstructure for Phase One of the Liverpool Science Park – a £9.4m, purpose-built Incubator Centre – is due to by the second quarter of 2005.
	    A £20m Oncology Research Centre at the University of Liverpool was opened in 2004.

	Liverpool Hope University College The University intends to build on its Investor In People status to create ever more opportunities for staff and student development, while increasing student numbers to 7000 by 2005.
	Liverpool John Moores University The John Moores University is planning to develop accommodation in the northern part of Liverpool. It is also to work with the University of Liverpool on the new Business Science Park, which is set to open in the next few years.
Campus room rental	Minimum Maximum £50 £99
Yield range	5.3–6%

Type of property	3 bed house (i.e. 2 bed upstairs + 1 converted other)	4 bed house	5 bed house	6 or more bed house
Entry price	£120,000	£145,000	£185,000	£210,000
Median room rate	£45	£42	£45	£45
Average yield B*	5.3%	5.4%	5.7%	6%
B – Estimated annual profit	−£324	−£208	£135	£702

Financial scores	Capital growth (out of 5)	Yield (out of 5)	Total (out of 10)
	2.5	5	7.5

Description	Liverpool is one of the UK's most happening cities. Since it received the Culture Capital award for 2008 there has been much interest and hype surrounding Liverpool. The city is rich in culture and the arts and is renowned for its association with the Beatles and Liverpool FC. It was once a clubbing mecca – a reason why many students chose to study there. The city now has a more pub-going atmosphere, in tune with the professionals working in the city. The rejuvenation of the city is likely to attract further investment and opportunties.
Websites to advertise on	Liverpool student housing: www.liverpoolstudenthouses.co.uk Local and national student listings: www.student-accom.com City information for students: www.accommodationforstudents.com Liverpool and Wirral: www.liverpoolpropertyrentals.co.uk Liverpool online guide: www.myliverpool.org

Estate agents	Address	Tel	Web
Bradford & Bingley Estate Agents	11 Broad Green Road, Old Swan, Liverpool L13 5SD	0151 220 4443	www.bbg.co.uk
Halifax Property Services	30 Allerton Road, Mossley Hill, Liverpool L18 1LN	0845 602 2710	www.halifax.co.uk
Roberts Edwards & Worrall	3 Allerton Rd, Mossley Hill, Liverpool L18 1LQ	0151 733 7101	www.worrall.co.uk
Acumen Estates	40 East Prescot Road, Old Swan, Liverpool L14 1PW.	0151 228 4447	www.acumen estates.co.uk

Letting agents	Address	Tel	Web
Liverpool Homes Network	136 Smithdown Road, Wavertree, Liverpool L15 3JR	0151 222 5000	www.liverpool homesnetwork.co.uk
Collertons	50 Liverpool Road, Crosby, Liverpool L23 5SG	0151 286 9696	www.collertons.com
R House Lettings	44 Penny Lane, Liverpool L18 1DG	0151 291 5000	www.r-house.co.uk
Castle Estates	147 Allerton Road, Liverpool L18 2DD	0151 291 8250	www.liverpool.castle-estates.co.uk
Sutton Kersh	102 County Road, Walton, Liverpool L4 3QN	0151 521 7383	www.suttonkersh.co.uk

Loughborough

University	Loughborough University
Population	153,461

	Student population	Undergraduate	Postgraduate	Total
		10355	4740	15090
	Campus capacity	4508	500	5308
	Size of market	5847	4240	9782

Drop-out rates	7%
Student areas	Central location, Golden Triangle, off Ashby Road, Toot Hill

University	Accommodation officer contacts			
	Tel	Address	Web	Landlord accreditation scheme?
Loughborough University	01509 222258	Student Accommodation Services, Loughborough University, Loughborough LE11 3TU	www.lboro.ac.uk	Yes

Planned development for city	The city's plans to develop Loughborough Wharf have been adjusted to appease opponents. The development involves an upgrade of the wharf area including office buildings, private flats, shops and a cafe bar. One of the main concerns had been the presence of student accommodation, which the developers have now removed.
Planned development for universities	The East Midlands Development Agency (EMDA) has confirmed a £3m contribution to the Lachesis Fund, greatly enhancing the region's ability to generate new businesses from the leading edge science and technology capabilities of its Universities. The Lachesis Fund is a partnership of the Universities of De Montfort, Leicester, Loughborough, Nottingham and Nottingham Trent and Quester, an independent venture capital company. By 2010 the expanded £7m fund will have contributed to the birth of some 50 businesses employing highly-skilled scientists and graduates, aiding the development of a culture of entrepreneurship and innovation within the region.

Campus room rental**	Minimum	Maximum
	£40	£109

Yield range	7.1–9.8%

Type of property	3 bed house (i.e. 2 bed upstairs + 1 converted other)	4 bed house	5 bed house	6 or more bed house
Entry price	£80,000	£105,000	£150,000	£200,000
Median room rate	£52	£55	£52	£50
Average yield B*	9.2%	9.8%	8.1%	7.1%
B – Estimated annual profit	£2,266	£3,547	£3,026	£2,280

Financial scores	Capital growth (out of 5)	Yield (out of 5)	Total (out of 10)
	3	3	6

Description	Loughborough is about as near to the centre of the United Kingdom as you can be. It is a great combination of a thriving market town and a prominent high-technology centre for the East Midlands – a magnet for inward investment. Close neighbours are the cities of Derby, Leicester and Nottingham, with many other cities such as London reachable within one and a half hours by train. The town centre is pedestrianised. For entertainment there is a wide selection of pubs, bars, clubs and restaurants to choose from as well as a cinema.
Websites to advertise on	Local and national student listings: www.student-accom.com City information for students: www.accommodationforstudents.com Easy roommate: http://uk.easyroommate.com

Estate agents	Address	Tel	Web
Andrew Granger & Co	3 Wards End, Loughborough LE11 3HA	01509 235534	www.andrewgranger.co.uk
Bradford & Bingley Marketplace Ltd	3 Swan Street, Loughborough LE11 5BJ	01509 218006	www.bbg.co.uk
Connells Estate Agents	22–23 Swan Street, Loughborough LE11 5BL	01509 268831	www.connells.co.uk
Your Move	Cattle Market, Loughborough LE11 3DN	01509 231731	www.your-move.co.uk

Letting agents	Address	Tel	Web
Hartley Estates	5 High Street, Loughborough LE11 2PY	01509 611119	www.hartleyestates.co.uk
Taylors Estate Agents	65–66 Baxter Gate, Loughborough LE11 1TH	01509 218362	www.taylors-ea.co.uk

Letting agents	Address	Tel	Web
William H Brown – Loughborough	13–14 Market Street, Loughborough LE11 3EP	01509 214686	www.sequencehome. co.uk
Sinclair Estate Agents	63 Baxter Gate, Loughborough LE11 1TH	01509 611887	www.sinclairestate agents.co.uk
Moore and York	18 Devonshire Square, Loughborough LE11 3DT	01509 214546	www.moore-york.co.uk

Manchester

Universities	University of Manchester, UMIST, Manchester Metropolitan University, Royal Northern College of Music, University of Salford
Population	392,819

Student population	Undergraduate	Postgraduate	Total
University of Manchester	20185	7830	28015
UMIST	4685	2845	7530
Manchester Metropolitan University	24785	6910	31690
Royal Northern College of Music	425	185	610
University of Salford	15655	3540	19200
Total	65735	21310	87045
Campus capacity	24357	–	24357
Size of market	41378		62688

Drop-out rates	University of Manchester	8%
	UMIST	8%
	Manchester Metropolitan University	15%
	University of Salford	15%
	Royal Northern College of Music	11%

Student areas	Birch-in-Rusholme, Blackley, Burnage, Buttress, central, Chorlton, Crumpsall, Didsbury, Eccles, Failsworth, Fallowfield, Heaton Moor, Hulme, Levenshulme, Longsight, Moss Side, Openshaw, Prestwich, Rushlome, Sale, Salford, Swinton, Urmston, Victoria Park, Whalley Range, Withington, Wythenshawe

Accommodation officer contacts

University	Tel	Address	Web	Landlord accreditation scheme?
University of Manchester	0161 275 2888	Accommodation Office, Precinct Centre, Oxford Road, Manchester M13 9RS	www.man.ac.uk	Yes
UMIST	0161 275 2888	Accommodation Office, The Precinct Centre, Oxford Road, Manchester M13 9RS	www.umist.ac.uk	Yes
Manchester Metropolitan University	0161 247 2958	Accommodation Office, First Floor, Loxford Tower, Lower Chatham Street, Oxford Road, Manchester M15 6BS	www.mmu.ac.uk	Yes

Royal Northern College of Music	0161 907 5219	Senior Assistant (Registrations), 124 Oxford Road, Manchester M13 9RD	www.rncm.ac.uk	Yes
University of Salford	0161 295 5457	Accommodation Office, Allerton Building, University of Salford, Salford M6 6PU	www.salford.ac.uk	Yes
Planned development for city	Up to 160,000 jobs could be created in Greater Manchester during the next ten years, according to a report by a research consultancy group. It said many jobs will be in financial and professional services. It does however point out the recent withdrawal of government funding for the Metrolink tram network is a blow to the region's economy.			

Planned development for universities	University of Manchester
	UMIST and the University of Manchester have recently merged. It has become the biggest university in Europe. As part of the merger UMIST and the University of Manchester received a £20m grant from the Higher Education Funding Council for England (HEFCE).
	   UMIST reopened a unique world-class research facility in 2003 after a £6.6m overhaul. The refurbished chemical engineering laboratory has been renamed The Morton Laboratory.
	   The building of the world-leading 4GLS in Daresbury will cost £11.5m for an exploratory phase of the project.			

	Manchester Metropolitan University October 2003 saw Manchester Metropolitan University being selected to run the North West arm of the new National Science Learning Centre, created to reignite interest in learning about science. The Science Learning Centre North West will be run in collaboration with St Martin's College, Lancaster and Greater Manchester SETPOINT, and is one of seven consortia in an innovative £51m government-charity initiative to boost science teaching.			

	University of Salford
	A brand new £16m building next to Salford Crescent station will house students of nursing, midwifery, physiotherapy, radiography, social work and complementary medicine.
	   An estimated £28m will provide a new state-of-the-art building for students of Art and Design and Media, Music and Performance. The transformation of the former factory site opposite the Adelphi Building will be a major contribution to the rapidly evolving Arts and Media Quarter in the City of Salford.
	   The creation of an Innovation Hub building is being spearheaded by the University, alongside the City of Salford and the Regional Development Agency. The growth in the student population in Salford has led to new accommodation initiatives.			

	Royal Northern College of Music The College offers brilliant facilities including a state-of-the-art library, an electro-acoustic studio, performance spaces and rehearsal studios, with RNCM providing an extremely supportive environment with a very relaxed and friendly atmosphere.			
Campus room rental	Minimum £40		Maximum £75	
Yield range	7.7–11%			
Type of property	3 bed house (i.e. 2 bed upstairs + 1 converted other)	4 bed house	5 bed house	6 or more bed house
Entry price**** Median room rate Average yield B* B – Estimated annual profit	£55,000 £43 11% £2,376	£72,000 £42 11% £3,077	£130,000 £43 7.8% £2,234	£165,000 £45 7.7% £2,727
Financial scores	Capital growth (out of 5) 3.5	Yield (out of 5) 5	Total (out of 10) 8.5	

Description	As the UK's second largest city, Manchester is the capital of the north and, in many ways, is just as buzzing as London.
	    The universities are spread over several sites. The majority of these are situated in or near town and most students are based near the city. There are many options for social life in Manchester – there are pubs, clubs, restaurants and bars for virtually all tastes.
	    With the biggest news in the northern academic circles being the uniting of Manchester University and UMIST, forming the biggest University in Europe, times are looking good for the city with more research money and students heading its way.			

Websites to advertise on	Local and national student listings: www.student-accom.com City information for students: www.accommodationforstudents.com Easy roommate: http://uk.easyroommate.com Links to Manchester rooms: www.roomsforlet.com/links.asp Student accommodation approved by the University: www.accommodation.man.ac.uk Student lets: www.rivershill.co.uk Student village: www.thestudentvillage.com			

Estate agents	Address	Tel	Web	
Bradford & Bingley	715 Wilmslow Road, Disbury, Manchester M20 6WF	0161 4481234	www.bbg.co.uk	

Estate agents	Address	Tel	Web
Bridgfords	416 Wilmslow Road, Withington, Manchester M20 3BW	0161 445 0580	www.bridgfords.co.uk
Savills	Fountain Court, 68 Fountain Street, Manchester M2 2FE	0161 244	www.savills.co.uk
Mark Warren Estates	1150 Rochdale Road, Blackley, Manchester M9 6FQ	0161 7208800	www.markwarren estates.com
Letting agents	Address	Tel	Web
Halifax Property Services	1 Cross Street, Manchester M2 1HX	0161 2530208	www.halifax.co.uk
Leslie Fink Ltd	121 Princess Street, Manchester M1 7AD	0161 2286561	
Aubrey Lee and Company	1170 Rochdale Road, Blackley, Manchester M9 6ER	0161 7208108	www.aubreylee.net
Beresford Adams – Didsbury	722 Wilmslow Road, Didsbury, Manchester M20 2DW	0161 4457809	www.beresfordadams. co.uk
Buxton Lane Estates	341 Manchester Road, Droylsden, Manchester M43 6GE	0161 3703023	www.homesonview. co.uk

Middlesbrough

University	University of Teesside
Population	134,847

	Student population	Undergraduate	Postgraduate	Total
		17605	2175	19780
	Campus capacity	1285	–	1285
	Size of market	16320	2175	18495

Drop-out rates	12%
Student areas	Gresham, Linthorpe, Longlands, Marton, Southfield, town centre

	Accommodation officer contacts			
University	Tel	Address	Web	Landlord accreditation scheme?
University of Teesside	01642 342255	Accommodation Office, University of Teeside, Middlesbrough TS1 3BA	www.tees.ac.uk	Yes

Planned development for city	Ambitious £500m plans to develop a redundant area of Teesside into a landscape featuring apartments, hotels, a theatre and restaurants were revealed in 2004. They include a hotel in the shape of a champagne bottle and a Space Invader-inspired Museum of Digital Media. It is hoped the scheme will raise the town's profile and attract investment.
Planned development for universities	The University of Teesside has been awarded £3.1m from the Higher Education Funding Council for England (HEFCE) to support knowledge transfer from universities and colleges across England to business and the wider community.

Campus room rental**	Minimum		Maximum	
	£33		£60	

Yield range	5.8–8.9%

Type of property	3 bed house (i.e. 2 bed upstairs + 1 converted other)	4 bed house	5 bed house	6 or more bed house
Entry price	£60,000	£80,000	£140,000	£170,000
Median room rate	£38	£35	£35	£35
Average yield B*	8.9%	8.2%	5.9%	5.8%
B – Estimated annual profit	£1,587	£1,664	£280	£246

Financial scores	Capital growth (out of 5)	Yield (out of 5)	Total (out of 10)
	2.5	3.5	6

▶

Description	Middlesborough, in common with most of the north of the country, suffered a period of decline with the reduction in the traditional industries. Today, however, evidence of investment is notable throughout the town. Students will find really good shopping, three cinemas, five or more theatres as well as plenty of pubs, clubs, restaurants and all the usual paraphernalia of a decent sized town. Very typically northern in appearance, the town is also right on the Yorkshire Moors. The University is situated on a campus that is within easy walking distance of Middlesborough town centre. The campus has recently undergone a multi-million pound redevelopment, which has created some new buildings and renovated old ones.
Websites to advertise on	Local and national student listings: www.student-accom.com City information for students: www.accommodationforstudents.com Student properties postings for North East students: www.stud-lets.co.uk Local and national student listings: www.pastures-new.co.uk

Estate agents	Address	Tel	Web
Bairstow Eves	93 Albert Road, Middlesbrough TS1 2PA	01642 227827	www.bairstoweves countrywide.co.uk
Bradford & Bingley Marketplace Ltd	50 High Street, Stokesley, Middlesbrough TS9 5AX	01642 711555	www.bbg.co.uk
Halifax Property Services	148 High Street, Eston, Middlesbrough TS6 9EN	01642 465246	www.halifax.co.uk
Michael Poole	64–66 Borough Road, Middlesbrough TS1 2JH	01642 254222	www.michaelpoole.co.uk

Letting agents	Address	Tel	Web
Manners and Harrison	121 Albert Road, Middlesbrough TS1 2PQ	01642 231100	www.sequencehome. co.uk
Thirlwells	75 Borough Road, Middlesbrough TS1 3AA	01642 245796/24	www.thirlwell-estates. co.uk
Whitegates	155 Albert Road, Middlesbrough TS1 2PX	01642 218704	www.whitegates.co.uk

Letting agents	Address	Tel	Web
Sanderson Taylor Partnership	15 High Street, Stokesley, Middlesbrough TS9 5AD	01642 711355	www.sandersontaylor. co.uk
Keith Pattinson	129 Albert Road, Middlesbrough TS1 2PQ	01642 219119	www.pattinson.co.uk

Newcastle	
Universities	University of Newcastle upon Tyne, University of Northumbria at Newcastle
Population	259,573

	Student population Undergraduate Postgraduate Total
	University of
	   Newcastle upon Tyne 12850 6065 18915
	University of Northumbria
	   at Newcastle 19705 4575 24280
	Total 32555 10640 43195
	Campus capacity 7418 900 8318
	Size of market 25137 9740 34877

Drop-out rates	University of Newcastle upon Tyne 8% University of Northumbria at Newcastle 10%
Student areas	City centre, Fenham, Gosforth, Heaton, Jesmond, Sandyford, Spital Tongues, West Jesmond

	Accommodation officer contacts			
University	**Tel**	**Address**	**Web**	**Landlord accreditation scheme?**
University of Newcastle upon Tyne	0191 222 6360	Accommodation Office, University of Newcastle upon Tyne, 19/20 Windsor Terrace, Newcastle upon Tyne NE1 7RU	www.ncl.ac.uk/accommodation	Yes
University of Northumbria at	0191 227 4209	Accommodation Office, Ellison Place, Newcastle upon Tyne NE1 8ST	www.unn.ac.uk	Yes

Planned development for city	A major upset in the local elections of 2004 saw the Liberal Democrats taking control of Newcastle City Council. It meant the end of more than 30 years of Labour control of the city council.
	    Plans to bulldoze hundreds of homes have been reversed by councillors in Newcastle. The controversial £200m regeneration project was dubbed Going For Growth. In 2003 there were also plans to build a new £27m library in Princess Square and the council was seeking lottery money to help fund the creation of a £36m Museum of the North, in partnership with Tyne & Wear Museums, the University, One NorthEast and others.
	    The council was also planning to spend £150m on extensions and improvements to the Eldon Square shopping centre.			

Planned development for universities	University of Newcastle upon Tyne More and better sports facilities are on the wish list but there are as yet no fixed plans for improvements.			

	In 2003 Newcastle University received a £21m funding boost – its share of a £1bn investment in scientific excellence.			
	University of Northumbria at Newcastle The University is to spend £60m on demolishing a cinema complex to make way for a city campus. Northumbria University says it needs the site for expansion plans and as space for some of its 2,600 staff. Another £11.5m plan is to expand student accommodation in Newcastle, providing about 460 state-of-the-art units for University of Northumbria students. The development marks the second phase of student accommodation in the Camden Street area of the city, following the completion of 345 similar units.			
Campus room rental	Minimum £39		Maximum £70	
Yield range	6.3–7.9%			
Type of property	3 bed house (i.e. 2 bed upstairs + 1 converted other)	4 bed house	5 bed house	6 or more bed house
Entry price Median room rate Average yield B* B – Estimated annual profit	£80,000 £45 7.9% £1,476	£120,000 £43 6.7% £1,068	£160,000 £43 6.3% £884	£200,000 £45 6.3% £1,152
Financial scores	Capital growth (out of 5) 4	Yield (out of 5) 2.5	Total (out of 10) 6.5	
Description	Newcastle is home to two universities, the University of Newcastle and the University of Northumbria. It has a reputation as a fantastic student city. There are numerous pubs, clubs and restaurants to suit a range of tastes and budgets. Shopping facilities are excellent and there is a vibrant cultural scene. The regenerated Newcastle of today provides students with some of the most vibrant city living in the UK. It has the same problems as any big city and you should expect it to be very cold and wet for a large proportion of the year but other than that you could do a great deal worse. The students have a good relationship with the city's residents.			
Websites to advertise on	Student properties postings for North East students: www.stud-lets.co.uk Local and national student listings: www.pastures-new.co.uk Local and national student listings: www.student-accom.com City information for students: www.accommodationforstudents.com Student lettings management: www.rm-accommodation.co.uk Letting agents students: www.johnparish.co.uk			

Estate agents	Address	Tel	Web
Your Move	6 Shopping Centre, Chapel House, Newcastle Upon Tyne NE5 1DT	0191 2641411	www.your-move.co.uk
Reeds Rains	31 Front Street, Whickham, Newcastle Upon Tyne NE164EA	0191 4883610	www.reedsrains.co.uk
Bradford & Bingley Marketplace Ltd	121 St Georges Terrace, Jesmond, Newcastle Upon Tyne NE2 2DN	0191 2810744	www.bbg.co.uk
Bairstow Eves Estate Agents	92 Grey Street, Newcastle Upon Tyne NE1 6AG	0191 2327471	www.bairstoweves.co.uk
Letting agents	**Address**	**Tel**	**Web**
David Dumble and Associates	12 Coast Road, Newcastle Upon Tyne NE28 8QT	0191 2635519	www.daviddumble.co.uk
Groves Residential	38 Acorn Road, Jesmond, Newcastle Upon Tyne NE2 2DJ	0191 2120400	www.groves.co.uk
Halifax Property Services	Bishops Court, Front Street, Whickham, Newcastle Upon Tyne NE16 1JH	0191 4887968	www.halifax.co.uk
Keith Pattinson – Forest Hall	17a Station Road North, Forest Hall, Newcastle Upon Tyne NE12 7AR	0191 2150677	www.pattinson.co.uk
Newcastle Building Society	Portland House, New Bridge Street, Newcastle Upon Tyne NE1 8AL	0191 244 2000	www.newcastle.co.uk

Newport

Universities	Harper Adams University College, University of Wales College, Newport
Population	137,017

	Student population	Undergraduate	Postgraduate	Total
	Harper Adams University College	1440	125	1565
	University of Wales College, Newport	7305	1675	8980
	Total	8745	1800	10545
	Campus capacity	960	170	1130
	Size of market	7785	1630	9415

Drop-out rates	Harper Adams University College	11%
	University of Wales College, Newport	18%

Student areas	Caerleon, Edgmond, Newport

	Accommodation officer contacts			
University	**Tel**	**Address**	**Web**	**Landlord accreditation scheme?**
Harper Adams University College	01952 815286	Student Services, Student Union Building, Edgmond, Newport TF10 8NB	www.harper-adams.ac.uk	Yes
University of Wales College, Newport	01633 432042	Accommodation Office, PO Box 179, Newport NP18 3YG	www.newport.ac.uk	No

Planned development for city	Newport was unveiled as the newest city in Wales in 2002 after winning a competition to celebrate the Queen's Golden Jubilee. There was much controversy over the decision to award city status to Newport as opposed to Wrexham, apparently further increasing the north-south divide in Wales. However, this recognition will help the city get back on its feet after the widespread steel job losses in 2001. Some good news for golf fans is that the town's Celtic Resort is to host the 2010 Ryder Cup.
Planned development for universities	Harper Adams University College As part of the Higher Education Funding Council for England (HEFCE) drive, Harper Adams University College won £1.4m in 2004 to develop its work with rural businesses. The cash injection will work on current projects whilst opening up new initiatives.
	University of Wales College, Newport Plans are underway for a new £60m city centre campus to house the School of Art, Media and Design, Business and Management and Computing and Engineering. There will also be accommodation for an extra 500 students and a new Students' Union building.

	The city status will also aid the development of UWCN since research shows that students prefer to study in a city rather than a town.		
Campus room rental**	Minimum £45		Maximum £60
Yield range	4.1–5.6%		
Type of property	3 bed house (i.e. 2 bed upstairs + 1 converted other)	4 bed house 5 bed house	6 or more bed house
Entry price Median room rate Average yield B* B – Estimated annual profit	£120,000 £35 4.1% −£1,452	£135,000 £175,000 £40 £40 5.6% 5.4% −£59 −£355	£220,000 £38 4.9% −£1,327
Financial scores	Capital growth (out of 5) 4	Yield (out of 5) 1.5	Total (out of 10) 5.5
Description	Newport is close to all the obvious benefits of Cardiff but often students find late night taxis back from the city to be a drag. Newport itself has some good pubs to offer to students and some live music, but you'll want to take advantage of Cardiff before long.		
Websites to advertise on	Local and national student listings: www.student-accom.com City information for students: www.accommodationforstudents.com Student accommodation: www.spot-property.co.uk Lettings agent: www.telfordmobiles.co.uk		
Estate agents	**Address**	**Tel**	**Web**
Dixon Fenwick and Co	12 Market Street, Telford TF1 1DT	01952 260888	www.dixon-fenwick.co.uk
Evans Estates	12 Hazledine House, Central Square, Telford TF3 4JL	01952 291444	
Farrar Gough	10 Market Street, Wellington, Telford TF1 1DT	01952 410064	
Hamels	17 Church Street, Wellington, Telford TF1 1DD	01952 641515	www.hamels.co.uk

Letting agents	Address	Tel	Web
Estate Lettings	119a Trench Road, Trench, Telford TF2 7DP	01952 610600	www.telford mobiles.co.uk
Temperton & Temperton	25 High Street, Newport TF10 7AT	01952 812519	www.tempertons. co.uk
Davies, White & Perry	45–47 High Street, Newport TF10 7AT	01952 811003	www.davies whiteperry.co.uk
Barbers	30 High Street, Newport TF10 7AQ	01952 820239	www.barbers-online.co.uk
D. Roberts & Partners	4 Hazledine House, Central Square, Telford TF3 4JL	01952 291722	www.dbroberts.co.uk

Northampton

University	University College Northampton
Population	194,477

	Student population	Undergraduate	Postgraduate	Total
		9860	1130	10990
	Campus capacity	1360	240	1600
	Size of market	8500	890	9390

Drop-out rate	14%
Student areas	Northampton

University	Accommodation officer contacts			
	Tel	Address	Web	Landlord accreditation scheme?
University College Northampton	01604 735500	Accommodation Services, Boughton, Green Road, Northampton NN2 7AL	www.nene.ac.uk	No

Planned development for city	More than £24m is to be spent on providing affordable homes for people in Northampton. The funding is partly stimulated by the aim of providing cheaper homes to attract key workers to the area. The government, council and housing corporation are together allocating funds to ten housing associations to produce 592 affordable homes.
Planned development for university	University College Northampton's Business Bridge office has been named as an official outlet for the Department of Trade and Industry's (DTI) Knowledge Transfer Partnerships (KTP) programme. It is the only one in Northamptonshire. KTPs allow businesses with a long-term strategic challenge to tap the resources of a university in order to find a solution.

Campus room rental**	Minimum £50	Maximum £80

Yield range	7.5–10.3%

Type of property	3 bed house (i.e. 2 bed upstairs + 1 converted other)	4 bed house	5 bed house	6 or more bed house
Entry price	£79,000	£87,000	£104,000	£115,000
Median room rate	£42	£44	£44	£42
Average yield B*	7.5%	9.5%	9.9%	10.3%
B – Estimated annual profit	£1,183	£2,703	£3,592	£4,301

Financial scores	Capital growth (out of 5)	Yield (out of 5)	Total (out of 10)
	3	3.5	6.5
Description	University College Northampton is a lively, medium-sized institution which has been located on its attractive parkland campus in Northampton for over 25 years and involved in the town's education for nearly a century. It combines academic strengths and superb facilities with a friendly and dynamic atmosphere.		
Websites to advertise on	Local and national student listings: www.student-accom.com City information for students: www.accommodationforstudents.com Guidance from University and links: http://oldweb.northampton.ac.uk/stu/accom Northampton letting: www.northamptonletting.co.uk		

Estate agents	Address	Tel	Web
Bairstow Eves	4 Mercers Row, Northampton NN1 2QL	01604 232222	www.bairstoweves.co.uk
Bonds Estate Agents	6 Bridge Street, Northampton NN1 1NW	01604 633877	www.bondshomes.co.uk
Haart	6–7 George Row, Northampton NN1 1DF	01604 637282	www.spicerhaart.co.uk
Harrison Murray	3 George Row, Northampton NN11DY	01604 622205	www.harrisonmurray.co.uk

Letting agents	Address	Tel	Web
Kelly Estate Agents	4 George Row, Northampton NN1 1DF	01604 622888	www.kelly-estate-agents.co.uk
Merrys Estate Agents	14 Bridge Street, Northampton NN1 1NW	01604 632266	www.merrys.co.uk
O'Riordan Bond	13 Market Square, Northampton NN1 2DU	01604 231007	www.oriordanbond.co.uk
Taylors	53 Harborough Road, Kingsthorpe, Northampton NN2 7SH	01604 720077	www.taylorsestateagents.co.uk
Your Move	81 Harborough Rd, Northampton NN2 7SL	01604 718392	www.your-move.co.uk

Norwich

Universities	University of East Anglia, Norwich School of Art and Design
Population	121,553

	Student population **Undergraduate** **Postgraduate** **Total**
	University of East Anglia 10710 3440 14150
	Norwich School of Art
	and Design 615 70 685
	Total 11325 3510 14835
	Campus capacity 2708 420 3158
	Size of market 8617 3090 11677

Drop-out rates	University of East Anglia	8%
	Norwich School of Art and Design	9%

Student areas	Bowthorpe, Dereham Road, Golden Triangle, West City, West Earlham, West Norwich

Accommodation officer contacts

University	Tel	Address	Web	Landlord accreditation scheme?
University of East Anglia	01603 592092	Accommodation Office, University of East Anglia, Norwich NR4 7TJ	www.uea.ac.uk	No
Norwich School of Art and Design	01603 773059	Student Services Centre, City College, Ipswich Road, Norwich NR2 2LJ	www.nsad.ac.uk	No

Planned development for city	Property prices soared by 26% in 2003 – 5% above the national average rise. This can be attributed partly to increasing demand for white-collar staff by service industry employers. Job prospects are good in the financial services industry. Norwich Union, with 8500 staff, is by far the area's biggest employer.
Planned development for universities	University of East Anglia (UEA) A new hall of residence is planned to replace some that already exist. There is also talk of doubling the size of the Union building, but as of yet there are no dates or final plans for this. The University of East Anglia is to receive a £1.55m funding boost for its business and knowledge transfer activities. The funding is the result of a successful bid by the University to the Higher Education Innovation Fund (HEIF).
	Norwich School of Art and Design The HEIF has awarded £375,000 to the Norwich School of Art and Design to develop links with business and the community. The School will receive this money for two years in order to set up a Centre for Innovation, Business and the Community.

	The School will also receive funding from a joint project in film and digital media which is led by the University of Hertfordshire with Norwich School of Art and Design, the University of East Anglia and Anglia Polytechnic University.			
Campus room rental**	Minimum £50		Maximum £70	
Yield range	5.2–7.8%			
Type of property	3 bed house (i.e. 2 bed upstairs + 1 converted other)	4 bed house	5 bed house	6 or more bed house
Entry price	£90,000	£120,000	£160,000	£270,000
Median room rate	£50	£47	£50	£50
Average yield B*	7.8%	7.4%	7.4%	5.2%
B – Estimated annual profit	£1,590	£1,669	£2,200	-£870
Financial scores	Capital growth (out of 5) 3	Yield (out of 5) 2.5	Total (out of 10) 5.5	
Description	Norwich is a good sized city which is big enough not to be boring. The city seems to thrive on students, who make up a large proportion of the population. In terms of nightclubs and nightlife, Norwich does well but London is not too far away should the students fancy partying elsewhere.			
Websites to advertise on	Local listings as affiliated by Norwich School of Art and Design: www.edp24.co.uk Specialists in residential lettings: www.topcitylettings.co.uk Residential letting agents and property managers: www.norfolk.castle-estates.co.uk Residential letting agent: www.norwich-accommodation.co.uk			

Estate agents	Address	Tel	Web
Elliots Estate Agents	37 St Andrews Street, Norwich NR2 4TP	01603 61 45 45	www.elliots estateagents.co.uk
Howards Estate Agents	28 St Andrews Street, Norwich NR2 4AE	01603 612664	www.howards.co.uk
Keys Estate Agents	8 Market Place, Aylsham, Norfolk NR11 6EH	01263 733195	www.gakey.co.uk
Bradford & Bingley Estate Agents	43 Exchange Street, Norwich NR2 1DJ	01603 219606	www.bbg.co.uk

Letting agents	Address	Tel	Web
Savills	8–10 Upper King Street, Norwich NR3 1HB	01603 229229	www.savills.co.uk
Watsons Residential	Wendene Main Centre, Bowthorpe, Norwich NR5 9HA	01603 748911	www.watsons-ea.co.uk
Arnolds	34/36 Prince of Wales Road, Norwich NR1 1LH	01603 620551	www.arnolds.uk.com
Brown & Co Estate Agents	Old Bank of England Court, Queen Street, Norwich NR2 4TA	01603 629871	www.brown-co.com
Tops Property Services	15–17 Princes Street, Norwich NR3 1AF	01603 767050	www.tops-property.com

Nottingham

Universities	University of Nottingham, Nottingham Trent University
Population	748,503

Student population	Undergraduate	Postgraduate	Total
University of Nottingham	22990	8175	31165
Nottingham Trent University	18665	4775	23440
Total	41655	12950	54605
Campus capacity	5600	1000	6600
Size of market	36055	11950	48005

Drop-out rates	University of Nottingham 4% Nottingham Trent University 10%
Student areas	Arboretum, Basford, Beeston, Rylands, Wollaton, Bobbers Mill, Bulwell, Carrington, Castle View, city centre, Clifton, Dunkirk, Forest Fields, Hyson Green, Lenton, Mapperley, Meadows, Radford, Sherwood, Sneinton, Wollaton

Accommodation officer contacts

University	Tel	Address	Web	Landlord accreditation scheme?
University of Nottingham	0115 951 3643	Accommodation Office, University of Nottingham, Nottingham NG7 2RD	hamish.adams@ nottingham.ac.uk	Yes
Nottingham Trent University	0115 848 2894	Accommodation Services, Burton St, Nottingham NG1 4BU	cor.web@ntu.ac.uk	Yes

Planned development for city	The city's growth industries include media, telecommunications and financial services. Retail has been a huge success story, with Nottingham ranked the third best shopping destination in the UK.
	    The capital of the East Midlands is also Britain's fastest-growing city – employment rose by 14% in one recent five-year spell – and has the third-highest gross domestic product in the country, according to the government's annual employment survey.
	    The development of Nottingham has been impressive and shows no signs of slowing. Major sites include the Nottingham Waterside, a 250-acre area adjoining the world famous Trent Bridge. Other prime sites include the former Royal Ordnance Factory, now Queensgate, and the Nottingham Business Park, all set to become one of the UK's most prestigious office locations. On the Eastside of the City there will be many changes set in motion by the success of Nottingham's landmark £40m National Ice Centre.

Planned development for universities	University of Nottingham The University of Nottingham is to take part in a joint venture with the

	Wanli Education Group (WEG) to develop a purpose-built university campus in the city of Ningbo, in Zhejiang province of China.		
	The new campus will be the first to be opened in China by a UK university and follows new legislation approved by the Chinese government on Sino-Foreign educational enterprises.		
	The University plans to open a veterinary school for 100 students in 2006. It will be the UK's first new vet school for half a century. The school aims to meet a national demand for well-qualified veterinary science graduates.		

	Nottingham Trent University
	Through a strategic plan encompassing six key 'strategic platforms', the University intends to instigate change and improvements throughout. The implementation of these six platforms are detailed on www.ntu.ac.uk (Nottingham Trent University website). They aim to deliver education and research that 'makes a difference'.

Campus room rental	Minimum	Maximum
	£53	£93

Yield range	11.1–14.1%			

Type of property	3 bed house (i.e. 2 bed upstairs + 1 converted other)	4 bed house	5 bed house	6 or more bed house
Entry price	£55,000	£85,000	£105,000	£135,000
Median room rate	£55	£50	£52	£59
Average yield B*	14.1%	11.1%	11.6%	12.3%
B – Estimated annual profit	£3,729	£3,695	£5,051	£7,236

Financial scores	Capital growth (out of 5)	Yield (out of 5)	Total (out of 10)
	4.5	5	9.5

Description	Nottingham is a famous city with plenty to do and see. However, like any city it has its no-go areas, but has plenty of shopping, cinemas, theatres and clubs. You won't get bored here. Being the East Midland's largest city, there is good access to all the UK via the M1 and decent trains to London and elsewhere.

Websites to advertise on	National and local student accommodation: www.student-accom.com Nottingham student housing website: www.fblproperty.co.uk Nottingham student lettings: www.ms-estates.co.uk Nottinghamshire housing website: www.accomnotts.f9.co.uk/student.htm Nottingham students website: www.housingstudents.com

Estate agents	Address	Tel	Web
Bradford & Bingley	24 High Road, Beeston, Nottingham NG9 2JP	0115 9225712	www.bbg.co.uk mpe@market place.co.uk
Robin Thomson	53 Mansfield Road, Nottingham NG1 3FH	0115 941 8712	enquiries@rthomson 22.fsbusiness.co.uk www.robinthomson .co.uk
Nottingham Property Services	32/34 High Road, Nottingham NG9 2JP	0115 925 1685	www.the nottingham.com sales-development@ thenottingham.com
Spencer Birch	10 Kings Walk, Trinity Square, Nottingham NG1 2AE	0115 941 3678	info@spencer-birch.co.uk www.spencer birch.co.uk
Letting agents	**Address**	**Tel**	**Web**
Michael Vernon	65 High Road, Beeston, Nottingham NG9 2JQ	0115 922 4521	info@michael-vernon.fsbusiness.co.uk www.michael-vernon.com
Robert Ellis	92 High Road, Beeston, Nottingham NG9 2LF	0115 922 9090	beeston@ robertellis.co.uk www.robertellis.co.uk
CP Walker & Son	107 High Road, Beeston, Nottingham NG9 2JU	0115 925 4062	http://cpwalker.co.uk lettings@ cpwalker.co.uk
Accommodation Link	65 Castle Boulevard, Nottingham NG7 1FD	0115 985 9383	nottingham@ belvoirlettings.com www.accomlink.co.uk
Whitegates Estate Agency	156 High Road, Beeston, Nottingham NG9 2LN	0115 922 2222	nottinghamlettings@ whitegates.co.uk www.whitegates.co.uk

Oxford

Universities	University of Oxford, Oxford Brookes University
Population	134,248

Student population	Undergraduate	Postgraduate	Total
University of Oxford	16035	6980	23020
Oxford Brookes University	12385	6100	18485
Total	28420	13080	41505
Campus capacity	9707	3500	13207
Size of market	18713	9580	28298

Drop out rates	University of Oxford	3%
	Oxford Brookes University	11%

Student areas	Botley, Cowley, Grandpont, St Clements, West Oxford

Accommodation officer contacts

University	Tel	Address	Web	Landlord accreditation scheme?
University of Oxford	01865 280803	Ewert House, Ewert Place, Banbury Road, Summertown, Oxford OX2 7DD	www.ox.ac.uk	Yes
Oxford Brookes University	01865 484660	Accommodation Office, Gypsy Lane, Headington, Oxford OX3 0BP	www.brookes.ac.uk	Yes

Planned development for city	Oxfordshire County Council has quelled reports that a link road between the M40 and Oxford Road in Banbury has been agreed. The council has been quick to point out that the road was merely a suggestion and that nothing had been put on paper. It said if such a road was incorporated in future plans, it would be at least 2016 before it could be built.
	A University college has bought the Acland Hospital for £10.75m to develop cheap accommodation for students who currently have to pay for expensive private housing in Oxford. It will initially use the 1.7-acre site for research and teaching, as well as study bedrooms for 100 students, but it plans to redevelop the Banbury Road-based hospital to provide double the amount of accommodation.
Planned development for university	University of Oxford
	There are some plans to increase the social role of the Oxford University Students' Union. Currently most activities are organised by the colleges.
	The Said School of Business has now opened and intends attracting the best students.
	There are occasional rumours that Oxford University will be buying the engineering department but this isn't confirmed yet.

	Oxford Brookes University New halls of residences are currently under construction with over 1,000 new study bedrooms being developed. These will mostly be on the main Gypsy Road site. Oxford Brookes has become the first university in the world to be awarded Fairtrade status, providing a platform for raising awareness of international trade issues amongst students, staff and the wider public.			
Campus room rental**	Minimum £62		Maximum £120	
Yield range	7.4–8.1%			
Type of property	3 bed house (i.e. 2 bed upstairs + 1 converted other)	4 bed house	5 bed house	6 or more bed house
Entry price **Median room rate** **Average yield B*** **B – Estimated** ** annual profit**	£130,000 £68 7.4% £1,837	£150,000 £65 8.1% £3,026	£180,000 £60 7.8% £3,180	£210,000 £60 8.1% £4,086
Financial scores	Capital growth (out of 5) 4	Yield (out of 5) 3	Total (out of 10) 7	
Description	The city of Oxford is beautiful. Aside from the architecture there are some great places to shop and the combined student population is pretty high so there are plenty of student friendly places. There are pubs galore for students and tourists. Although most of the colleges have fairly limited social facilities for late nights, the local area is all there for real night owls.			
Websites to advertise on	Local and national student listings: www.student-accom.com City information for students: www.accommodationforstudents.com Lettings listings: www.accomm-let.co.uk Specialising in student lets: www.north-oxford-property.co.uk Student agent: www.pastures-new.com Oxford area room rental: www.rentaflat.co.uk			

Estate agents	Address	Tel	Web
Savills	Wytham Court, 11 West Way, Botley, Oxford OX2 0QL	01865 269000	www.savills.co.uk
David Tompkins	6 Chapel Way, Botley, Oxford OX2 9LS	01865 436455	www.david tompkins.co.uk
James C Penny	113 Walton Street, Oxford OX2 6AJ	01865 554422	www.jamesc penny.co.uk

Estate agents	Address	Tel	Web
Breckon & Breckon	5 King Edward Street, Oxford OX1 4HN	01865 244735	www.breckon.co.uk

Letting agents	Address	Tel	Web
Bradford & Bingley	114–116 St Aldates, Oxford OX1 1BD	01865 241019	www.bbg.co.uk
Simon Fraser	57 Lonsdale Road, Summertown, Oxford OX2 7ES	01865 311541	www.simon fisher.co.uk
Knight Frank	2 Worcester Street, Oxford OX1 2BX	01865 790077	www.knightfrank.com
RMA Properties	116a Cowley Road, Oxford OX4 1JE	01865 251025	www.rma properties.co.uk
Fairfax and Co	22 The Parade, Kidlington OX5 1DB	01865 377744	www.johnfairfax.co.uk

Paisley

University	University of Paisley
Population	172,850

		Undergraduate	Postgraduate	Total
	Student population	9050	1540	10590
	Campus capacity	800	0	800
	Size of market	8250	1540	9790

Drop-out rate	18%
Student areas	Paisley, Ayr campus

Accommodation officer contacts

University	Tel	Address	Web	Landlord accreditation scheme?
University of Paisley	0141 848 3158	High Street, Paisley PA1 2BE	www.paisley.ac.uk	No

Planned development for city	Details have been announced of a £500m development to regenerate the south bank of the River Clyde from Braehead to Renfrew. The Renfrew Riverside project is expected to create 8,000 jobs and attract new businesses into the area. Included in the plans are more than one million square feet of business space, 2,000 new homes and leisure facilities. A public park and riverside walkway will be put in place along with an indoor real snow ski centre. Restaurants, shops and a cinema are also planned.
Planned development for university	The University of Paisley opened its new state-of-the-art Students' Union in 2003. The £5m Union, designed by award-winning architects Page and Park, is one of the University's most significant contributions to the regeneration of Paisley centre and offers students a unique facility radically different from the traditional concept of a Student Union building.

Campus room rental**	Minimum £35	Maximum £43

Yield range	9.1–11.2%

Type of property	3 bed house (i.e. 2 bed upstairs + 1 converted other)	4 bed house	5 bed house	6 or more bed house
Entry price	£50,000	£75,000	£110,000	£140,000
Median room rate	£40	£42	£46	£45
Average yield B*	11.2%	10.5%	9.8%	9.1%
B – Estimated annual profit	£2,262	£2,942	£3,698	£3,852

Financial scores	Capital growth (out of 5)	Yield (out of 5)	Total (out of 10)
	3	4	7
Description	Paisley is the largest town in Scotland, but its scale and colourful character make it a friendly place to study and live.　There is an excellent variety of shops, restaurants, bars and nightclubs. The Lagoon Leisure Centre includes saunas, solarium and an Olympic sized ice rink. Paisley was given its university status in 1992. Its history dates back to 1897, when it was founded to offer vocational courses.		
Websites to advertise on	Local and national student listings: www.student-accom.com　City information for students: www.accommodationforstudents.com　Easy roommate: http://uk.easyroommate.com　Link to Stirling listings online: www.letting-in-scotland.co.uk		

Estate agents	Address	Tel	Web
Allen and Harris	16 Causey Street, Paisley PA1 1UN	0141 8897222	www.allenandharris. co.uk
Countrywide Estate Agents	5 Causeyside Street, Paisley PA1 1UW	0141 8481155	www.sequencehome. co.uk
The Robb Agency	Paisley Office, Glasgow PA1 1YW	0141 8898883	www.onemoveforyou. co.uk
MSM Solicitors & Estate Agents	51 Moss Street, Paisley PA1 1DR	0141 8896244	

Letting agents	Address	Tel	Web
Graham Miller Estate Agents	31 Gauze Street, Paisley PA1 1ES	0141 8480707	www.teamprop.co.uk
Thistle Property Services	417 Paisley Road West, Glasgow G51 LS	0141 419 9777	www.s1homes.com
Slater Hogg and Howison	17–19 Gauze Street, Paisley PA1 1ES	0141 8877921	www.slaterhogg.co.uk
Allen and Harris	16 Causey Street, Paisley PA1 1UN	0141 8897222	www.allenandharris. co.uk
Castlehead Properties	Unit 33, The Paisley Centre, 23 High Street, Paisley PA1 2AQ	0141 8481856	www.rightmove.co.uk

Plymouth

Universities	College of St Mark and St John, University of Plymouth
Population	240,718

	Student population	Undergraduate	Postgraduate	Total
	University of Plymouth	22495	4525	27020
	College of St Mark and St John	2965	1775	4740
	Total	25460	6300	31760
	Campus capacity	2961	0	2961
	Size of market	22499	6300	28799

Drop-out rates	University of Plymouth	12%
	College of St Mark and St John	12%

Student areas	Central Plymouth, Freedom Fields, Greenbank, Lipson, Mutley, North Hill, Pennycomequick, Peverall, Prince Rock, St Judes

Accommodation officer contacts

University	Tel	Address	Web	Landlord accreditation scheme?
University of Plymouth	01752 232062	Accommodation Office, Drake Circus, Plymouth PL4 8AA	www.plymouth .ac.uk	Yes
College of St Mark and St John	01752 636711	Accommodation Office, Derriford Road, Plymouth PL6 8BH	www.marjon.ac.uk	No

Planned development for city	Plymouth's historic Grade One listed Royal William Yard has been undergoing redevelopment for 11 years. The Plymouth Development Corporation spent between £20m and £30m on it and the South West Regional Development Agency is looking at spending £35m. The site is being turned into shops, apartments and an exhibition centre.
Planned development for universities	University of Plymouth The University will receive a £2.4 million share of the awards made under the second round of funding from the Higher Education Funding Council for England's Higher Education Innovation Fund (HEIF2), a scheme that forms a major part of the government's strategy to increase prosperity and provide high-quality job opportunities.
	College of St Mark and St John Exeter University awards the degrees for this institute. Students benefit from a good degree whilst enjoying their studies in a small, friendly environment.

Campus room rental**	Minimum £45	Maximum £70
Yield range	8.1–8.9%	

Type of property	3 bed house (i.e. 2 bed upstairs + 1 converted other)	4 bed house	5 bed house	6 or more bed house
Entry price	£90,000	£110,000	£145,000	£165,000
Median room rate	£52	£52	£54	£50
Average yield B*	8.1%	8.9%	8.8%	8.5%
B – Estimated annual profit	£1,816	£2,871	£3,627	£3,855

Financial scores	Capital growth (out of 5)	Yield (out of 5)	Total (out of 10)
	3	3	6

Description	Plymouth is the second largest city on the south coast of England and, after Bristol, the largest in the South West, with a resident population of 241,000 and a further 100,000 in its travel-to-work area.
	Sites for campuses are located at Plymouth, Exeter, Exmouth and near Newton Abbot. Plymouth itself, which seems to be the party town whichever campus you're staying in, is a large and diverse place with plenty to amuse even the most picky of students.
	The general atmosphere is heavily influenced by surfers and other watersports enthusiasts. This is heaven for many of Plymouth's students and a welcome escape from the stuffy atmosphere of Exeter or Bath.

Websites to advertise on	Local and national student listings: www.student-accom.com City information for students: www.accommodationforstudents.com Student accommodation central Plymouth: http://ourworld.compuserve.com/homepages/mjs2nivit Plymouth student housing: www.plymouthstudentaccommodation.co.uk Links from University of Plymouth: www.plym.ac.uk

Estate agents	Address	Tel	Web
Bettisons – Plymouth	52 North Hill, Plymouth PL4 8EU	01752 202121	www.bettisons.co.uk
Bradford & Bingley Marketplace Ltd	133 Milehouse Road, Plymouth PL3 4AG	01752 559106	www.bbg.co.uk
Bradleys	55 Mutley Plain, Plymouth PL4 6JH	01752 251251	www.beagroup.co.uk
Your Move	4 Mannamead Road, Plymouth PL4 7AA	01752 220401	www.your-move.co.uk

Letting agents	Address	Tel	Web
Connells Estate Agents	159 The Ridgeway, Plympton, Plymouth PL7 3HJ	01752 345135	www.connells.co.uk
Fulfords	91–93 Ridgeway, Plymouth PL7 2AA	01752 347347	www.fulfords.co.uk
Miller	151 Ridgeway, Plympton, Plymouth PL7 2HJ	01752 336675	www.miller.co.uk
Darlows	39 Mutley Plain, Plymouth PL4 6JQ	01752 202055	www.tmxdarlows.com
Taylor Son and Creber Ltd	Frianon House, 6 Mannamead Road, Plymouth PL4 7AA	01752 202035	www.taylorcreber.co.uk

Pontypridd

University	University of Glamorgan
Population	33,500

	Student population	Undergraduate	Postgraduate	Total
		16620	3200	19820
	Campus capacity	1100	200	1300
	Size of market	15520	3000	18520

Drop-out rate	16%
Student areas	Treforest, Merthyr, Senghenydd, Pontypridd

University	Accommodation officer contacts			
	Tel	Address	Web	Landlord accreditation scheme?
University of Glamorgan	01443 482044	Accommodation Services, University of Glamorgan, Pontypridd CF37 1DL	www.glam.ac.uk	Yes

Planned development for city	Plans for a £7m office and car parking complex which could lead to the creation of 100 jobs in Pontypridd have been submitted. If approved, a high quality building for new office accommodation would be constructed on a site near to St Catherine's Church within the town centre. A car park with about 350 spaces could also be built for use by shoppers and visitors.
Planned development for university	The Students' Union is looking to develop considerably in the next few years. Nothing is confirmed yet but a larger Union building and more activities are on the cards.

The issue of housing also needs to be addressed as it doesn't look as if the situation is going to get better soon, as the university is closing down two of its five halls – Maes-Yr-Eglwys and the catered Forest Hall. |

Campus room rental**	Minimum	Maximum
	£51	£81

Yield range	4.6–8.3%

Type of property	3 bed house (i.e. 2 bed upstairs + 1 converted other)	4 bed house	5 bed house	6 or more bed house
Entry price	£80,000	£100,000	£150,000	£250,000
Median room rate	£43	£44	£41	£41
Average yield B*	7.6	8.3%	6.4%	4.6%
B – Estimated annual profit	£1,251	£2,118	£958	−£2,000

Financial scores	Capital growth (out of 5)	Yield (out of 5)	Total (out of 10)
	2.5	3	5.5

Description	The University is in the middle of the sleepy village of Treforest. This is a picturesque little place and has a few nice pubs to drink in. Pub crawls are laughably easy due to them all being within about a square mile! The local community doesn't exactly welcome Glamorgan's 17,000 students with open arms but they seem to grudgingly accept that without the University there wouldn't be a Treforest. There are some English-Welsh tensions but nothing to get in a pickle about. Cardiff is about 20 minutes away and easily accessible.		
Websites to advertise on	Local and national student listings: www.student-accom.com City information for students: www.accommodationforstudents.com University links: www.glamorgan.org.uk Housing links: www.taffhousing.co.uk/links.html		

Estate agents	Address	Tel	Web
Halifax Property Services	85 Taff Street, Pontypridd CF37 4SL	01443 400111	www.halifax.co.uk
Allen & Harris	83 Talbot Road, Talbot Green, Pontyclun CF728AE	01443 237667	
Barbara Rees	103 Dunraven Street, Tonypandy CF40 1AR	01443 442444	www.barbararees.net
Durbin Estate Agents	5 The Precinct, Main Road Tonteg, Pontypridd CF381SB	01443 204240	www.durbins.co.uk

Letting agents	Address	Tel	Web
Darlows Ltd	43 Dunraven Street, Tonypandy CF40 1AL	01443 436445	www.tmxdarlows.com
Leek and Weston	29 Gelliwastad Road, Pontypridd CF37 2BN	01443 492229	www.leekandweston.com
Peter Alan Ltd	94 Taff Street, Pontypridd CF37 4SL	01443 485600	www.peteralan.co.uk
Peter Mulcahy	5 Taff Vale Centre, Pontypridd CF37 4TG	01443 407917	www.pmea.co.uk
Seward and Co	Woodfield House, Main Road, Llantwit Fardre, Pontypridd, CF38 2LT		

Portsmouth

Universities	University of Portsmouth, University College Chichester
Population	186,704 (Portsmouth)

	Student population	Undergraduate	Postgraduate	Total
	University of Portsmouth	15070	4325	19395
	University College Chichester	3175	1800	4975
	Total	18245	6125	24370
	Campus capacity	2550	450	3000
	Size of market	15695	5675	21370

Drop-out rates	University of Portsmouth	12%
	University College Chichester	12%

Student areas	Eastney, Fratton, North End, Southsea

University	Accommodation officer contacts			
	Tel	Address	Web	Landlord accreditation scheme?
University of Portsmouth	023 9284 3214	Student Housing, The Nuffield Centre, St Michael's Road, Portsmouth PO1 2ED	www.port.ac.uk	No
University College Chichester	01243 816045	Accommodation Office, University College Chichester, Upper Bognor Road, Bognor Regis PO21 1HR	www.ucc.ac.uk	No

Planned development for city	Portsmouth Football Club has been given the go-ahead to redevelop their stadium to a capacity of 35,000 at a cost of about £125m. The development will include 500 houses, shops, restaurants and leisure facilities at Fratton Park with 14% of the homes being social housing.
Planned development for universities	University of Portsmouth The University and Students' Union get on very well. This close relationship has meant that the SU has been able to negotiate and persuade the University to implement future plans quite quickly. In recent years the students have benefited from a brand new Students' Union building and modern halls of residence. The University has internet access in most of its halls of residence and also plans to install this in many of the student houses around town. Having completed so much, the University is probably taking a well-earned break before deciding what to do next.
	University College Chichester University College Chichester, or UCC, is a small and very friendly University College based on two campuses, the Bishop Otter Campus in Chichester and the Bognor Regis Campus.

Campus room rental**	Minimum £63		Maximum £99	
Yield range	7.7–9.8%			
Type of property	3 bed house (i.e. 2 bed upstairs + 1 converted other)	4 bed house	5 bed house	6 or more bed house
Entry price	£90,000	£105,000	£140,000	£190,000
Median room rate	£57	£55	£52	£52
Average yield B*	8.9%	9.8%	8.7%	7.7%
B – Estimated annual profit	£2,380	£3,547	£3,476	£3,182
Financial scores	Capital growth (out of 5) 3	Yield (out of 5) 3	Total (out of 10) 6	
Description	Portsmouth University is split up around the city but most of the sites are within walking distance of one another. The University is actually right in the middle of the city so the students are well-placed to take full advantage of city life. Many students come to Portsmouth for the naval connection – it is the home of the British Navy. Many famous ships are docked here, for example *HMS Victory*, the *Mary Rose* and *HMS Warrior*. Another great attraction is Southsea and the beach. Southsea not only has a beach, which is crowded with students in the summer, but it also has the Common which stretches for miles along the seafront. All summer long people sunbathe and play and there are a variety of events like the Moscow State Circus. Southsea also has a fun-fair and a shopping centre.			
Websites to advertise on	Local and national student listings: www.student-accom.com City information for students: www.accommodationforstudents.com Room lets: www.thesublet.com/Index4/PortsmouthRoomsForRent.html AC property: www.portsnet.com/acpropertys			

Estate agents	Address	Tel	Web
Bradford & Bingley Marketplace Ltd	2 Elm Grove, Hayling Island, Portsmouth PO11 9EF	023 92465941	www.bbg.co.uk
Your Move	154 London Road, North End, Portsmouth PO2 9DJ	023 92668811	www.your-move.co.uk
Network Homes	21 Spur Road, Cosham, Portsmouth PO6 3DY	023 92210360	www.networkhomes. co.uk

Estate agents	Address	Tel	Web
Mann and Co	127 London Road, North End, Portsmouth PO2 9AA	023 92666611	www.mann countrywide.co.uk

Letting agents	Address	Tel	Web
Burlingtons	52 Kingston Road, Portsmouth PO2 7PA	023 92668111	www.burlingtons estateagents.co.uk
Fox & Sons	126 London Road, Portsmouth PO2 9DE	02392671110	www.rightmove.co.uk
Halifax Property Services	10 Middle Road, Park Gate, Portsmouth SO31 7GH	01489 582323	www.halifax.co.uk
Jeffries and Partners	196 Havant Road, Drayton, Portsmouth PO6 2EH	023 92373341	www.jeffries.uk.com
Wyatt and Son	3 Exchange House, 122 London Road, North End, Portsmouth PO2 9DD	023 92661213	www.wyattandson. co.uk

Preston

University	University of Central Lancashire
Population	129,642

	Student population	Undergraduate	Postgraduate	Total
		25500	2705	28205
	Campus capacity	1500	–	1500
	Size of market	24000	2705	26705

Drop-out rate	14%
Student areas	Ashton, Avenham, Billsborrow, Bilsborrow, Burrowbank, Deepdale, Firbank, Fulwood, Plungington, Ribbleton

University	Accommodation officer contacts			
	Tel	Address	Web	Landlord accreditation scheme?
University of Central Lancashire	01772 892520/ 31	Accommodation Service, Preston PR1 2HE	s.accommodation @uclan.ac.uk www.uclan.ac.uk	No

Planned development for city	After 26 towns in England had bid for the title, Preston was awarded city status in April 2002 by the Queen in celebration of her Golden Jubilee. In light of this status, an initiative was taken to target key UK business leaders and decision makers, as well as thousands of national and international travellers, as part of the campaign which aims to increase investment in the city. The key points that are being focused on include Preston's new-found city status, excellent location, transport links, skilled workforce and quality higher education providers.
Planned development for university	In January 2004, The Northwest Development Agency (NWDA) announced funding of £2.5m for a three-year initiative to raise the profile of the Contact Centre Sector as one of the most important employers in England's North West. The project CallNorthWest is hosted by the University of Central Lancashire (UCLan) in Preston, and brings together large, medium and small businesses as well as academics, councils, government agencies and trades unions, who will unite behind a 'skills agenda' for the region. The initiative aims to ensure that England's North West continues to be a preferred location for World Class Contact Centres due to the infrastructure in place to support the sector.

Campus room rental	Minimum	Maximum
	£52	£68

Yield range	7.9–11.2%

Type of property	3 bed house (i.e. 2 bed upstairs + 1 converted other)	4 bed house	5 bed house	6 or more bed house
Entry price	£65,000	£85,000	£125,000	£160,000
Median room rate	£47	£43	£42	£41
Average yield B*	11.2%	10.5%	8.7%	7.9%
B – Estimated annual profit	£2,941	£3,331	£3,111	£3,034

Financial scores	Capital growth (out of 5)	Yield (out of 5)	Total (out of 10)
	4	4	8

Description	Preston is the second largest city in Lancashire and unlike Lancashire's largest city, Blackpool, which lights up the North East, Preston actually has some style.
	There are many beautiful buildings including the city's library. There are plenty of pubs and other entertainment. Preston has easy access to Scotland, London and nearby Manchester.
Websites to advertise on	This is Preston: www.thisislancashire.co.uk/lancashire/preston Student accommodation service: www.uclan.ac.uk/other/hs/saccomm/private.htm Accomodation for students: www.accommodationforstudents.com Preston letting: www.prestonletting.co.uk Easy roommate: http://uk.easyroommate.com

Estate agents	Address	Tel	Web
Dickson Haslam	12 Chapel Street, Preston PR1 8BU	01772 883100	www.dickson haslam.com enquiries@ dicksonhaslam.com
Bairstow Eves	89 Fishergate, Preston PR1 2NJ	01772 252921	www.rightmove.co.uk
Your Move Estate Agents	82 Fishergate, Preston PR1 2NJ	01772 561 188	preston1@your-move.co.uk www.your-move.co.uk
Bradford & Bingley	91a Fishersgate, Preston PR1 2NJ	01772 823021	www.bbg.co.uk

Letting agents	Address	Tel	Web
Charles Parker Bennett & Co	17/18 Cannon Street, Preston PR1 3NR	01772 253 977	www.parker bennett.co.uk surveyors@ parkerbennett.co.uk

Letting agents	Address	Tel	Web
Farrell Heyworth	48 Lune Street, Preston PR1 2NN	01772 203345	preston@farrell heyworth.co.uk www.farrell heyworth.co.uk
Reeds Rains	80 Fishergate, Preston PR1 2UH	01772 561666	preston@ reedsrains.co.uk www.reedsrains.com
Countrywide Residential Lettings	89 Fishergate, Preston PR1 2NJ	01772 258317	www.crldirect.co.uk
Garside Waddingham Pinder	Fleet House, 8–10 Fleet Street, Preston PR1 2UT	01772 883188 / 201117	info@garside waddingham.co.uk www.garside waddingham.co.uk

Sheffield	
Universities	University of Sheffield, Sheffield Hallam University
Population	513,234
	Student population Undergraduate Postgraduate Total University of Sheffield 18650 6855 25505 Sheffield Hallam University 20190 6290 26480 Total 38840 13145 51985 Campus capacity 6304 900 7204 Size of market 32536 12245 44781
Drop-out rates	University of Sheffield 4% Sheffield Hallam University 10%
Student areas	Abbeydale, Broomhill, Central Sheffield, Crookes, Crookesmoor, Ecclesall, Highfields, Hunters Bar, Nether Edge, Netherthorpe, off Ecclesall Road, Sharrow, Walkley

Accommodation officer contacts

University	Tel	Address	Web	Landlord accreditation scheme?
University of Sheffield	0114 222 6041	Accommodation and Campus Services, The University of Sheffield, Sorby Hall, Endcliffe Vale Road, Sheffield S10 3ES	www.shef.ac.uk/ housing	Yes
Sheffield Hallam University	0114 225 4503	Accommodation Centre, 38–40 Howard Street, City Campus, Sheffield S1 1WB	www.shu.ac.uk	Yes

Planned development for city	A former South Yorkshire coalfield is to be transformed into a £100m business park, creating at least 2,000 jobs. The 84-acre Brookfields Park has appointed brownfield regeneration specialist St Paul's Developments to lead the scheme. It is a key step in the regeneration of the Dearne Valley, where 10,000 jobs have been created in the past decade.
Planned development for universities	University of Sheffield Half of the University's residential accommodation is to be privatised. The University had wanted to do this for a long time, but had encountered fierce reaction from the Students' Union in the past. The news did cause some outrage from the Students' Union. The University has decided that two halls of residence should be sold on the open market over a period of at least five years from 2003. Student representatives say this could result in a massive hike in rent for students.

	Sheffield Hallam University A £50m investment has recently been made in new learning facilities including the prize-winning and renowned Adsetts Learning Centre. The Centre is open 24 hours per day and combines library, lecture theatres and other facilities including state of the art network facilities. There are more than 1600 workspaces and IT resources and access to modern journals, books, videos, live TV, video conferencing and CD-ROMs.

Campus room rental**	Minimum	Maximum
	£42	£100

Yield range	5.5–8%			
Type of property	3 bed house (i.e. 2 bed upstairs + 1 converted other)	4 bed house	5 bed house	6 or more bed house
Entry price	£100,000	£110,000	£175,000	£235,000
Median room rate	£45	£47	£47	£46
Average yield B*	6.3%	8%	6.3%	5.5%
B – Estimated annual profit	£576	£2,119	£961	–£197

Financial scores	Capital growth (out of 5)	Yield (out of 5)	Total (out of 10)
	2.5	4	6.5

Description	The universities are woven into the fabric of the west of the city with departments dotted here and there and the space in between filled with student housing, sports facilities and shops. Out of town there is the vast Meadowhall shopping centre. Sheffield is one of the Midlands' major cities and despite its decline during the late 70s and early 80s it has undergone some considerable redevelopment. Nightlife is quite good with some swanky new bars and cafes. The sheer number of students in the city means that scholars form a major part of the population.

Websites to advertise on	Sheffield University official portal: http://portland.shef.ac.uk/housingfinder Local online classifieds: www.sheffnet.co.uk National student listings: www.studentaccommodationuk.com Local and national student listings : www.accommodationforstudents.com Easy roommate: http://uk.easyroommate.com

Estate agents	Address	Tel	Web
Blundells	84 Queen Street, Sheffield S1 2DW	0114 2721091	www.blundells.co.uk

Estate agents	Address	Tel	Web
Eadon Lockwood & Riddle	501 Glossop Road, Broomhill, Sheffield S10 2QE	0114 2660061	www.elr.co.uk
Halifax Property Services	5 Market Street, Chapeltown, Sheffield S35 2UW	0114 2570696	www.halifax.co.uk
Winkworth	City Centre Office, 66 Campo Lane, Sheffield S1 2EG	0114 2765715	www.winkworth.co.uk
Letting agents	Address	Tel	Web
Haybrook Property Services	Crystal Peaks, 4 Peak Square, Sheffield S20 7PH	0114 251 1710	www.haybrook.com
Lewis Wadsworth	19 Figtree Lane, Sheffield S1 2DJ	0114 2731121	www.lewiswadsworth.co.uk
Property Plus	34 Dronfield, Sheffield S18 2XB	01246 412000	www.pplus.co.uk
Reeds Rains	936 Ecclesall Road, Banner Cross, Sheffield S11 7TR	0114 2670150	www.reedsrains.co.uk
William H Brown – Sheffield	37–39 Church Street, Sheffield S1 2GL	0114 2769062	www.rightmove.co.uk

St Andrews

University	University of St Andrews
Population	14,695

	Student population	Undergraduate	Postgraduate	Total
		6405	1430	7835
	Campus capacity	2736	465	3101
	Size of market	3669	965	4734

Drop-out rate	5%
Student areas	Central, East Sands, Kinaldy Farm, North Haugh, off Lamond Drive

Accommodation officer contacts

University	Tel	Address	Web	Landlord accreditation scheme?
University of St Andrews	01334 462510	Accommodation Office, University of St Andrews, 79 North Street, St Andrews KY16 9AJ	www.st-and.ac.uk	Yes

Planned development for city	More than £100m is to be invested in the key commitments by Fife council from 2003 to 2006. The programme will target resources at seven key themes. These are: promoting stronger safer communities, safeguarding and improving Fife's environment, community regeneration and social inclusion, promoting a strong, diverse Fife economy, encouraging a well-educated and skilled Fife, promoting health and leisure and modernising Fife.
	£53 million will also be invested through the Public Private Partnership to build ten new primary schools across Fife.
	A five-year housing plan aimed at securing an adequate number of affordable houses in Fife has been launched. Proposals were unveiled against a backdrop of soaring house prices in the Fife region. Rocketing costs and the right to buy legislation have led to a significant increase in homelessness. The Housing Strategy aims to boost sheltered housing in the region.
Planned development for university	The Universities of St Andrews and Edinburgh are to collaborate on medical teaching and research, providing 50 more doctors per year for the NHS in Scotland and offering more opportunities for Scottish students to train as doctors.
	The University of St Andrews is to seek planning permission for a major new town centre building, which will provide much needed teaching and research space for the Faculty of Arts and a new home for the School of International Relations. The proposed multi-million pound building of architectural distinction will be located next to the University Library in North Street and will include a new lecture theatre, seminar rooms and office space.

	At the time of writing, the University of St Andrews Court was planning to hike up campus rents to come into line with those of other universities, at an estimated average of 27%.			
Campus room rental**	Minimum £50		Maximum £100	
Yield range	5.6–8.3%			
Type of property	3 bed house (i.e. 2 bed upstairs + 1 converted other)	4 bed house	5 bed house	6 or more bed house
Entry price Median room rate Average yield B* B – Estimated annual profit	£160,000 £64 5.6% £20	£175,000 £63 6.8% £1,601	£190,000 £60 7.4% £2,730	£205,000 £60 8.3% £4,311
Financial scores	Capital growth (out of 5) 2.5	Yield (out of 5) 3	Total (out of 10) 5.5	
Description	St Andrews is located about an hour from Edinburgh and 20 minutes from Dundee. The University makes up much of the seaside town and is its largest employer – hence the place takes on ghost-town status during the holidays. As for pubs, there are more per area than in any other town in the UK.			
Websites to advertise on	Local and national student listings: www.student-accom.com City information for students: www.accommodationforstudents.com Easy roommate: http://uk.easyroommate.com Link to St Andrews listings online: www.letting-in-scotland.co.uk Online listings: www.ukwebfind.co.uk/standrews.html			

Estate agents	Address	Tel	Web
Bennetts	52 Crossgate, Cupar KY15 5JX	01334 655150	www.rben.net
Bradburne and Company	139 South Street, St Andrews KY16 9UN	01334 479479	www.bradburne.co.uk
Rollo Davidson Mc Farlane	6 Bell Street, St Andrews KY16 9UX	01334 477700	www.rollos.co.uk

Letting agents	Address	Tel	Web
Pagan Osborne	106 South St, St Andrews KY16 9QD	01334 475001	www.paganproperty.co.uk

Letting agents	Address	Tel	Web
Mc Llroy Hipwell	147 Market Street, St Andrews KY16 9PF	01334 472740	
Murray Donald and Caithness	17 Bell Street, St Andrews KY16 9UR	01334 474455	www.md-c.co.uk
Drummond Cook & Mackintosh	33 Bell Street, St Andrews KY16 9UR	01334 472152	www.drummond cook.co.uk

Stafford

University	Staffordshire University			
Population	120,653			
	Student population	Undergraduate	Postgraduate	Total
		13110	2315	15425
	Campus capacity	1800	300	2100
	Size of market	11310	2015	13325
Drop-out rate	13%			
Student areas	Beaconside, Littleworth, Castletown, Holmcroft, Baswich, Queensville, Rising Brook			

University	**Accommodation officer contacts**			
	Tel	Address	Web	Landlord accreditation scheme?
Staffordshire University	01782 294217/ 8/9	Accommodation Office, Staffordshire University, College Road, Stoke On Trent ST4 2DE	www.staffs.ac.uk/ accommodation/	No

Planned development for city	The Great British Kitchen plan is to create a centre for culinary arts, which will provide 1,000 new jobs in Stafford on a 28-acre site. The £40m centre will provide a wide range of food-related activities for day visitors and staying guests: attractions, shopping and restaurants; leisure learning, education and training; shows, functions and special events.
	The plans announced by the government in 2004 to open a private toll motorway linking Birmingham to Manchester could affect large areas of housing in Stafford and other nearby areas.
Planned development for university	A new commercial centre with a travel shop and general store at the Stoke site is the other big news. As part of an official visit to the University, new Chancellor Sir Bill Morris officially opened the University's premier business learning and conference facilities at the Stoke campus.

Campus room rental**	Minimum	Maximum
	£52	£68

Yield range	6.8–8.1%			
Type of property	3 bed house (i.e. 2 bed upstairs + 1 converted other)	4 bed house	5 bed house	6 or more bed house
Entry price	£98,000	£108,000	£130,000	£200,000
Median room rate	£50	£45	£45	£48
Average yield B*	7.2%	7.8%	8.1%	6.8%
B – Estimated annual profit	£1,230	£1,908	£2,610	£1,829

Financial scores	Capital growth (out of 5)	Yield (out of 5)	Total (out of 10)
	3	3	6
Description	Stafford is quite a countryside town and has plenty of good pubs and a good atmosphere. Stoke is a little more built up but the Leek Road site has more of a campus feel to it. At Stoke a number of the major chain pubs have moved in meaning that the Union has some competition. Decent DJs and functions keep the students from wandering.		
Websites to advertise on	Local and national student listings: www.student-accom.com City information for students: www.accommodationforstudents.com University residential services: http://crntpro1.staffs.ac.uk/ResServs/stafford_results.asp Easy roommate: http://uk.easyroommate.com		

Estate agents	Address	Tel	Web
Bradford & Bingley Marketplace	Bank House, 40 Greengate Street, Stafford ST16 2JB	01785 242426	www.bbg.co.uk
Halifax Property Services	5 Eastgate Street, Stafford ST16 2NQ	01785 259321	www.halifax.co.uk
Jayman	6–7 Church Lane, Stafford ST16 2AW	01785 250095	www.jayman.co.uk
Clothier and Day Estate Agents	1 Eastgate Street, Stafford ST16 2NQ	01785 225205	www.rightmove.co.uk

Letting agents	Address	Tel	Web
Michael Stokes	43 Mill Street, Stafford ST16 2AJ	01785 241329	www.teamprop.co.uk
Nicolsons	7 Market Street, Stafford ST16 2JZ	01785 214214	www.nicolsons.co.uk
Reeds Rains	11 Mill Street, Stafford ST16 2AJ	01785 258888	www.reedsrains.co.uk
Owen Bennion and Son	41 Mill Street, Stafford ST16 2AS	01785 252137	www.bennionl.freeserve.co.uk
John German Estate Agents	4 Eastgate Street, Stafford ST16 2NQ	01785 236600	www.johngerman.co.uk

Stirling

University	University of Stirling
Population	86,200

	Student population	Undergraduate	Postgraduate	Total
		7095	1880	8975
	Campus capacity	2500	600	3100
	Size of market	4595	1280	5875

Drop-out rate	11%
Student areas	Bridge of Allan, Stirling

University	Accommodation officer contacts			
	Tel	Address	Web	Landlord accreditation scheme?
University of Stirling	01786 467060/1	Accommodation Office, University of Stirling, Stirling FK9 4LA	www.stir.ac.uk	Yes

Planned development for city	Stirling was granted city status by the Queen to mark her Golden Jubilee in 2002. The new city beat off competition from Ayr, Paisley and Dumfries, in Scotland. Scottish ministers have committed £30m towards the reopening of a rail link between Stirling and Kincardine. The investment will meet more than 80% of the £37.5m cost of the project. It is hoped that the Alloa line will be open by the end of 2005.
Planned development for university	The MacRobert on-campus cinema and theatre complex has recently received a large lottery grant resulting in an upgrade. Facilities constructed include a new 140-seat cinema, children's theatre, and modern dining room and cafe area.

Campus room rental**	Minimum	Maximum
	£46	£60

Yield range	5.1–8.5%

Type of property	3 bed house (i.e. 2 bed upstairs + 1 converted other)	4 bed house	5 bed house	6 or more bed house
Entry price***	£75,000	£100,000	£160,000	£250,000
Median room rate	£45	£45	£45	£45
Average yield B*	8.5%	8.5%%	6.6%	5.1%
B – Estimated annual profit	£1,701	£2,268	£1,260	-£1,098

Financial scores	Capital growth (out of 5)	Yield (out of 5)	Total (out of 10)
	3	3	6

Description	Stirling is situated in the centre of Scotland surrounded by snow-topped mountains, with Stirling Castle overlooking the campus from its impressive location on the cliff. The numerous lochs nearby provide an arena for lazy days or water sports during the summer. Both the town and the campus have a small, friendly feel, and as a result many students never leave. It has been known for students to arrive once and depart once, while four years go by in the middle. If you do venture out into Stirling then there is an indoor shopping centre with all the essential shops (larger shops can be found in Glasgow and Edinburgh, a short train journey away). Many of the local pubs are 'student friendly'.
Websites to advertise on	Local and national student listings: www.student-accom.com City information for students: www.accommodationforstudents.com Easy roommate: http://uk.easyroommate.com Link to Stirling listings online: www.letting-in-scotland.co.uk

Estate agents	Address	Tel	Web
Clyde Property	39 Allan Park, Stirling FK8 2LT	01786 471777	www.clydeproperty.co.uk
Collins & Co Property Services and Estate Agents	43 Glasgow Road, Stirling FK7 0PA	01786 451234	www.collinsandco.net
L H Melville Ltd	21 Upper Craigs, Stirling FK8 2DG	01786 450378	www.lhmel.co.uk
Manor Management Services	PO Box 21092, Stirling FK9 5WA	01786 463313	www.scottishrelocation popertyservices.com

Letting agents	Address	Tel	Web
Hill and Robb	3 Pitt Terrace, Stirling FK8 2EY	01786 450985	www.hillandrobb.co.uk
Muirhead Buchanan	8 Allan Park, Stirling FK8 2QE	01786 450944	www.muirboxs.co.uk
Slater Hogg and Howison	66–68 Upper Craigs, Stirling FK8 2DS	01786 470286	www.slaterhogg.co.uk
P F S Estate Agents	2 Alloa Road, Stirling FK9 5LT	01786 463311	www.pfsestateagents.co.uk
Heritage Estates	92 Glasgow Road, Stirling FK7 0PQ	01786 815577	

Sunderland

University	University of Sunderland
Population	280,807

	Student population	Undergraduate	Postgraduate	Total
		13795	2315	16115
	Campus capacity	2150	350	2500
	Size of market	11645	1965	13615

Drop-out rate	17%
Student areas	Ashbrooke, city centre, Millfield, Mowbray Park, off Chester Road, Pallion, Thornhill, Tyne and Wear

University	Accommodation officer contacts			
	Tel	Address	Web	Landlord accreditation scheme?
University of Sunderland	0191 515 2943	Accommodation Service, Johnson Building, Chester Road Campus, Sunderland SR1 3SD	www.sunderland. ac.uk	Yes

Planned development for city	Sunderland Area Regeneration Company (ARC) plans to carry out a £135m development with a department store, restaurants, shops and apartments. The development could create up to 1,200 jobs on Wearside.
	The extension of the Metro line into Sunderland has unlocked property hot spots and allowed more scope for growth on Wearside. The housing market in Sunderland has been rising steadily but property experts say stock in the city centre is still undervalued. This means there is affordable housing for first-time buyers.
Planned development for university	A key part of the University's development programme is a major new purpose-built campus on the banks of the River Wear, new student accommodation and a major project to refurbish the main block of Edinburgh Building. The £2.5m project, which has been substantially funded by the Higher Education Funding Council for England (HEFCE) will provide upgraded teaching rooms and offices in the building.
	Edinburgh Building's exterior and interior are being completely refurbished to give a modern, more welcoming appearance, and create a better teaching and working environment.
	Work on a £7m Digital Media Centre at St Peter's Campus is the first phase of a plan to create a centre of excellence for the arts, design and media. It will house studios, workshops, edit suites and facilities for TV/video, radio, journalism and multi-media.

Campus room rental**	Minimum	Maximum
	£48	£55

Yield range	7.9–16.1%			
Type of property	3 bed house (i.e. 2 bed upstairs + 1 converted other)	4 bed house	5 bed house	6 or more bed house
Entry price	£35,000	£45,000	£80,000	£140,000
Median room rate	£40	£38	£38	£39
Average yield B*	16.1%	15.6%	11.1%	7.9%
B – Estimated annual profit	£2,937	£3,691	£3,544	£2,499

Financial scores	Capital growth (out of 5)	Yield (out of 5)	Total (out of 10)
	5	3	8

Description	The University of Sunderland is based within the heart of the modern centre of the City of Sunderland, in North East England. The University has a large mix of courses, covering engineering, technology, business, management, life sciences and the creative arts.
	Facilities are constantly being improved and updated and include a modern library, language laboratories, media centre, an art gallery and specialist research centres including the Industry Centre and the Ecology Centre.
	Sunderland is a much redeveloped town in the grip of more redevelopment. A spectacular amount of money has been and is being spent. The centre is heavily pedestrianised and all the usual chain stores are present. A new Metro link is now in place, which allows easy access to Newcastle.

Websites to advertise on	Local and national student listings: www.student-accom.com City information for students: www.accommodationforstudents.com Student accommodation Sunderland: www.studentpad.co.uk Sunderland university links: http://restal.sunderland.ac.uk/_html2/accommodation.cfm

Estate agents	Address	Tel	Web
Andrew Craig	18 John Street, Sunderland SR1 1HT	0191 5653377	www.andrewcraig.co.uk
Halifax Property Services	4a Athenaeum Street, Sunderland SR1 1QX	0191 5674095	www.halifax.co.uk
Keith Pattinson	51 Fawcett Street, Sunderland SR1 1RS	0191 5652615	www.pattinson.co.uk
Murray Humphrey	8 Woods Terrace, Sunderland SR7 9AA	0191 5170988	www.mhlegal.com

Letting agents	Address	Tel	Web
Whitegates Estate Agency Ltd	Frederick Street, Sunderland SR1 1NA	0191 5675161	www.whitegates.co.uk
Kimmitt and Roberts	42 Church Street, Seaham, Sunderland SR7 7EJ	0191 5813213	www.kimmittand roberts.com
Peter Heron	20 Fawcett Street, Sunderland SR1 1RH	0191 5103323	www.peterheron.co.uk
Chadwick Airey	5 Athenaeum Street, Sunderland SR1 1QX	0191 5145777	www.chadwickairey. co.uk
Dowen Estate Agents	21 Athenaeum Street, Sunderland SR1 1DH	0191 5142299	www.dowen.co.uk

Swansea

Universities	Swansea Institute of Higher Education, University of Wales Swansea			
Population	223,293			
	Student population	Undergraduate	Postgraduate	Total
	Swansea Institute of Higher Education	4775	695	5470
	University of Wales, Swansea	10500	2975	13480
	Total	15275	3670	18950
	Campus capacity	2654	350	3004
	Size of market	12621	3320	15946
Drop-out rates	Swansea Institute of Higher Education 13% University of Wales, Swansea 8%			
Student areas	Brynmill, Hendrefolian, Mount Pleasant, Sketty, The Mumbles, Uplands			

Accommodation officer contacts

University	Tel	Address	Web	Landlord accreditation scheme?
Swansea Institute of Higher Education	01792 481208	Accommodation Office, Swansea Institute of HE, Townhill Road, Swansea SA2 0UT	www.sihe.ac.uk	No
University of Wales, Swansea	01792 295101	Accommodation Office, University of Wales, Swansea, Singleton Park, Swansea SA2 8PP	www.swan.ac.uk/ accommodation	No

Planned development for city	A new casino is set to open in Swansea, with the potential of creating 500 new jobs. They will move into the new £30m Salubrious Place leisure development in the Wind Street area of Swansea.
Planned development for universities	Swansea Institute of Higher Education Swansea University's School of Health Science and its neighbouring School at Swansea Institute of Higher Education have joined forces. The merger will build on the strengths in health education of the two already successful departments, and will provide world-class courses structured according to students' needs.
	University of Wales, Swansea A £10m funding for the AutoTechnium business innovation centre has been driven forward by the Welsh Assembly Government, the Welsh Development Agency, Swansea University, Swansea Institute and Carmarthenshire County Council with support from the automotive industry and the Welsh Automotive Forum. AutoTechnium will become a hub for high performance engineering, automotive and motorsport business development in Wales.

Campus room rental**	Minimum £42		Maximum £72	
Yield range	6.6–9.1%			
Type of property	3 bed house (i.e. 2 bed upstairs + 1 converted other)	4 bed house	5 bed house	6 or more bed house
Entry price	£65,000	£85,000	£140,000	£175,000
Median room rate	£42	£40	£42	£41
Average yield B*	9.1%	8.8%	7.1%%	6.6%
B – Estimated annual profit	£1,813	£2,191	£1,596	£1,375

Financial scores	Capital growth (out of 5) 3.5	Yield (out of 5) 3	Total (out of 10) 6.5
Description	Swansea is the second city of Wales and has all the resources you would expect. It is also in parts quite a pretty place with grey slate houses and plenty of greenery. There are some good pubs and clubs in the city which attract people from a wide area.		
Websites to advertise on	Local and national student listings: www.student-accom.com City information for students: www.accommodationforstudents.com Links from the Swansea University Students' Union: www.swansea-union.co.uk Let a property : www.let-a-property.info/letting-agents/Mid%20Glamorgan		

Estate agents	Address	Tel	Web
Ashley Jones & Partners	24 Woodfield Street, Swansea SA6 8AB	01792 700456	www.teamprop.co.uk
Darlows	Sketty, Swansea SA6 8AL	01792 204057	www.tmxdarlows.com
David Jones	73 High Street, Gorseinon, Swansea SA4 4BP	01792 896868	www.teamprop.co.uk
Peter Alan	496 Mumbles Road, Mumbles, Swansea SA3 4BX	01792 361581	www.peteralan.co.uk

Letting agents	Address	Tel	Web
Dawsons	Killay Office, 419 Gower Road, Killay, Swansea SA2 7AN	01792 298014	www.dawsonsproperty.co.uk
John Francis	Mumbles Office, Swansea SA1 5NE	01792 360060	www.johnfrancis.co.uk
Taylors	Swansea SA6 8AQ	01792 643686	www.taylorsestagent.co.uk
Simpson Evans and Partners	21 Walter Road, Swansea SA1 5NQ	01792 476111	www.simpsonevans.co.uk
Roberts Homes	18 Station Road Ystradgynlais, Swansea SA91NT	01639 842013	www.teamprop.co.uk

Winchester

University	University College Winchester
Population	107,213

		Undergraduate	Postgraduate	Total
	Student population	4515	965	5480
	Campus capacity	1000	–	1000
	Size of market	3515	965	4480

Drop-out rate	11%
Student areas	Bar End, Highcliffe, Stanmore, Winnall

Accommodation officer contacts

University	Tel	Address	Web	Landlord accreditation scheme?
University College Winchester	01962 827301	Sparkford Road, Winchester SO22 4NR	www.wkac.ac.uk	Yes (soon)

Planned development for city	Cala Homes has proposed an outline planning application to Winchester City Council for 2,000 homes at Barton Farm, Winchester, the area that has been identified as the Winchester City North Major Development Area reserve-housing site.
Planned development for university	University College Winchester is one of the newest higher education institutions as of 2004 when it acquired taught Degree Awarding Powers and changed from being King Alfred's College.

Campus room rental**	Minimum £65	Maximum £93

Yield range	6–7%

Type of property	3 bed house (i.e. 2 bed upstairs + 1 converted other)	4 bed house	5 bed house	6 or more bed house
Entry price	£140,000	£180,000	£230,000	£310,000
Median room rate	£65	£67	£65	£65
Average yield B*	6.5%	7%	6.6%	6%
B – Estimated annual profit	£1,032	£1,977	£1,870	£714

Financial scores	Capital growth (out of 5) 3	Yield (out of 5) 2.5	Total (out of 10) 5.5

Description	The College is situated on a wooded hillside overlooking the beautiful cathedral city of Winchester, and within ten minutes' walk of the city centre. Winchester is ideally placed for travel to other parts of the country and mainland Europe. Direct services link Winchester with many

	major towns and cities. By road on the M3 motorway, Winchester is 64 miles from London.		
Websites to advertise on	Local and national student listings: www.student-accom.com City information for students: www.accommodationforstudents.com Winchester classifieds: www.winchesterontheweb.com National listings: www.upmystreet.com		
Estate agents	**Address**	**Tel**	**Web**
Belgarum Estate Agents	72a High Street, Winchester SO23 9DA	01962 844460	www.belgarum.com
Bradford & Bingley Marketplace Ltd	11a Southgate Street, Winchester SO23 9DZ	01962 866422	www.bbg.co.uk
Complete Property Service	15 Southgate Street, Winchester SO23 9DZ	01962 831831	www.complete365.com
Fox & Sons	70 High Street, Winchester SO23 9DA	01962 862121	www.sequencehome.co.uk
Letting agents	**Address**	**Tel**	**Web**
Connells Estate Agents	Westgate Chambers, 82 High Street, Winchester SO23 9AP	01962 864444	www.connells.co.uk
Dreweatt Neate – Winchester	9a Jewry Street, Winchester SO23 8RZ	01962 842742	www.dreweatt-neate.co.uk
Savills	Jewry Chambers, 44 Jewry Street, Winchester SO23 8RW	01962 841 842	www.savills.co.uk
Halifax Property Services	7 Southgate Street, Winchester SO23 9DY	01962 868551	www.halifax.co.uk
Knight Frank	14 Jewry Street, Winchester SO23 8RZ	01962 850333	www.knightfrank.com

Wolverhampton

University	University of Wolverhampton
Population	236,573

	Student population	Undergraduate	Postgraduate	Total
		19130	3875	23005
	Campus capacity	2029	358	2387
	Size of market	17101	3517	20618

Drop-out rate	14%
Student areas	Blakenhall, Darlaston, Dunstall, Heath Town Palfrey, Pennfields, Whitmore Reans

University	Accommodation officer contacts			
	Tel	Address	Web	Landlord accreditation scheme?
University of Wolverhampton	01902 321040	Residential Services Office, University of Wolverhampton, Lomas Street, Wolverhampton WV1 1QU	www.wlv.ac.uk/ accomm	Yes

Planned development for city	Wolverhampton City Council has approved a £50m programme of improvements to libraries, galleries and museums, parks, sports centres, community centres and other leisure and cultural facilities. These improvements will be undertaken up to March 2009. In some cases applications have either been made or need to be made to external sources to complete the schemes.
Planned development for university	The Business Process Modernisation Project was launched in February 2001. It seeks to identify and implement improvements of key processes such as student administration across the University in order to better meet the needs of all the stakeholders: schools, students, learning centres, registry and other departments. The New Horizons Project is a £60m development plan. It involves the building of several more buildings and facilities at the University including the Millennium Building and housing a 300-seat lecture theatre, an informal study area, an exhibition hall, a refectory, 1,300 students and 200 academic staff. It is being built on the site of the old psychology building. The project also involves the creation of a lottery funded centre for the British Judo Association, a new sports hall at the Telford Campus and some post-graduate business courses at the Compton Campus.

Campus room rental**	Minimum	Maximum
	£45	£60
Yield range	6.1–8.1%	

Type of property	3 bed house (i.e. 2 bed upstairs + 1 converted other)	4 bed house	5 bed house	6 or more bed house
Entry price	£78,000	£110,000	£155,000	£180,000
Median room rate	£45	£40	£40	£40
Average yield B*	8.1%	6.8%	6.1%	6.3%
B – Estimated annual profit	£1,566	£1,066	£625	£924

Financial scores	Capital growth (out of 5)	Yield (out of 5)	Total (out of 10)
	3	2.5	5.5

Description	Wolverhampton is often considered to be part of Birmingham, but is actually a large town in its own right. During the last century the town became famous as part of the Black Country, so-called because of the pollution associated with its thriving industrial areas. While Wolverhampton retains its reputation as a major manufacturing centre, today it is equally well known for its excellent shopping centres, nightlife and sporting venues. The University is growing, innovative and friendly with five campuses located throughout the West Midlands and Shropshire.
Websites to advertise on	Local and national student listings: www.student-accom.com City information for students: www.accommodationforstudents.com Student listings: www.studentpad.co.uk West Midlands portal: www.roomsforlet.co.uk/student-accommodation Landlord postings: www.studenthousehunt.com

Estate agents	Address	Tel	Web
Oliver Ling	74 Darlington Street, Wolverhampton WV1 4LY	01902 427041	www.oliverling.com
Bradford & Bingley Marketplace	13 Wolverhampton Road, Cannock WS11 1AP	01543 503678	www.bbg.co.uk
Connells	20 Darlington Street, Wolverhampton WV1 4HW	01902 885133	www.connells.co.uk
David Berriman	15 High Street, Tettenhall, Wolverhampton WV6 8QS	01902 747744	www.david berriman.co.uk

Letting agents	Address	Tel	Web
Skitts Estate Agents	16 Darlington Street, Wolverhampton WV1 4HW	01902 685208	www.skitts.net

Letting agents	Address	Tel	Web
Lawson & Company	66 Chapel Ash, Wolverhampton WV3 0TT	01902 428008	www.lawsonandcompany.com
Whitegates	76 Darlington Street, Wolverhampton WV1 4LY	01902 429035	www.whitegates.co.uk
Sanders Wright & Freeman	13 Waterloo Road, Wolverhampton WV1 4DJ	01902 575556	www.swfestateagents.co.uk
Martin & Co	85 Darlington Street, Wolverhampton WV1 4EX	01902 574910	www.martinco.com

Worcester

University	University College Worcester			
Population	93,358			
	Student population	Undergraduate	Postgraduate	Total
		6065	1130	7195
	Campus capacity	576	0	576
	Size of market	5489	1130	6619
Drop-out rate	13%			
Student areas	Broadmore Green, St Johns			

University	Accommodation officer contacts			
	Tel	Address	Web	Landlord accreditation scheme?
University College Worcester	01905 855137	Accommodation Office, University of Worcester, Henwick Grove, Worcester WR2 6AJ	www.worc.ac.uk	No

Planned development for city	Plans to refurbish Worcester city centre were given the go-ahead in summer 2003. Worcester City Council has approved the plans to transform the High Street. The council will oversee the project with the help of a steering group which will include council officials, education leaders, the police and shopping centre managers.
Planned development for university	University College Worcester (UCW) has been awarded a £10 million grant from the Strategic Development Fund of the Higher Education Funding Council for England (HEFCE) towards the first phase of the redevelopment of the former Worcester Royal Infirmary site in Castle Street. This grant is the largest ever awarded in UCW's history.

Campus room rental**	Minimum		Maximum	
	£41		£55	

Yield range	7.1–8%			
Type of property	3 bed house (i.e. 2 bed upstairs + 1 converted other)	4 bed house	5 bed house	6 or more bed house
Entry price	£105,000	£125,000	£175,000	£210,000
Median room rate	£55	£53	£53	£53
Average yield B*	7.4%	8%	7.1%	7.1%
B – Estimated annual profit	£1,479	£2,347	£2,089	£2,507

Financial scores	Capital growth (out of 5)	Yield (out of 5)	Total (out of 10)
	3	2.5	5.5

Description	Worcester is a thriving cathedral city, set in beautiful riverside surroundings. Its modern amenities offer a first class quality of life. Worcester enjoys excellent access by road, rail and air. The city has retained its traditional half-timbered buildings and character, with a street plan dating back to medieval times. The River Severn flows through the heart of the city.
Websites to advertise on	Local and national student listings: www.student-accom.com City information for students: www.accommodationforstudents.com Good information provided by the university: http://cook.worc.ac.uk/cgi-bin/accommodation/2004/query2004.cgi Student network: www.studentlandlord.org.uk Worcester listings: www.torent.co.uk/aaregion/aarea/aauni/WORCESTER.html

Estate agents	Address	Tel	Web
Allan Morris	Worcester Office, Worcester WR1	01905 612266	www.allan-morris.co.uk
Andrew Grant	59–60 Foregate Street, Worcester WR1 1DX	01905 24477	www.andrew-grant.co.uk
Humberts	4 Foregate Street, Worcester WR1 1DB	01905 611066	www.humberts.co.uk

Letting agents	Address	Tel	Web
Carter Jonas	Croome Estate Office, High Green, Severn Stoke, Worcester WR8 9JS	01905 371261	www.carterjonas.co.uk
G. Herbert Banks	The Estate Office, Hill House, Great Witley, Nr Worcester WR6 6JB	01299 896968	www.gherbertbanks.co.uk
Michael Tuck	Brindley Road, Warndon Villages, Worcester WR4 9SB	01905 757577	www.michaeltuck.co.uk
Parkinson Wright	Haswell House, St Nicolas Street, Worcester WR1 1UN	01905 726789	www.parkinsonwright.co.uk
Oaklands Estate Agents	45 Foregate Street, Worcester WR1 1EE	01905 723307	www.remarks-worcester.com

Wrexham

University	The North East Wales Institute of Higher Education
Population	128,477

		Undergraduate	Postgraduate	Total
Student population		5220	595	5815
Campus capacity		506	–	506
Size of market		4714	595	5309

Drop-out rate	15%
Student areas	The Dunks, Hightown, Wrexham Centre

Accommodation officer contacts

University	Tel	Address	Web	Landlord accreditation scheme?
The North East Wales Institute of Higher Education	01978 293305/2	The Accommodation Office, NEWI, Plas Coch, Mold Road, Wrexham LL11 2AW	www.newi.ac.uk	Yes

Planned development for city	Councillors have approved proposals to redevelop a rundown part of Wrexham town centre. The Bridge Street regeneration scheme gained a £1.6m package from the Welsh Assembly Government in 2003 to upgrade the area and attract investment. They also approved the first application to build new houses in the area since the scheme began.

Planned development for university	The University of Wales has recommended that the North East Wales Institute of Higher Education (NEWI) be invited to become a full member of the University, after years of associate membership.
	    This is seen by staff at NEWI as a recognition of the commitment shown to providing excellent higher education for the local community. The new status will be regarded as a reward for efforts in attracting people who would not otherwise have considered studying at university.
	    It is hoped that the news will provide a further boost to the North Wales economy as businesses seek NEWI's help in creating a knowledge driven economy across the region.

Campus room rental**	Minimum	Maximum
	£42	£59

Yield range	6.5–8.3%

Type of property	3 bed house (i.e. 2 bed upstairs + 1 converted other)	4 bed house	5 bed house	6 or more bed house
Entry price	£75,000	£100,000	£135,000	£190,000
Median room rate	£44	£42	£43	£44
Average yield B*	8.3%	7.9%	7.5%	6.5%
B – Estimated annual profit	£1,589	£1,817	£2,009	£1,377

Financial scores	Capital growth (out of 5)	Yield (out of 5)	Total (out of 10)
	3	2.5	5.5
Description	Wrexham has been a bustling market town for 300 years. It is Wales' fourth largest town and home to its oldest football team. The centre is full of character and charm as well as having two indoor shopping centres. It has many pubs, which serve real ale and have a real atmosphere. There are also some lively restaurants and clubs in the town. Wrexham is in the heart of the Welsh borderlands and acts as a gateway to North Wales. The surrounding countryside is amongst the most beautiful in Britain. There are beaches and mountains located within a short driving distance from Wrexham. Opposite the Plas Coch campus a retail park has been developed. This complex contains a six-screen cinema as well as a major supermarket.		
Websites to advertise on	Local and national student listings: www.student-accom.com City information for students: www.accommodationforstudents.com Easy roommate: http://uk.easyroommate.com University guide: www.newi.ac.uk/students/student_guide_web/accommodation.htm Letting for students: http://andrewspms.co.uk/smith		

Estate agents	Address	Tel	Web
G and A Estates	41 King Street, Wrexham LL11 1HR	01978 312800	
Jones Peckover	33 High Street, Wrexham LL13 8LD	01978 364283	www.jonespeckover. com
Seth Hughes and Son	St Georges Crescent, Wrexham LL13 8DA	01978 265123	
Wingetts	29 Holt Street, Wrexham LL13 8D	01978 353553	www.wingetts.co.uk

Letting agents	Address	Tel	Web
Kent Jones	47–49 King Street, Wrexham LL11 1HR	01978 266789	www.homesonview. co.uk
Molyneux	35–37 King Street, Wrexham LL11 1LG	01978 262275	www.molyneux-estate agents.co.uk
Swetenhams	43 King Street, Wrexham LL11 1HR	01978 265678	www.sequencehome. co.uk

Letting agents	Address	Tel	Web
Thomas C Adams – Wrexham	19 King Street, Wrexham LL11 1HF	01978 290000	www.thomascadams.com
Whitegates – Wrexham	2 King Street, Wrexham LL11 1LE	01978 312123	www.whitegates.co.uk

York

Universities	University of York, York St John College
Population	181,131

	Student population	Undergraduate	Postgraduate	Total
	University of York	7955	2055	11240
	York St John College	5030	870	5905
	Total	12985	2925	17145
	Campus capacity	3807	690	4497
	Size of market	9178	2235	12648

Drop-out rates	University of York	6%
	York St John College	11%

Student areas	Bishopthorpe Road, Bootham, Central, Clifton, Fulford, Heslington, Heworth, Melrosegate, Osbaldwick, South Bank, University Road

Accommodation officer contacts

University	Tel	Address	Web	Landlord accreditation scheme?
University of York	01904 432165	Accommodatation Office, Heslington, York YO10 5DD	accommodation@ york.ac.uk www.york.ac.uk/ admin/accom	Yes
York St John College	01904 716661	The Accommodation Office, Lord Mayor's Walk, York YO31 7EX	accommodation@ yorksj.ac.uk	No

Planned development for city	The main priorities are York Pride and Safe City. York Pride motivates residents to take pride in their own street, neighbourhood and city, making a difference to the condition of the physical environment. Safe City is about making people feel safer on the streets and in their homes. It means visibly tackling anti-social behaviour such as criminal damage, graffiti and nuisance offences, in and around York.
Planned development for universities	University of York Plans for a large extension to the University of York's main campus at Heslington were released in 2003. The masterplan for the site, known as Heslington East, shows a green, landscaped site edged with woodland and a large lake, and served by environmentally friendly transport systems. The project will enable the University to respond to the increased pressures on it to grow and will have enormous benefits for the city and region.
	York St John College The Princess Royal officially opened the Fountains Learning Centre, Foss

| | and Skell Buildings at York St John College in 2004. The new buildings, key elements in a £27 million development project, demonstrate the College's commitment to providing top quality learning and teaching facilities for its students and staff and for the wider community. | | | |

Campus room rental	Minimum £50		Maximum £85	
Yield range	4.9%–8.3%			

Type of property	3 bed house (i.e. 2 bed upstairs + 1 converted other)	4 bed house	5 bed house	6 or more bed house
Entry price	£100,000	£145,000	£200,000	£290,000
Median room rate	£55	£55	£51	£50
Average yield B*	8.3%	7.1%	6%	4.9%
B – Estimated annual profit	£2,156	£1,747	£588	−£1,770

Financial scores	Capital growth (out of 5) 3	Yield (out of 5) 2.5	Total (out of 10) 5.5

Description	York is a great city famous for its churches and tight cobbled lanes, not unlike parts of Cambridge. The University, however, is slightly different. It is anything but historic, established in 1963 two miles south-east of the city centre in a village called Heslington. With the exception of a stately manor, the University seems to be made entirely of concrete and it looks as if the builders used the same plans for most of the campus. Its saving grace, however, are the well kept gardens.
Websites to advertise on	Local and national student listings: www.student-accom.com City information for students: www.accommodationforstudents.com National listings: www.upmystreet.com

Estate agents	Address	Tel	Web
Bairstow Eves	72 Low Petergate, York YO1 7HZ	01904 643264	www.bairstoweves countrywide.co.uk
Bradford & Bingley Marketplace Ltd	6–7 Bridge Street, York YO1 6DD	01904 649999	www.bbg.co.uk
Hunters	18 & 19 Colliergate, York YO1 8BN	01904 621026	www.huntersnet.co.uk
R M English and Son	2 Railway Street, Pocklington, York YO4 2QZ	01759 303202	www.rmenglish.co.uk

Letting agents	Address	Tel	Web
Savills	13–15 Micklegate, York YO1 6JH	01904 617 800	www.savills.co.uk
Halifax Property Services	31 High Petergate, York YO1 2HP	01904 629333	www.halifax.co.uk
Hudson Moody	5 High Petergate, York YO1 7EN	01904 629629	www.hudson-moody.com
Reeds Rains	29 Micklegate, York YO1 1JH	01904 655546	www.reedsrains.co.uk
William H Brown	48 Goodramgate, York YO1 7LF	01904 621138	www.sequencehome.co.uk

Universities in the London Area

The information for London area universities has been condensed as no one borough returns a decent yield! I've included them only for completeness. The sheer size of the London student market requires a chapter in its own right. There are no defined student quarters for each individual university or college in London[1], so if you can find cheap property[2] within the student vicinity, presenting good potential yields, good access to the transport, then it may be worth a look. I use the term cheap property very loosely here!

Borough	Barking and Dagenham			
University	University of East London			
	Student population	Undergraduate 10165	Postgraduate 4140	Total 14305
Drop-out rate	18%			
Accommodation officer contacts	University	Tel	Address	Web
	University of East London	020 8223 4445	Residential Services, University Way, Romford Road, London E15 4LZ	www.uel.ac.uk

---

1   University of London campuses may have locations in multiple places across Greater London. When possible, the main campus is used as the principal location.

2   London has many flats on offer, but this has generally been excluded from this criteria as we require a property which can accommodate three or four bedrooms.

Borough	Camden		
Universities	Central School of Speech and Drama, Royal Veterinary College		
	Student population Central School of Speech	**Undergraduate**	**Postgraduate**	**Total**
	and Drama	430	385	815
	Royal Veterinary College	690	245	1065
	Total	1120	630	1880
Drop-out rates:	Central School of Speech and Drama		16%	
	Royal Veterinary College		4%	
Accommodation officer contacts	**University**	**Tel**	**Address**	**Web**
	Central School of Speech and Drama	020 7722 8183	Central School of Speech and Drama, Embassy Theatre, Eton Avenue, London NW3 3HY	www.cssd.ac.uk
	Royal Veterinary College	020 7468 5000	The Registry, Royal College Street, London NW1 0TU	www.rvc.ac.uk

Borough	City of London		
University	London School of Economics (LSE)		
	Student population	**Undergraduate** 3535	**Postgraduate** 4735	**Total** 8275
Drop-out rate	London School of Economics (LSE)		9%	
Accommodation officer contacts	**University**	**Tel**	**Address**	**Web**
	London School of Economics (LSE)	020 7955 7531	Accommodation Office, E294 East Building, LSE, Houghton Street, London WC2A 2AE	www.lse.ac.uk

Borough	**Ealing**			
University	Thames Valley University			
	Student population	Undergraduate	Postgraduate	Total
		14690	1640	16330
Drop-out rate	20%			
Accommodation officer contacts	University	Tel	Address	Web
	Thames Valley University	020 8579 5000	Ealing Campus, St Mary's Road, Ealing, London, W5 5RF	www.tvu.ac.uk

Borough	**Greenwich**			
Universities	University of Greenwich, Trinity College of Music			
	Student population	Undergraduate	Postgraduate	Total
	University of Greenwich	14675	5520	20195
	Trinity College of Music	355	135	490
	Total	15030	5655	20685
Drop-out rates	University of Greenwich	19%		
	Trinity College of Music	7%		
Accommodation officer contacts	University	Tel	Address	Web
	University of Greenwich	020 8331 8884	Accommodation Services, M069 Queen Mary Court, 30 Park Row, London SE10 9LS	www.gre.ac.uk
	Trinity College of Music	020 7487 9608	Student Services, Trinity College of Music, 11–13 Mandeville Place, London W1M 6AQ	www.tcm.ac.uk

Borough	**Hammersmith and Fulham**			
University	Imperial College, University of London			
	Student population	Undergraduate 7365	Postgraduate 4375	Total 11745
Drop-out rate	4%			
Accommodation officer contacts	University	Tel	Address	Web
	Imperial College	020 7594 9444	Student Accommodation Office, Imperial College, 15 Prince's Gardens, London SW7 1NA	www.ic.ac.uk

Borough	**Haringey**			
University	Middlesex University			
	Student population	Undergraduate 18115	Postgraduate 4780	Total 22895
Drop-out rate	15%			
Accommodation officer contacts	University	Tel	Address	Web
	Middlesex University	020 8411 6121	Central Accommodation Office, Building 4, North London Business Park, Oakleigh Road South, New Southgate, London N11 1QS	www. mdx.ac.uk

Borough	**Hillingdon**			
University	Brunel University			
	Student population	**Undergraduate** 10760	**Postgraduate** 4370	**Total** 15135
Drop out rate	10%			
Accommodation officer contacts	**University**	**Tel**	**Address**	**Web**
	Brunel University	020 8891 0121	Accommodation Office, Twickenham Campus, First Floor Gordon House, Room G244, 300 St Margaret's Road, Twickenham, Middlesex TW1 1PT	www. brunel.ac.uk

Borough	**Islington**			
Universities	City University, London Metropolitan University[3]			
	Student population	**Undergraduate**	**Postgraduate**	**Total**
	City University	13155	8270	21425
	London Metropolitan University	25020	6575	31595
	Total	38175	14845	53020
Drop-out rates:	City University	16%		
	London Metropolitan University	29%&19%		
Accommodation officer contacts	**University**	**Tel**	**Address**	**Web**
	City University	020 7477 8033	Accommodation Office, City University, Northampton Square, London EC1V 0HB	www.city.ac.uk
	London Metropolitan University	020 7133 4288	London Metropolitan University, 166–220 Holloway Road, London N7 8DB	www.london met.ac.uk

3   London Guildhall University and the University of North London have merged to form London Metropolitan University.

Borough	**Kingston-upon-Thames**			
University	Kingston University			
	Student population	Undergraduate 14555	Postgraduate 4045	Total 18600
Drop-out rate	14%			
Accommodation officer contacts	University	Tel	Address	Web
	Kingston University	020 8547 2000	River House, 53–57 High Street, Kingston upon Thames, Surrey KT1 1LQ	www.kingston. ac.uk

Borough	**Merton**			
University	Wimbledon School of Art			
	Student population	Undergraduate 510	Postgraduate 125	Total 635
Drop-out rate	11%			
Accommodation officer contacts	University	Tel	Address	Web
	Wimbledon School of Art	020 8408 5000	Main Building, Merton Hall Road, London SW19 3QA	www. wimbledon .ac.uk

Borough	**Richmond-upon-Thames**			
University	St Mary's College, University of Surrey			
	Student population	Undergraduate 2445	Postgraduate 550	Total 2995
Drop-out rate	13%			
Accommodation officer contacts	University	Tel	Address	Web
	St Mary's College	020 8240 4034	Accommodation Office, Waldegrave Road, Twickenham, Middlesex TW1 4SX	www.smuc. ac.uk

Borough	**Southwark**			
University	London South Bank University			
	Student population	Undergraduate 15395	Postgraduate 4735	Total 20130
Drop-out rate	26%			
Accommodation officer contacts	University	Tel	Address	Web
	London South Bank University	020 7815 6417	Accommodation Office, South Bank University, Room G1, London SE1 0AA	www.sbu.ac.uk

Borough	**Tower Hamlets**			
University	Queen Mary, University of London			
	Student population	Undergraduate 7550	Postgraduate 2350	Total 9900
Drop-out rate	16%			
Accommodation officer contacts	University	Tel	Address	Web
	Queen Mary	020 7882 5522	Residence Office, Mile End Road, London E1 4NS	www.qmw.ac.uk

Borough	Wandsworth			
Universities	St George's Hospital Medical School, University of Surrey Roehampton			
	Student population	**Undergraduate**	**Postgraduate**	**Total**
	St George's Hospital Medical School	2865	720	3585
	University of Surrey Roehampton	10440	1690	8080
	Total	13305	2410	15715
Drop-out rates	St George's Hospital Medical School 7% University of Surrey Roehampton 16%			
Accommodation officer contacts	**University**	**Tel**	**Address**	**Web**
	St George's Hospital Medical School	020 8725 0497	Accommodation Office, Cranmer Terrace, London SW17 0RE	www. sghms.ac.uk
	University of Surrey Roehampton	020 8392 3300	Froebel College, Roehampton Lane, London SW15 5PJ	www. roehampton .ac.uk

Borough	Westminster		
Universities	Kings College of London, University College London (UCL), the London Institute, Royal College of Music, School of Pharmacy, School of Oriental and African Studies (SOAS), University of Westminster		
	Student population **Undergraduate**	**Postgraduate**	**Total**
	Kings College of London (KCL) 14345	6125	20475
	University College London (UCL) 11820	7080	18900
	The London Institute 9765	1735	11505
	Royal College of Music 375	225	600
	School of Pharmacy 655	555	1210
	School of Oriental and African Studies (SOAS) 1990	1855	3845
	University of Westminster 17525	8250	25780
	Total 56475	25825	82315
Drop-out rates	Kings College of London (KCL)	7%	
	University College London (UCL)	2%	
	The London Institute	10%	
	Royal College of Music	6%	
	School of Pharmacy	11%	
	School of Oriental and African Studies (SOAS)	15%	
	University of Westminster	20%	

Accommodation officer contacts	University	Tel	Address	Web
	Kings College of London (KCL)	020 7848 2759	Accommodation Office, King's College London, Strand, London WC2R 2LS	www.kcl.ac.uk
	University College London (UCL)	020 7862 8880	Accommodation Office, University College London, Room B Basement, Senate House, Malet Street, London WC1E 7HU	www.ucl.ac.uk
	The London Institute	020 7514 6230	Accommodation Service, 65 Davies Street, London W1Y 2DA	www.linst.ac.uk
	Royal College of Music	020 8749 1134	Manager, College Hall, 220–238 Goldhawk Road, London W12 9PL	www.rcm.ac.uk
	School of Pharmacy	020 7753 5800	Accommodation Office, School of Pharmacy, 29–39 Brunswick Square, London WC1N 1AX	www. ulsop.ac.uk
	School of Oriental and African Studies (SOAS)	020 7837 7163	Accommodation Office, Dimwiddy House, 189–205 Pentonville Road, London N1 9NF	www.soas.ac.uk
	University of Westminster	020 7911 5000	Student Housing Services, University of Westminster, 35 Marylebone Road, London NW1 5LS	www. westminster .ac.uk

Universities near London

Area	Cranfield			
University	University of Cranfield			
	Student population	Undergraduate 515	Postgraduate 4280	Total 4790
Drop-out rate	16%			
Accommodation officer contacts	University	Tel	Address	Web
	University of Cranfield	01234 754347	Accommodation Office, Mitchell Hall, Cranfield University, Cranfield MK43 0AL	www.cranfield.ac.uk

Area	Egham			
University	Royal Holloway, University of London			
	Student population	Undergraduate 4855	Postgraduate 1570	Total 6425
Drop-out rate	10%			
Accommodation officer contacts	University	Tel	Address	Web
	Royal Holloway	01784 443338	Accommodation Office, Royal Holloway, Egham, Surrey TW20 0EX	www.rhul.ac.uk

Area	Luton			
University	University of Luton			
	Student population	Undergraduate 9845	Postgraduate 1910	Total 11755
Drop-out rate	15%			
Accommodation officer contacts	University	Tel	Address	Web
	University of Luton	01582 743921	Accommodation Services, University of Luton, Park Square, Luton LU1 3JU	www. luton.ac.uk

Area	Maidstone			
University	Kent Institute of Art and Design			
	Student population	Undergraduate 1930	Postgraduate 130	Total 2060
Drop-out rate	11%			
Accommodation officer contacts	University	Tel	Address	Web
	Kent Institute of Art and Design	01622 757286	Oakwood Park, Maidstone, Kent ME16 8AG	www.kiad.ac.uk

Area	Reading			
University	University of Reading			
	Student population	Undergraduate 10440	Postgraduate 4810	Total 15250
Drop-out rate	8%			
Accommodation officer contacts	University	Tel	Address	Web
	University of Reading	0118 931 8055/56	Accommodation Services, Whiteknights House Annexe, Whiteknights, Reading RG6 6AH	www.rdg.ac.uk

Area	High Wycombe			
University	Buckinghamshire Chilterns University College			
	Student population	Undergraduate 9160	Postgraduate 605	Total 9765
Drop-out rate	14%			
Accommodation officer contacts	University	Tel	Address	Web
	Buckinghamshire Chilterns University College	01494 603017	Accommodation Office, BCUC, Queen Alexandra Road, High Wycombe, HP11 2JZ	www.bcuc.ac.uk

Scores for main student areas in London

There is not necessarily a link between a university campus and the area it is situated in. For example, not every student from the Royal Veterinary College may live in Camden, and a student from Kings College London may choose to live in Camden.

In descending order of yields calculated:

Student area(s)	Entry price (3 or 4 bed)[4]	Median room rate	Yield range	Estimated annual profit
Woolwich, Charlton	£145,000–£170,000	£90	8.7%–9.9%	£3,627–£5,886
Catford, Lewisham	£150,000–£185,000	£95	8.9%–9.6%	£3,966–£5,963
Ealing	£180,000–£215,000	£110	8.6%–9.6%	£4,308–£6,869
Wimbledon, Tooting	£195,000–£230,000	£110	7.9%–8.9%	£3,633–£6,194
Bow, Bethnal Green, Hackney	£185,000–£215,000	£100	7.6%–8.7%	£2,955–£5,365
Reading	£130,000–£140,000	£65	7.1%–8.7%	£1,482–£3,476
Willesden, Harlesden	£185,000–£230,000	£105	8%–8.6%	£3,519–£5,442
New Southgate	£205,000–£230,000	£105	7.2%–8.6%	£2,619–£5,442
Hendon, Golders Green, Colindale, Finchley	£220,000–£240,000	£110	7%–8.6%	£2,508–£5,744
Wood Green, Haringey, Hornsey, South Tottenham	£180,000–£205,000	£90	7.1%–8.2%	£2,052–£4,311
Barking, Stratford, Brick Lane, East Ham	£130,000–£140,000	£65	7.1%–8.1%	£1,482–£2,724

4   Houses specifically chosen, as the 2 bedroom and 3 bedroom houses are most desired by students i.e. 3 bedroom house = {3 bed + converted lounge = 4 bed total} and so on.

Student area(s)	Entry price (3 or 4 bed)	Median room rate	Yield range	Estimated annual profit
Greenwich, Deptford	£200,000–£220,000	£95	6.7%–8.1%	£1,716–£4,388
Leyton, Stratford, Newham	£160,000–£200,000	£85	7.5%–8%	£2,388–£3,784
Clapham, Clapham Common	£280,000–£320,000	£135	6.8%–7.9%	£2,628–£5,904
Brixton, Streatham, West Norwood, Norbury	£190,000–£215,000	£90	6.7%–7.9%	£1,602–£3,861
Walthamstow, Wanstead, South Woodford	£180,000–£200,000	£85	6.6%–7.9%	£1,488–£3,784
Hammersmith, Kensington, Fulham, Putney, Shepherds Bush, Earls Court, Battersea, Marble Arch	£270,000–£345,000	£135	7.1%–7.4%	£3,078–£4,779
Wandsworth, Roehampton	£195,000–£215,000	£85	6.1%–7.4%	£813–£3,109
Hampstead, West Hampstead	£330,000–£360,000	£140	5.9%–7.3%	£942–£4,856
Islington	£240,000–£295,000	£110	6.5%–7%	£1,608–£3,269
Camden, St Johns Wood	£290,000–£380,000	£135	6.5%–6.7%	£2,178–£3,204
Bayswater, Notting Hill, Queensway	£300,000–£365,000	£130	6.1%–6.7%	£1,164–£3,127
Tuffnell Park, Upper Holloway, Gospel Oak	£265,000–£290,000	£100	5.3%–6.5%	−£645–£1,990
Finsbury, Stoke Newington	£195,000–£250,000	£85	6.1%–6.4%	£812–£1,534
Southwark, Bermondsey, Camberwell	£220,000–£260,000	£85	5.4%–6.1%	−£312–£1,084
Greenford, Southall	£185,000–£230,000	£70	5.3%–5.7%	−£429–£178
Stepney, Mile End	£245,000–£290,000	£85	4.9%–5.5%	−£26–£266

Students' Unions

University	Website
Aberdeen, University of	www.abdn.ac.uk/union
Aberystwyth, University of	union.aber.ac.uk
Anglia Polytechnic University	www.asu.anglia.ac.uk
Bath Spa University College	www.bathspa.ac.uk/su
Bath, University of	www.bath.ac.uk/busu
Birkbeck College, London	www.bbk.ac.uk/su
Birmingham, University of	www.bugs-bham.co.uk
Bournemouth University	www.subu.org.uk
Bradford, University of	www.ubu.brad.ac.uk
Brighton, University of	www.bton.ac.uk/ubsu
Bristol, University of	www.ubu.org.uk
Brunei University	www.ubsonline.net
Buckinghamshire Chilterns University College	www.bcsu.org.uk
Buckinghamshire, University of	www.buckingham.ac.uk/su
Cambridge University	www.cusu.cam.ac.uk
Cardiff University	www.cardiffstudents.com
Central England in Birmingham,	www.uce.ac.uk/union
University of Central Lancashire, University of	www.yourunion.co.uk
Cheltenham and Gloucester College	www.chelt.ac.uk/su
Chester College	www.chester.ac.uk/studentsunion
Coventry University	www.coventry.ac.uk/sandf/s_union
Cranfield University	www.cranfield.ac.uk/socs/csa
Derby, University of	www.derby.ac.uk/udsu

University	Website
Dundee University	www.dusa.dundee.ac.uk
Durham, University of	www.dsu.org.uk
East Anglia, University of	www.stu.uea.ac.uk
East London, University of	www.uelsu.org.uk
Edge Hill College of Higher Education	www.ehce.ac.uk/about/su.htm
Edinburgh University	www.eusa.ed.ac.uk./su
Essex, University of	www.essex.ac.uk
Exeter, University of	www.guild.ex.ac.uk
Glamorgan, University of	www.itc.glam.ac.uk/union
Glasgow University	www.guu.co.uk
Goldsmiths College, London	www.su.gold.ac.uk
Greenwich, University of	www.gre.ac.uk/suug
Harper Adams University College	www.wmhea.ac.uk
Heriot-Watt University	www.trioch.net
Hertfordshire, University of	uhsu.herts.ac.uk
Hull University	www.hull.ac.uk/su
Imperial College of Science, Technology and Medicine	www.su.ic.ac.uk
Keele University	www.kusu.net
Kent at Canterbury, University of	www.su.ukc.ac.uk
King's College London	www.kclsu.org
Kingston University	www.kingston.ac.uk/guild
Lampeter, University of	www.lamp.ac.uk/su
Lancaster University	www.lusu.co.uk
Leeds Metropolitan University	www.lmusu.org.uk
Leeds, University of	www.leeds.ac.uk/union
Leicester University	www.le.ac.uk/su
Limerick, University of	www.ulsu.ul.ie
Lincolnshire and Humberside, University	www.hul.ac.uk/su
Liverpool John Moores University	www.isu.livjm.ac.uk
Liverpool, University of	www.l-s-u.com
London Metropolitan University	www.londonmet.ac.uk
London School of Economics	www.lse.ac.uk/su
London Union, University of	www.ulu.ucl.ac.uk

University	Website
Loughborough University	www-lsu.lboro.ac.uk
Luton, University of	students.luton.ac.uk
Manchester Metropolitan University	www.mmsu.com
Manchester, University of	www.umu.man.ac.uk
Middlesex University	www.musu.mdx.ac.uk
Napier University	www.napierstudents.com
National Ireland, Galway	www.su.nuigalway.ie
Newcastle, University of	www.ncl.ac.uk/~nunion
North East Wales Institute of H.E.	www.newi.ac.uk/sunion
Northumbria, University of	www.unsu.co.uk
Nottingham Trent University	www.su.ntu.ac.uk
Nottingham, University of	www.su.nottingham.ac.uk
Oxford Brookes University	www.brookes.ac.uk/student/union
Oxford, University of	www.ousu.org
Plymouth, University of	www.upsu.plym.ac.uk
Portsmouth University	www.upsu.net
Queen Mary and Westfield College, London	www.qmsu.org
Queen's University Belfast	www.qubsu.org
Reading, University of	www.rusu.co.uk
Rose Bruford College, Kent	www.rbcsu.org.uk
Royal Academy of Music	www.ram.ac.uk/pages/3.htm
Royal Holloway	www.su.rhbnc.ac.uk
Salford University	www.salford.ac.uk/susu
School of Oriental and African Studies	www.soasunion.org
Sheffield Hallam University	hallamunion.com
Sheffield, University of	www.shef.ac.uk/union
South Bank University	www.sbsu.org.uk
Southampton Institute	www.solent.ac.uk/sisul
Southampton, University of	www.soton.ac.uk/-susu
St Andrews, University of	www.st-andrews.ac.uk/union
St Georges Hospital Medical School	www.sghms.ac.uk/student
St Martin's College	www.thestudentsunion.org.uk
St Mary's College	www.smuc.ac.uk/studentsunion
St Bartholomew's & the Royal London School of Medicine and Dentistry	www.mds.qmw.ac.uk/assoc

University	Website
Staffordshire University	www.staffs.ac.uk/studentsunion
Stirling, University of	www.stir.ac.uk/theuni/suinfo/susa
Strathclyde, University of	www.theunion.strath.ac.uk
Sunderland, University of	www.sunderiand.ac.uk/-rsOweb
Surrey, Roehampton, University of	www.roehampton.ac.uklrsu/su.htm
Surrey, University of	www.ussu.co.uk
Sussex, University of	www.ussu.net
Swansea, University of	www.swansea-union.co.uk
Teesside, University of	www.utu.org.uk
Thames Valley University	www.tvu.ac.uk/su
Trinity and All Saints College	www.tasc.ac.uk/su
Trinity College Carmarthen	www.trinity-cm.ac.uk
Ulster, University of	www.ulst.ac.uk/surf
UMIST	www.su.umist.ac.uk
University College London	www.uci.ac.ukluci-union
University College, Safford	www.ucsalf.ac.uk/su
University College Cork	www.ucc.ie/ucc/su
University College Dublin	www.ucd.ie/facgen.htm
University College Worcester	www.worcsu.com
University of the West of England, Bristol	www.uwe.ac.uk/union
Victoria Manchester, University of	www.umu.man.ac.uk
Wales Bangor, University of	www.undeb.bangor.ac.uk
Wales College of Medicine, University of	www.uwcm.ac.uk
Wales College, Newport, University of	su.newport.ac.uk
Welsh College of Music and Drama	www.wcmd.ac.uk
West of England, university of	www.uwe.ac.uk/union
Westminster, University of	www.uwsu.com
Wolverhampton, University of	www.wiv.ac.uk/su/welcome.html
York St John College	www.ysjsu.co.uk
York, University of	www.york.ac.uk/student/su

Index